D0147050

DEC 2 0 2010

Culture and Customs of Turkey

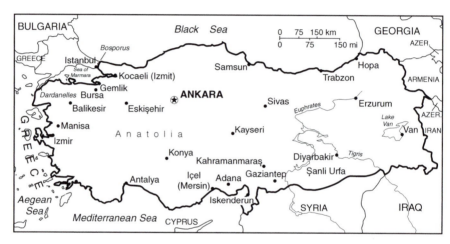

Turkey. Courtesy of Bookcomp, Inc.

Culture and Customs of Turkey

RAFIS ABAZOV

Culture and Customs of Europe

GREENWOOD PRESS
Westport, Connecticut • London

Library of Congress Cataloging-in-Publication Data

Abazov, Rafis.
    Culture and customs of Turkey / Rafis Abazov.
        p.   cm.—(Culture and customs of Europe)
    Includes bibliographical references and index.
    ISBN 978–0–313–34215–8 (alk. paper)
    1. Ethnology—Turkey.   2. Turkey—Social life and customs.   I. Title.
    GN635.T82A33   2009
    306.09561—dc22   2008040214

British Library Cataloguing in Publication Data is available.

Copyright © 2009 by Rafis Abazov

All rights reserved. No portion of this book may be
reproduced, by any process or technique, without the
express written consent of the publisher.

Library of Congress Catalog Card Number: 2008040214
ISBN: 978–0–313–34215–8

First published in 2009

Greenwood Press, 88 Post Road West, Westport, CT 06881
An imprint of Greenwood Publishing Group, Inc.
www.greenwood.com

Printed in the United States of America

The paper used in this book complies with the
Permanent Paper Standard issued by the National
Information Standards Organization (Z39.48–1984).

10 9 8 7 6 5 4 3 2 1

Every reasonable effort has been made to trace the owners of copyright materials in this book, but in some instances this has proven impossible. The author and publisher will be glad to receive information leading to more complete acknowledgments in subsequent printings of the book and in the meantime extend their apologies for any omissions.

Contents

Series Foreword

THE OLD WORLD and the New World have maintained a fluid exchange of people, ideas, innovations, and styles. Even though the United States became the de facto world leader and economic superpower in the wake of a devastated Europe in World War II, Europe has remained for many the standard bearer of Western culture.

Millions of Americans can trace their ancestors to Europe. The United States as we know it was built on waves of European immigration, starting with the English who braved the seas to found the Jamestown Colony in 1607. Bosnian and Albanian immigrants are some of the latest new Americans. In the Gilded Age of one of our great expatriates, the novelist Henry James, the Grand Tour of Europe was de rigueur for young American men of means, to prepare them for a life of refinement and taste. In a more recent democratic age, scores of American college students have Eurailed their way across Great Britain and the Continent, sampling the fabled capitals and bergs in a mad, great adventure, or have benefited from a semester abroad. For other American vacationers and culture vultures, Europe is the prime destination. What is the New Europe post–Cold War, post–Berlin Wall in a new millennium? Even with the different languages, rhythms, and rituals, Europeans have much in common: They are largely well educated, prosperous, and worldly. They also have similar goals and face common threats and form alliances. With the advent of the European Union, the open borders, and the Euro and considering globalization and the prospect of a homogenized Europe, an updated survey of the region is warranted.

Culture and Customs of Europe features individual volumes on the countries most studied and for which fresh information is in demand from students and other readers. The Series casts a wide net, inclusive of not only the expected countries, such as Spain, France, England, and Germany, but also countries such as Poland and Greece that lie outside western Europe proper. Each volume is written by a country specialist, with intimate knowledge of the contemporary dynamics of a people and culture. Sustained narrative chapters cover the land, people, and brief history; religion; social customs; gender roles, family, and marriage; literature and media; performing arts and cinema; and art and architecture. The national character and ongoing popular traditions of each country are framed in an historical context and celebrated along with the latest trends and major cultural figures. A country map, chronology, glossary, and evocative photos enhance the text.

The historied and enlightened Europeans will continue to fascinate Americans. Our futures are strongly linked politically, economically, and culturally.

Preface

BOTH THE OTTOMAN Empire and the Turkish Republic have always attracted the Western audience with their magnificent cultural accomplishments, oriental mysticism, and their roles as a doorstep to the thundering Muslim universe. Probably no other country in the world has been depicted by writers, scholars, and politicians in more polarized ways and controversial writings. In times of crisis, Turkey was regularly flooded by the influx of spies, adventurers, and warriors who often portrayed this land as an imminent threat to stability and prosperity in western Europe. In times of peace, hordes of tourists and art lovers inundated the streets and roads of Turkey, admiring the hospitality and openness of the Turkish people and the magnificence of their culture.

Indeed, the culture of Turkish land and of Turkish people seamlessly stitched together the greatest achievements of Asian and European arts, the enchanting mysticism of the Golden Christendom with the simple and rough beauty of the universalism of Turkic-speaking nomads. The unforgettable, brilliantly crafted poems of the greatest mystic of the Turkish land—Jellaladin Rumi—called for unity, universal love, and harmony in the souls of people. This harmony is well-symbolized in the peaceful coexistence of the greatest masterpieces of the world—Grand Sultan Akhmed Mosque and Hagia Sofia—in Istanbul.

When one walks along the narrow passages between and around these two monumental buildings surrounded by visitors literally from every corner of the world, it is easy to believe in the eternity of unruffled life. The reality, however, was not always kind to the people of Anatolia and to the state that was once described as the "magnificent Empire." For about two hundred years the Ottoman Empire had been devastated by an endless series of wars and conflicts that culminated in World War I (1914–1918). Those wars knocked on the doors of every family in Turkey, and spring boarded horrible atrocities against many communities in many areas of the Empire. In the end, not only did the Empire experience utter defeat but it also collapsed under the combination of numerous internal and external factors. It looked as if the Turkish State might disappear from the political map forever. Yet, Clio, the Greek muse and goddess of history, spanned another turn for the country as a group of young military officers led by Mustafa Kemal fiercely launched a war of independence. This four-year long war (1919–1922) ultimately resulted in the establishment of the modern and secular Turkish Republic in 1923.

Both politically and culturally, the Turkish Republic manifested the establishment of a new paradigm in the history of Turkey as it emphasized secularism, Turkish nationalism, and democracy. This process, though, was not simple and straightforward. It was dotted with economic downturns, military coups, and deep conflicts between political and social groups. In a cultural sphere, the republic declared itself guarantor of the cultural legacy of the Turkish land from eastern Anatolia and Black Sea region to eastern Thrace. The Turkish intellectuals and artists used comprehensively, although selectively, the rich cultural heritage of the past to interweave it with the Western influences of the present to create their own modern and uniquely distinctive cultural universe.

At the beginning of the twenty-first century, Turkey emerged as an energized, diverse, and rapidly changing country. A journey through various regions of Turkey would help a curious traveler discover the rich diversity of local communities, each with its own unique elements of folklore, cuisine, costumes, and everyday customs. For decades, these communities were accustomed to the slow pace of life with leisurely hours of talks over cups of Turkish coffee. The 1990s, however, turned the familiar life upside-down, as the government freed entrepreneurial spirit and abandoned its paternalistic policies and many of the economic, political, and cultural restrictions. Suddenly the whole society went in search of a new way of life, chasing business opportunities and wealth. These changes were particularly profound between 2002 and 2008. Along with the forces of globalization they began making an impact not only on Turkish society but also on Turkish culture and Turkish identity.

This book is not an attempt to make a snapshot of the culture and customs of Turkey today, but rather it is a journey into the rich and fast-changing cultural universe of Turkey and the Turkish people. It is also an attempt to introduce the Western audience to the peculiarities of modern Turkish culture and give an overview of the most important and far-reaching changes that would influence the country for many years to come. Additionally, it is an attempt to look at the essence of the intellectual and artistic life in contemporary Turkey and to discuss the most important issues that move the Turkish public and that are hotly debated, read, and cared for by the intellectuals, politicians, artists, and ordinary people.

The research and writing of this book required passionate listening to many individuals and groups that enriched my knowledge about the country and various topics related to the themes of the book. There is a large body of work produced by Western academia that discusses the history, religion, and culture of Turkey from different angles. Many of them represent competing views and ideas and many authors disagree with each other on a number of occasions. A curious reader can also find a huge body of literature written in Turkish and available for scholars who would like to learn more about the country and various issues related to the country.

Being severely limited by space and time, however, I focused on surveying the most recognizable and distinctive elements of Turkish culture and on the most profound recent changes and trends. For those readers who would like to enrich their knowledge about major scholarly discussions and works on various issues, the endnotes and bibliography section will be of great help.

Acknowledgments

CULTURE AND CUSTOMS of Turkey was written with a single objective: to introduce the complexity of the cultural dynamics, modernization, building of a nation-state, and national identity in this country. This attempt to bring the most important information and most relevant discussion into a single volume requires a certain degree of generalization. It also requires a certain degree of selection in reviewing the rich cultural and historical heritage of Turkey. I tried my best selecting the most noteworthy facts and most seminal information for this book through discussions and consultations with my colleagues and friends both in the United States and Turkey. I am fully aware that this is not a concise survey of the culture and customs of Turkey, and I hope that after reading this book, readers will seek out information, research, and discussions to enrich their understanding of Turkish culture. It is also my intention that this publication will be a useful guide to scholars and members of the general public to learn more about the subject.

This work emerged from several years of research on the history and culture of Turkey and it would have been impossible to complete without valuable contributions from many people around me. It is my pleasure to acknowledge the support of Dr. Catharine Nepomnyashchy, Alla Rachkov, and all my colleagues at the Harriman Institute, as well as Rashid Khalidi, David Cuthell and, Ahmet Kuru at the Middle East Institute at Columbia University for providing me with their trust and creating the intellectual environment that supported my long journey in writing this book. I would like to express special appreciation to Haldun Yavas, Executive Director, and Mehmet Kalyoncu,

Director of the Office of Academic and Global Initiatives, both of the Turkish Cultural Center in New York, for all their support and help in gathering information and materials for this work and arranging the field study trip to Turkey. I am also indebted to my students, whose curiosity, understanding, and numerous questions encouraged me to look at many issues from different angles.

A number of individuals from different parts of the world have supplied me with interesting facts and publications and have read the early chapters of this book, contributing their constructive critical comments and corrections: Etem Erol, Isyk Kuscu, Mustafa Dogru, Kamil Yilmaz, Jeanene Mitchell, Osman Oztoprak, Umut Unal, Gokce Ulken, and many others. I tried my best to incorporate all their suggestions and to correct all unfortunate inaccuracies in the course of the work on this book. Any errors or floaters, however, are the author's sole responsibility.

I would like to thank my wife for all her support and understanding and for her interest in the volumes and volumes of early and advanced drafts that I wrote while working on the manuscript. She was always my first and critical reader, who encouraged my intellectual writing and editing odyssey.

I would also like to thank Wendi Schnaufer, Senior Acquisition Editor at Greenwood Publishing Group, Kaitlin Ciarmiello, Acquisitions Editor, and Peggy M. Rote, Editor, for entrusting me with this fascinating work and dealing patiently with my anarchic working and writing style. They carefully read my manuscript section by section and provided valuable comments.

Note on Transliterations

Modern Turkish uses the Latin alphabet, modified to reflect the peculiarities of the Turkish sound system. The Turkish alphabet has 29 letters, which are pronounced approximately as follows:

Turkish Alphabet (*Turk Alfabesi*)

	Letters		Pronounciation
1	A	a	As *a* in *father*
2	B	b	As *b* in *Istanbul*
3	C	c	As *j* in *jinni*
4	Ç	ç	As *ch* in *chat*
5	D	d	As *d* in *dervish*
6	E	e	As *e* in *red*
7	F	F	As *f* in *Sufi*
8	G	G	As *g* in *Georgia*
9	Ğ	ğ	silent—lengthens preceding vowel
10	H	h	As *h* in *history*
11	İ	i	As *e* in open
12	I	ı	As *i* in *hit*
13	J	J	As *g* in *montage*
14	K	k	As *k* in *Ankara*
15	L	L	As *l* in *Anatolia*
16	M	m	As *m* in *Marmara*

(*cont.*)

(*cont.*)

	Letters		Pronounciation
17	N	n	As *n* in **nay**
18	O	o	As a shortened *o* in **no**
19	Ö	ö	As *e* in *her*
20	P	p	As *p* in **pasha**
21	R	r	As the *r* in **Rome**
22	S	s	As *s* in **sultan**
23	Ş	ş	As *s* in **sugar**
24	T	t	As *t* in **Turkey**
25	U	u	As *u* in **full**
26	Ü	ü	As ew in **few**
27	V	v	As *v* in **Vienna**
28	Y	y	As *y* in **yes**
29	Z	z	As *z* in **Zagreb**

In this book, most of the names of the cities and towns are given in accordance with the current English transliteration. All Turkish personal names are given in a standard form—first name followed by the family name. They are also given in accordance with the English language transliteration.

Chronology

329 B.C.	Alexander the Great conquered Anatolia on the way to Persia and Central Asia.
Third–Second centuries B.C.	Greco-Bactrian states in Asia Minor, Persia, and Central Asia.
Second century B.C.	The Great Silk Road starts to function, connecting China with Asia Minor and the Mediterranean.
447	Attila, the ruler of the Hun Empire (believed to be of Turkic origin), defeated the Roman Army on the Vid River and invaded southeastern Europe reaching the outskirts of Constantinople.
453	Attila unexpectedly died during his preparation for another campaign against Constantinople under suspicious circumstances; allegedly, his killing was arranged by the Roman Emperor.
454–455	The Hun Empire disintegrated because of internal strife and defeats in the hands of the Ostrogoths.
552–744	Turk Khanate established in Central Asia.
568–571	War between western Turks and Iran.
582–593	Civil strife between western and eastern Turks.
Seventh century (1st half)	Establishment of ancient Turk alphabet.

622	Beginning of Muslim (Hijra) calendar.
654–683	Muslim Arabs entered into the central Asian region for the first time and clashed with the Turkic armed forces.
751	Battle of Talas; Arab troops, with assistance from the Turkic confederation of Karluks, defeated the Chinese army, bringing central Asia under Muslim control.
861	Turkic slave soldiers killed Caliph al-Mutawakkil in Baghdad area, asserting their influence in the Caliphate.
993?–1063	Togrul Beg, founder of the Turkish Great Seljuk Empire, which at the time of Togrul's death included territories in central Asia, Iran, Iraq, and eastern Anatolia, reigned.
1035–1038	The Great Seljuks defeated the rival Ghaznavids dynasty and conquered Merv, expanding their control to northern Persia.
1055	Togrul Beg defeated the Buwayhids in Baghdad and forced the declining Abbasid Caliphate to accept the Seljuks as military protectors of the Caliphate.
1069–1070	Early Turk poet, Yusuf Balasaguni, created *Kutadgu Bilig* (Knowledge which brings happiness), one of the first literary works in the Turkic language.
1071	Battle of Manzikert (present-day eastern Anatolia); Seljuk Sultan Alp Arslan defeated the Byzantine troops, capturing Byzantine Emperor, Romanos IV Diogenes, and opening the roads for Turkish control in Asia Minor.
1072–1074	Creation of *Divan Lugat at-Turk* (Dictionary of Turk dialects) by Makhmud Kashagari.
1078	Turkish sultan made Nicaea the capital of the Turkish state in Anatolia, renaming it Iznik.
1097–1099	First Crusade; Crusaders defeated the Seljuk.
1176	Battle of Myriokephalon; the Seljuk army, led by Kilich Arslan, defeated the Byzantine army, led by Emperor Manuel I Komnenos.

1204	Fall of Constantinople in the Fourth Crusade, beginning of decline of the Byzantine Empire.
1219–1224	Genghis Khan (also spelled as Chingis Khan, first known as Temujin) turned his war campaign toward Central Asia.
1227	Genghis Khan died during one of his campaigns, but his successors continued the Mongol conquest of the Middle East and eastern Europe.
1243	Battle of Kose Dagh, Mongols defeated the Seljuks.
1299	Osman I declared his independence from the Seljuks and founded the Ottoman kingdom (*Osmanli davleti*), becoming the first sultan of the Ottoman dynasty.
1300	Sultan Osman I defeated Byzantine army.
1327	Sultan Orhan captured Bursa.
1330–1331	Ibn Batuta, great Arab geographer, visited Anatolia.
1370–1384	Central Asian Turkic ruler, Tamerlane (Timur, 1336–1405), attacked Mogulistan and invaded Khorasan.
1394	Ottoman Sultan Bayezid I the Thunderbolt unsuccessfully besieged Constantinople.
1396	Bayezid I defeated an alliance of Christian kings (sometimes referred as the Crusade of Nicopolis) at the Battle of Nicopolis.
1402	Battle of Ankara, Ottoman Sultan Bayezid I was defeated and captured by Tamerlane.
1421	Murad II unsuccessfully besieged Constantinople.
1453	Ottoman Sultan Mehmed II conquered Constantinople, making it the Ottoman capital.
1514	Battle of Caldiran, Ottoman Sultan Selim I defeated Shah Islmail of Persia (present-day Iran).
1517	Sultan Selim I completed conquest of Syria, Egypt, and the Arabian Peninsula.
1520–1566	Sultan Suleiman Magnificent the Lawgiver (*Kanuni* in Turkish) reigned, zenith of the Ottoman Empire.

1529	Ottoman army unsuccessfully besieged Vienna, and was forced to retreat.
1571	Battle of Lepanto; the fleet of the Holy League—an alliance of Spain, Venice, Genoa, and the Papal State formed by Pope Julius II—defeated the Ottoman navy.
1578–1590	War with Persia for control of Armenia, Azerbaijan and Transcaucasus.
1699	Treaty of Karlowitz signed, ending the Ottoman expansion in Europe.
1768–1774	War with Russia. Treaty of Kuchuk Kaynarca.
1773	Naval Technical Academy, which became the Istanbul Technical University in 1944, was founded.
1783	The Russian Empire conquered Crimea.
1789–1807	Sultan Selim III reigned.
1804–1813	Russian-Iranian war, which ended with the defeat of the Iranian army.
1808–1839	Sultan Mahmud II reigned, extensive legal and military reforms were launched.
1813	Russia and Iran signed a peace agreement in Gulistan. The Russian Empire officially acquired Georgia, Daghestan, and Azerbaijan.
1826	Janissaries corps were abolished.
1828–1829	Russo-Turkish War and defeat of the Turkish armies in the Balkans and the Caucasus. The war ended with the peace agreement between Russia and Turkey in Andrion.
1832	Battle of Konya, Egyptian army defeated the Ottomans.
1838–1842	First Anglo-Afghan war.
1839	Ottoman reforms (Tanzimat) initiated by the Rose Garden reform decree.
1839–1861	Sultan Abdulaziz reigned.
1856	Alliance of the Ottoman Empire, France, Great Britain, and the Kingdom of Sardinia defeated the Russian Empire in the Crimean War; the Treaty

	of Paris asserted Turkish control of Moldavia and Wallachia.
1856–1857	British-Persian (Iranian) war for control over Herat and the defeat of Persia. Persian Shah recognized the independence of Herat.
1863	Robert College, which became the Bogazici University in 1973, was founded in Istanbul.
1864	Provincial reorganization.
1869	The *Mecelle* Code was promulgated.
1875	Bosnian peasants rose against the Ottomans, Serbia and Chernogoria (Montenegro) declared war on the Ottomans.
1876	The first Ottoman constitution introduced, first Ottoman elections.
May–August	Sultan Murad V reigned.
1876–1909	Sultan Abdulhamid II reigned.
1877–1878	Russo-Turkish War.
1878	Sultan Abdulhamid II abolishes parliament. Constitution is suspended.
March	Treaty of San Stefano. Turkey recognized the independence of Serbia, Montenegro, Romania, and Bulgaria.
July	Congress of Berlin revised the terms of the Treaty of San Stefano. Austria-Hungary received mandate for two Ottoman provinces: Bosnia and Herzegovina.
1881	Mustafa Kemal (future Mustafa Ataturk) was born in Salonika.
1891	Influential liberal New Literature movement was founded in Istanbul.
1900	Ottoman Darulfunum, which became the Istanbul University in 1933, opened.
1908	The Young Turks Revolution began, Sultan Abdulhamid II restored the constitution.
December	National elections to parliament.

1909	Sultan Abdulhamid II deposed. The Dawn of the Future literary movement founded.
1909–1918	Sultan Mehmed V Resad reigned.
1911	The National Literature Movement founded.
1912–1913	First and Second Balkan Wars; the Ottoman armies defeated, losing its European possessions except Eastern Thrace.
1914–1918	World War I, the Ottoman Empire allied with Germany.
1915	British army landed at Dardanelles, clashed with the Ottomans in Eastern Anatolia.
1917	Sultan Mehmed V Resad hosted German Kaiser Wilhelm II.
	Russian Duma forced the abdication of Tsar Nicolas II, the last tsar of the Russian Empire; the entire Imperial family of Romanovs was executed the following year.
1918	Sultan Mehmed V Resad died.
1918–1922	Sultan Mehmed VI Vahideddin, the 36th and last Ottoman Sultan, reigned.
1919	Mustafa Kemal Pasha landed at Samsun, national congresses at Erzurum and Sivas, the National Pact was signed.
	The beginning of the Turkish War of Independence.
1920	The Anatolian News Agency (AA, *Anadolu Ajansi*) founded.
1921	The Turkish government welcomed Commander Mikhail Frunze sent by the Soviet government to assist the Turkish Republic in the War of Independence.
1922	
August	Battle of Sakarya; Turkish troops defeated the Greek army, reasserting Turkish control over Anatolia and Eastern Thrace.
November	Sultanate was abolished, Sultan Mehmed VI Vahideddin exiled along with the entire royal family.

December	Union of Soviet Socialist Republics (USSR) was established with the capital in Moscow.
1923	Population exchange between Turkey and Greece agreed to at the Lausanne Conference (Switzerland); it affected about two million people, followed by a smaller exchange with Bulgaria.
October	Turkish Republic was established with the capital in Ankara.
1924	Constitution of the Turkish Republic was introduced; first daily newspaper, *Cumhuriyet,* established; Caliphate abolished.
1925	Kurds, led by Sheikh Said, launched uprising in an attempt to gain independence but were defeated.
	Law introduced banning *fez,* religious orders, and some institutions associated with the Caliphate.
1926	Swiss civil code introduced.
1927	First public radio program broadcasted.
1928	New Turkish alphabet based on the Latin script introduced.
1930	Religious uprisings in and near Izmir suppressed.
1934	First five-year plan adopted.
	Turkish women received suffrage.
	Law requiring usage of family name introduced; Turkish Parliament granted the title Ataturk to Mustafa Kemal.
1936	Turkey took part in the Olympic Games for the first time.
1937	Kurdish rebellion in Tunceli suppressed.
1938	Mustafa Kemal (Ataturk) died; General Ismet Inonu elected as second president of the Turkish Republic.
1939–1945	World War II; Turkey declared its neutrality.
1940	Village Institutes, the cornerstones of the Turkish government's rural development project, opened to train teachers for rural schools in Anatolia.
1945	Turkey declared war against Germany and Japan.

1947	Truman Doctrine declared Turkey as area of special strategic interest for the United States against the Soviet threat; the Cold War began.
1948	The independent secular newspaper *Hürriyet* (*Liberty*) founded; it became one of the largest and most influential newspapers in Turkey.
1950	Democratic party won the national elections; Celal Bayar was elected third president of the Turkish Republic.
1952	Turkey joined NATO.
1954	Turkish national soccer team reached finals in the World Soccer Cup.
1955	Turkish writer, Yaşar Kemal, published his classic novel *Memed, My Hawk* (*İnce Memed*).
1959	Republic of Cyprus declared its independence.
	Turkey applied for associate membership in the European Economic Community.
1960	First military coup d'état, National Unity Committee (NUC) formed.
1961	New Turkish constitution adopted, beginning of the Second Republic.
1963	First war in Cyprus between Turkish and Greek Cypriots.
1967	Second war in Cyprus between Turkish and Greek Cypriots.
1970	Necmettin Erbakan founded his first pro-Islamic party in the history of the Republic.
1974	Coup in Cyprus, Turkish troops landed in Cyprus.
1978	
September–December	Mass riots led to sectarian killing of more than 200 people, martial law introduced.
1978	Abdullah Ochalan founded the *Partiya Karkerên Kurdistan* (PKK, Kurdistan Workers Party).
1979	Islamic Revolution in Iran, Soviet army entered Afghanistan.

1980	Military coup d'état, constitution and national parliament suspended.
1981	Military suspended activities of all political parties.
1982	New Turkish constitution adopted, beginning of the Third Republic.
1983	Turgut Ozal was appointed prime minister, beginning of the new economic policy.
1984	Bilkent University, the first private university in Turkey, opened its doors.
1986	The independent newspaper, *Zaman* (Time), founded in Istanbul; within two decades, it became one of the largest newspapers in Turkey.
1989	Turgut Ozal became president of the Republic.
1991	About 500,000 Iraqi Kurds sought refuge in Turkey after the beginning of the first Gulf War.
1992	The central Asian republics became members of the UN, the International Monetary Fund (IMF), and the World Bank. Turkey became one of the first countries to recognize their independence.
1993	Tansu Ciller became the first female prime minister in the history of the Republic.
1995	Pro-Islamic Welfare Party (*Refah Partisi* [*RP*]) won national elections.
1996	Necmettin Erbakan, a leader of the Welfare Party (*Refah Partisi*) became prime minister. The United Nations Educational, Scientific, and Cultural Organization (UNESCO) declared 1996/1997 as the year of Nasreddin Hoca.
1997	National Security Council publicly demanded that politicians strictly follow the secularist principles of the Republic; European Union (EU) rejected Turkey's application for full membership.
1999	Abdullah Ochalan, who led the PKK (Kurdistan Workers Party) activities for more than 20 years, arrested and brought for trial to Turkey.
August	More than 17,000 people died in massive earthquake in northwestern Turkey.

October   CNN TURK, the first Western-style cable news
                            channel, established by *Dogan Medya Grubu* and
                            Time Warner (USA).

2000   President Suleyman Demirel retired. Necdet Sezer
                            became president.

2001   Economic crisis in Turkey. Lira, the Turkish cur-
                            rency, collapsed and Turkish gross domestic product
                            declined more than 10 percent.

November   The Turkish government agreed to contribute troops
                            to the NATO-led International Security and Assis-
                            tance Force (ISAF) in Afghanistan.

2002   Government announced that it would ease some re-
                            strictions on the use of the Kurdish language.

June   The Turkish military took command over the In-
                            ternational Security and Assistance Force (ISAF) in
                            Afghanistan and increased their presence to about
                            1,300 military personnel.

November   The Justice and Development Party (AKP) came to
                            power, winning 34.3 percent of votes in the general
                            parliamentary elections.

2003

March   Turkish parliament rejected proposal to allow U.S.
                            troops to pass through Turkey and to open northern
                            front in the war against Saddam Hussein.

November   Terrorists discharged bombs in Istanbul against syn-
                            agogues, British consulate-general, and a London-
                            based bank.

2004   Turkey signed protocol banning death penalty in all
                            circumstances, thus moving toward harmonizing its
                            legislature with the legal system in the EU. First pri-
                            vate Kurdish language school opened in the town of
                            Batman.

March   The Justice and Development Party (AKP) won local
                            elections.

2006   Ferit Orhan Pamuk, Turkish writer and professor at
                            Columbia University (USA), won the Nobel Prize in
                            literature. Turkish government allowed private chan-
                            nels to air programs in Kurdish language.

June	The EU opened first "negotiating chapters" on Turkey's accession to the Union, which covered such areas as science and research. UNESCO awarded the King Sejong Literacy Prizes to the Turkish Mother–Child Education Foundation.
November	Pope Benedict XVI visited Turkey for the first time urging a "dialogue between Christians and Muslims."
2007	UNESCO celebrated the 800th anniversary of Mawlana Jalaladdin Rumi (1207–1273).
January	Prominent Armenian-Turkish journalist and human rights advocate, Hrant Dink, was assassinated in front of the office of the Armenian-language weekly, *Argos,* in Istanbul. Thousand of Turks demonstrated in Istanbul and Ankara condemning the act of violence.
July	The ruling Justice and Development Party (AKP), led by Prime Minister Recep Tayyip Erdogan, won parliamentary elections, securing 46.6 percent of the votes.
August	Abdullah Gul, of the ruling Justice and Development Party (AKP), was elected eleventh president of Turkey, becoming the first representative of the Islamic organization in this post in the history of the secular Turkish Republic.
November	U.S. President George W. Bush met Prime Minister Recep Tayyip Erdogan and called for expanding political and military cooperation between the two countries and offered to share with Turkey the U.S. intelligence on "terrorist organizations."
2008	
January	Draft of the new constitution of the Turkish Republic presented to the public; however, the head of the Constitutional Court warned that there was no need for introducing the new constitution. Turkey experienced one of the coldest winters in living memory with heavy snowfall in many areas of the country, including Ankara and Istanbul.
February	The Turkish Air Force crossed the border with Iraq and bombed targets allegedly controlled by the PKK groups.

March	The Sixth Bursa Book Fair organized in cooperation with the Turkish Publishers Association.
July	The Constitutional Court dismissed the legal case that alleged that the governing AK Party's (Justice and Development Party or *Adalet ve Kalkınma Partisi* in Turkish) actions have violated and undermined the secular Turkish constitution.
October	A trial began against eighty-six suspected members of an underground political group (so-called *Ergenekon*) accused of plotting a series of attacks and a military coup against the incumbent Turkish government.
2009	UNESCO celebrated the 400th anniversary of the birth of the Katip Çelebi (1609–1657), Turkish historian, scholar, writer.

1

Land, People, and History

Any great nation with an imperial past has much to regret and much to celebrate... But great empires were great because of their lasting achievements—
the Ottoman contribution to art, architecture, education, legal institutions, and
charitable foundations remains underappreciated.[1]
> —Prof. Gerald MacLean, historian

A PERSON STANDING on the Bosporus Bridge in Istanbul is actually standing
on a unique artery that connects two continents—Asia and Europe. This is a
great observation point to admire heavy European-style ancient and medieval
castles and palaces, colorful and magnificent mosques, the Ottoman Empire's
architectural masterpieces, and elegantly flying modern skyscrapers. This is
an important transportation corridor, which millions of cars and tens of millions of people cross to-and-fro every year. At the same time, it is a fragile
link because even the smallest accident can halt the whole route and stop the
movement of goods, passengers, and services and affect the lives of countless
numbers of people.

In a sense, the Bosporus Bridge is a symbol of modern Turkey—a new
country on an ancient land. At the beginning of the new millennium, Turkey
is a country of about 71 million people (2008, official est.) rapidly sailing to
the 100th anniversary of the establishment of the Turkish Republic, which
will be celebrated in 2023. It has one of the most dynamic economies in the
Mediterranean Sea basin and a bustling cultural environment that attracts
a speedily increasing number of tourists. Turkey connects Asia and Europe

Pamukkale is one of the natural wonders in Turkey: the mineral-rich waters drip down the hills, forming snow-white colored stalactites and numerous mineral water pools. Courtesy of the author, 2007.

through myriads of obvious and invisible links and personal ties, including large pipelines that pump central Asian, Russian, and Middle Eastern oil and gas to the Western markets. At the same time, it is a frontier state that borders restless war-torn Iraq and troublesome Iran. It is a largely Muslim country, where the government strongly supports the U.S.-led war on international terrorism, and where, at the same time, small political groups display their disapproval of the pro-Western policies and Western values. It is truly the land of contrasts and controversies. But most of all, Turkey is a country of rapid changes that constantly transform the social, economic, and cultural landscapes of the country. It is a country where one year of development is often equal to ten years of development in some other countries. To understand Turkey, one has to understand its diversity, its historical and cultural heritage, and the directions where the numerous changes take the country.

PEOPLE

The population of Turkey is estimated at about 71 million people (2008) up from about 14 million people in 1927 (1927 census). The population

Seaport in Antalya. Courtesy of the author, 2007.

is comparable in size to that of France or of the states of California, New York, and Texas combined. It is expected that the population figure will grow by about 30 million people within next twenty to thirty years, and so will exceed 100 million people around 2040, if the reproduction rate of the 1990s remains unchanged. If the current population were equally divided over the country, the average population density would be about 236 people per square mile (or about ninety-one per square kilometer). However, the average population density in eastern Anatolia is about one-quarter of the national average, while the Istanbul metropolitan area is the most densely populated area in southern Europe (about 16,500 people per square mile (or 6,600 per square kilometer).

A foreigner in the middle of Istanbul, Ankara, Izmir, Antalya, or any other large city would be overwhelmed by the diversity of the ethnic backgrounds, color, cultures, languages, and language dialects. His first questions would be: Who are the Turks? How does the country bring together people of so many unique cultures and regional backgrounds? What unites them and makes them distinctively Turkish?

One of the simplified perceptions of Turks is that of people of the ancient large and powerful nomadic empires of central Eurasia that, with triumph, marched through central Asia, the Caspian region, and Persia all the way to Anatolia while establishing their new homeland and a mighty empire that included Asia Minor, southeastern Europe, Caucasus, the Middle East and north Africa. A careful examination, however, of the formation of the Turkish nation reveals a more complex picture. The Turks did establish their kingdoms, such as the Seljuk State, and one of the most powerful empires in their era, the Ottoman Empire[2] and did form the core of the ruling class, military, and civil elite. At the same time, they displayed great skills and passion in incorporating numerous other tribes, ethnic and cultural groups, and local communities and elites in and around the Seljuk State and later in and around the Ottoman state.

As long as individuals and communities pledged loyalty to the Ottoman rulers and accepted the political system, they became a part of the "Ottoman family": this was not unusual when members of the ethnic and religious minorities and representatives of local elite achieved the highest positions in the Ottoman government, army, and administration. In this regard, for many centuries the Ottoman state was a melting pot, where people of central Asian, Middle Eastern, north African, and European origins interacted and lived with each other, married, befriended, quarreled, and competed to form a bubbling Ottoman society; in this regard, it was very similar to the United States in the twentieth century.

However, a series of political missteps in domestic affairs and devastating defeats in the international arena in the early twentieth century, combined with the polarization of the society and the rise of nationalism and religious intolerance among various ethnic groups, led to the most humiliating catastrophe in the Turkish history—the collapse of the empire. Not only was the political order threatened, but the very existence of the Turkish nation was in peril. The Turks managed to save their state and their nation by reestablishing many of their institutions, concepts, and identity on very different terms.

The national trauma of those days forced the founders of the Turkish Republic to emphasize the strengthening of the unity, the centralization of state control over all aspects of life, and the importance of a strong national identity bound around some important symbols, such as language, loyalty to the state and to the Turkish land, and to the founding principles. Under these conditions, throughout the twentieth century, Turkey accepted hundreds of thousands—some Turkish scholars claim millions—of refugees from the Balkans, Crimea, central Asia, the Caucasus, and the Middle East. Even today, Turkish schoolchildren start their days with the pledge to Turkishness, and every adult man is obliged to undergo a compulsory military service, where he pledges to defend every inch of Turkish land.

REGIONS AND REGIONAL IDENTITIES

A well-organized network of highways takes travelers to the heart of Turkey in western Anatolia and to the farthest corners of the country. Not only do these roads reveal the breathtaking scenery and beautiful landscapes, but also a remarkable regional diversity to which the souls and identities of many Turks are strongly attached.

Turkey, located just to the south of the Black Sea, almost 1,000 miles (about 1,400 kilometers) long from the east to the west; and more than 300 miles (about 500 kilometers) long from north to south. The size of the country is 300,847 square miles (or about 780,000 square kilometers), roughly the size of the state of Texas, or the combined areas of Spain and the United Kingdom. The Turkish borders were established only after the end of the War of Independence in 1923. Thus, many areas—that had for centuries been a part of the Ottoman Empire culturally and politically—were divided between different countries: Georgia and Armenia in the northeast, Iran in the east, Iraq in the southeast, Syria in the south, and Bulgaria and Greece in the northwest.[3]

Most of the territory of Turkey is located in the Asia Minor or Anatolia, which the Turks call Anadolu (from the Greek word *Anatole*—the land of the rising sun). A small area that constitutes about 3 percent of the Turkish territory is situated on the European continent. Hundreds of small and large mountains, rivers, lakes, and sea bays form its extremely diverse geographic topography. This diversity, in turn, is reflected in the regional dialects of the spoken Turkish language, the cuisines, the artistic styles, and the folk traditions. The seven major areas in Turkey from the west to the east are: (1) Eastern Thrace and the Sea of Marmara, (2) the Aegean, (3) western Anatolia, (4) Mediterranean, (5) Black Sea coast, (6) central Anatolia and Cappadoccia, and (7) eastern Anatolia.

The eastern Thrace region lies in the Balkan Peninsular, and it is separated from the rest of Turkey by the water chain of the Bosporus, the Sea of Marmara, and the Dardanelles. The proximity to the warm sea and the abundance of the drinking water in the Maritsa River, enhanced by the mild Mediterranean weather, makes this area highly suitable for agriculture, including high-quality grape production. It is also an attractive holiday destination for the inhabitants of Istanbul and international tourists. This region is where Istanbul is located; it is the largest metropolitan center not only in Turkey but also in southern Europe. Local people love to highlight that they live in "Europe" and are the guardians of the Turkey's European traditions.

The Aegean region is situated on the western coast of Anatolia. The mild climate formed by the Aegean Sea makes this region one of the most livable

The typical landscape in Cappadoccia. Courtesy of the author, 2007.

areas in the country. No wonder it is one of the most heavily populated regions in the country, and Izmir, the third largest city in Turkey, sits in the center of the region, right on the costal area. A series of mountain ranges that run from the east to the west form spectacular scenes and break the area into several broad valleys. The region's main attractions are the many ancient classical-era sites and picturesque villages and towns that attract art lovers and experts in antiquity.

Western Anatolia is located in the heart of the country on the semiarid plateau at an elevation between 1,000 and 2,000 feet above sea level (300–600 meters). The people of this area endure the dry continental climate with hot summers and cold winters. The region is home to Ankara, the nation's capital and second largest city, and to Konya, one of the capitals of the early Seljuk state. Large and dry valleys are suitable for animal husbandry, and many locals make a living herding cattle, sheep, and goats. An intensive irrigation system allows farmers to grow barley, corn, tobacco, fruit, poppies, and various vegetables.

The Mediterranean region is separated from other parts of Turkey by the Taurus Mountains that reach about 6,000 to 9,000 feet above the sea level (about 1,800–2,750 meters) protecting a long narrow strip of land from the

Fanciful churches and houses carved in the soft rock of the mountains of Cappadoccia. Courtesy of the author, 2007.

cold northern winds. Many Turks call this area "our tropical paradise," as the climate is very mild and pleasant; and it is excellent for growing various tropical and subtropical fruits, including bananas, figs, grapes, mandarins, and oranges. In fact, the city of Antalya—one of the most prominent tourist destinations in the area—adopted oranges as its regional symbol. Hot summers with temperatures ranging between 90°F and 100°F (32°C–37°C) attract people from all over Turkey and eastern Europe to its beaches and affordable resorts.

The Black Sea coast is stretched for about 500 miles (800 kilometers) from the east to the west and consists of long and narrow costal plains backed up by the heavily forested Pontic Ranges. This is an important agricultural area where Turkey's largest rivers—the Sakarya and the Kizilirmak—provide plenty of water for agricultural activities. This area is famous for its high-quality tobacco, tea, and hazelnuts.

Central Anatolia and Cappadoccia is a completely landlocked area in the central part of the country. Its average elevation is about 1,000 to 2,000 feet above sea level (300–600 meters). This is a traditionally agricultural area where people grow various cereal crops, sunflower, sugar beets, grapes, and various vegetables. Its population is scattered around small cities and towns, the largest of which is Kayseri (500,000 people), Yozgat (200,000 people), and Aksaray (150,000 people).

Eastern Anatolia, which borders Georgia, Armenia, and Iran, is the most sparsely populated area of Turkey east of central Anatolia. Moderately elevated mountains dominate this region, which has a relatively dry continental climate. The highest peak in the country—Mt. Agri Dagi (biblical Mt. Ararat) is located here, and it is a source of two greatest rivers of the Middle East— the Tigris and the Euphrates. This is a predominantly agricultural area with probably the lowest average incomes in the country, where people still rely on growing cereals and vegetables and on animal husbandry. Eastern Anatolia holds the Turkish record of being the coldest region in the country—snow and ice remain on the mountain peaks well into the middle of the summer. It is home to the largest ethnic minority in Turkey—the Kurds, and the area that they dominate is also sometimes called Kurdistan.

The regional affiliations and loyalties have traditionally played a significant role in Turkish politics and culture and in forming the Turkish regional identities. When friends and colleagues come together, they still start their conversations by discussing their regional origins or guessing the regional background of each other by their regional accents. Many Turkish anecdotes revolve around the regional cultural differences and identify some characters (e.g., entrepreneurship, slow thinking) with specific region. However, during the last decades, these regional identities have notably weakened because of the large migration from small cities and towns to large metropolitan areas and to foreign countries due to the increasing mobility of the Turkish society.

LANGUAGES

Modern Turkish language has played a great role in stitching together numerous regional and subregional groups and clans and in building and strengthening the modern Turkish identity.[4] Although many communities in Turkey speak different dialects and some of them, such as Arabs, Armenians, Greeks, Kurds, and many others might speak their own languages at home, all of them communicate with each other in the modern Turkish language.

Turkish language belongs to the Turkic group of the Altaic language family. All together, there are between 160 and 200 million people on the Eurasian continent who speak about thirty languages that belong to this group. Some of them—such as Azeri, spoken in Azerbaijan and northern Iran, and Turkmen, spoken in Turkmenistan and northern Iraq—are very close to the modern Turkish and can be easily understood by the Turks. Others—like Bashkir, Kazakh, Kyrgyz, Tatar, Uigur, and Uzbek—are distantly related to the Turkish and require significant effort for the Turks to understand. Some scholars claim that one of the most distant cousins of the Turkish language is Mongol; but it is as distant as classical Latin is from modern English.[5]

The Turkish language experienced significant transformation in the twentieth century through the changes of the script and codification of grammar and vocabulary. Until 1928, the Turkish language was based on modified Arabic script, often called Ottoman script. In fact, many members of the Ottoman royal family and poets of the Ottoman government (*Divan*) were traditionally fluent in Arabic and used Persian (Farsi language) in the palaces and in administration. The Ottoman-era Turkish used a lot of loanwords from Persian and Arabic in everyday conversations. Since the mid-nineteenth century, many military officials and members of the young westernized intelligentsia have brought in a number of expressions that are of French, German, Italian, and English origins. Turkey's first president Mustafa Kemal initiated radical reforms and established the Turkish Language Association (TDK, *Turk Dil Kurumu*) in 1932 that was probably modeled after the French Academy (*Académie Française*).

The main task of these reforms was the standardization of the modern Turkish language (as opposed to the traditional or "old" Ottoman language) through modification of the vocabulary by replacing Arabic and Persian loanwords with their Turkish equivalents, especially in technical, military, and everyday terminology. The TDK exercised significant power and influence, as it went as far as banning the usage of many words of the Arabic and Persian origin in the press, the government administration, and the public education system. During the first seventy years of its existence, the association succeeded in reshaping both everyday and technical vocabulary to such a degree that the first speech of the founding farther of the nation—Mustafa Kemal delivered in Turkish in 1920s had to be "translated" into modern Turkish in the 1990s. The general public and intelligentsia have sometimes rejected the TDK's artificial requests: for example, the Turkish word "firka" (political party) did not work well with the public and many people preferred to use the word "parti" instead. Some representatives of the older generation used the words inherited from the Ottoman era, while most of the younger Turks, who grew up learning and speaking the modern Turkish language, knew nothing better.

The association also succeeded in noticeably weakening the regional dialects by replacing them with the Istanbul dialect that was adopted as a backbone for the standardized modern Turkish language. The dialects do still exist in modern Turkey, for example, the strong Karadeniz dialect in the Black Sea region and Dogu spoken in eastern Anatolia. In a recent trend, young people in Istanbul and members of the Turkish immigrant communities in the United Kingdom and United States often heavily interpolate English words into their youth slang, creating colloquial "Turkinglish," while their counterparts in

Austria and Germany borrow German words, creating the so-called Turko-Deutsche slang.[6]

As was noted above, not all citizens of Turkey speak Turkish as their first language. The largest non-Turkish language spoken in the country is the Kurdish language. It belongs to the Indo-European language group and is mostly spoken in the southeastern provinces of Anatolia. For many decades, the Turkish government enforced the usage of Turkish language by Kurd minority. In fact, the demand for an education in the Kurdish language in Kurd-populated areas was among the driving forces that have been fueling the tensions between Turkish and Kurdish communities for many decades. Only in the 2000s did the Turkish government soften its stand allowing teaching and broadcasting in the Kurdish language in the Kurdish-dominated areas. There are no exact numbers, but several estimates claim that between 8 million and 15 million people or between 11 and 20 percent of the population of Turkey speak or understand Kurdish language.

There are also very small communities that speak Arabic, Armenian, Greek, Hebrew, Farsi, and some other languages. These communities are very small, and it is estimated that the population of each is between 5,000 and 25,000 people.

HISTORY

Intellectual debates about modern Turkish history and about the Turks very often selectively turn to the historical facts. As in many modern countries, the mainstream historians in Turkey glorify the historical achievements and write the history of their nation from their own perspective, because, in the words of British historian Gerald MacLean, "writing is always a political act, and this is seldom truer than in the case of writing about and in the Turkish Republic."[7] However, unlike in many Western countries, the central government in Ankara, for a long time, has been proactive in interpreting the past events and funding historical research as a part of its modern nation-state and identity building. Therefore, for many decades, the main emphasis was given to the history of the establishment of the modern Turkish Republic and the life and deeds of its founder.

In a recent trend, the intellectuals and the general public were freed of many imposed restrictions and began rediscovering Turkey's past. A quick trip to a popular bookstore in Istanbul will reveal a huge public interest in historical issues—the bookshelves are filled with the historical works both translated from other languages and written by local scholars and intellectuals. Turkey, with all of its architectural and historical monuments, is an open history textbook. The Turks, like people in many other developing countries, feel quite uneasy with the Western eurocentric interpretation of history.[8] After all, for the Turks, the defeat from the crusaders in the early eleventh century represents tragic pages in the Seljuk history, while the conquest of Constantinople and crash of the Byzantine Empire are the greatest achievements of the Ottoman Empire, and the Western textbooks often present opposite views of the same historical events.

By and large, the current intellectual debates and public interests in the history of Turkey revolve around four major issues: (1) the emergence and origin of the Turks; (2) the rise of the early Turkic kingdoms and establishment of the early Ottoman statehood; (3) the era of achievements of the "magnificent empire" of the Ottomans; and (4) the founding and building of the modern Turkish Republic.

EMERGENCE OF TURKS AND THE GREAT SILK ROAD

The history of early Turks began far from the territory of modern Turkey and in a very different setting. Most Turks trace their ancestor's homeland to central Eurasia, to the territory that is now on the crossroads of Russia's Altai and western Siberia, northern Mongolia, and northeastern China. This is a mystical land of Turan, where the early Turkic tribes emerged by fighting off their mortal enemies, as legends state, with support of Mother Earth and the Sky God. Gradually, they grew in numbers, strengthened, and began expanding by conquering close and far-away territories. Precise dates of ancient Turkic tribal confederations and their legendary khanates are still debated by scholars because the early Turks left very few written records, and archeologists have just begun discovering magnificent burial grounds of the early Turks' leaders. The prevailing scholarly views date the emergence of the early notable Turkic tribal protostates to around the third to fifth centuries A.D., although recently central Asian scholars argued that the early Turkic khanates can be dated between the second century B.C. and second century A.D.

The early Turks were engaged in nomadic and seminomadic animal husbandry in the enormous steppe and forested-steppe zone of Central Eurasia that was quite unsuitable for settled agriculture. The nomads domesticated and raised horses, sheep, goats, and probably bulls, which provided leather and wool for clothing and nomadic housing—*yurts* (traditional round tents), and meat and milk for everyday food staples. In addition, they were engaged in hunting and probably knew metalwork, may be even ironwork. The nomads have been very good horseback riders—they had to move around constantly because large herds quickly consumed the available grass and bushes.

These nomads had never been isolated from their settled neighbors and regularly traded and bartered goods with them. The expansion of this trade from China to Europe gave birth to the Great Silk Road, which was named after the silk exports that Chinese secretive producers had monopolized for centuries. Not only silk but jade, spices, and luxury goods were exported to many states and empires on the Eurasian continent, including the Byzantine Empire, the Persian Empire, and the Middle Eastern powers through this road. The Turks benefited from this trade in two ways. First, the Turks found themselves profiting immensely from the huge demand for horses, particularly for cavalry horses, as this demand spiraled with the rise of centralized states and large armies in China and Central Asia; and for horses and bulls for transportation purposes. Second, the Turks benefited from the trade by taxing the long-distance international and regional caravans, providing military convoys, buying or bartering advance weaponry, and accumulating knowledge about the world around them.

Between the second and fourth centuries A.D. or even earlier, the Turkic-speaking tribal confederations began their expansions by spreading out in all directions and increasing their control over vast territories captured from the neighbors. On some occasions, they moved temporarily into the conquered cities and towns and later returned to their familiar environment. On many occasions, however, they stayed. Scholars still debate the reasons that triggered and stimulated these moves of large groups of the population, including the usual suspects, such as demographic and environmental factors, changing social structures and military organizations, and the formation of classes. Sometimes, scholars also point out the exceptional military and political advantages of the nomadic states and the talents of individual rulers (khans and khagans). These migrations became particularly large between the fourth and seventh centuries, when numerous Turkic-speaking tribes reached the farthest corners of the Eurasian continent. One such tribe—the Huns—crossed the Eurasian steppe and established their stronghold in central Europe by defeating all their enemies on the Volga, Dnepr, and Danube rivers and by clashing with the most powerful empire of that era—the Romans. The Huns led by ambitious rulers defeated the Ostrogoths and the Wisigoths. Under the rule of the talented general and ruler Attila (?– 453 A.D.), the Huns threatened the very existence of the Byzantine Empire. Attila's troops crashed the best legions of the Empire on a number of occasions, and the Emperor was forced to agree on Attila's marriage to his daughter. It seemed inevitable that Constantinople, the capital of the Eastern Roman Empire, would fall to the Turkic-speaking Huns by the 450s. Only the sudden death of King Attila (who was allegedly poisoned by the Romans) in 453 and the consequent disintegration of the Huns' empire saved Constantinople from an imminent collapse.

The essence of the success of nomadic, seemingly "barbaric" and disorganized armies that relied on mounted warriors was in the enormous comparative advantage of the mobile cavalry in the military warfare of that era.

The ruins of the ancient Roman arena in western Turkey. Courtesy of the author, 2007.

They used both the high maneuverability of their light cavalry and the high effectiveness of their weaponry, namely composite curved bows. They had huge, practically professional, armies at their disposals because their societies were extremely militarized, and every nomad, from early childhood, learned horseback-riding, archery, and use of other military weaponry. In addition, the steppe provided a nearly endless supply of the equivalent of the military SUVs of that era—the horses. In a sharp contrast to professional troops in settled areas, these armies could be maintained cheaply because they were based on a compulsory enlistment and they were easy to dismantle upon completion of a campaign; though, once started, the khans were constantly pressed to continue their military operations by their ambitious and greedy generals.

Between the sixth and ninth centuries, the ruthless Turkic rulers began a systematic conquest of northern China, central Asia, and the Eurasian steppe between the Syr Darya and Volga rivers. More than a dozen of large and small nomadic empires emerged in these areas, and the Turks began moving into the conquered territories with their families and herds, setting up their temporary and permanent military bases in a close proximity to the major trading and political centers. By the ninth to the eleventh centuries, the Turkic-speaking groups firmly established themselves in central Asia and raided the Caucasus, Persia, and some areas in Asia Minor. Because the political situation in the homeland remained uncertain and many tribal leaders continued to fight each other for wealth, power, and influence, some Turks decided to settle in central Asia permanently, making it their new home.

Around the same time, one very important event radically changed the history of the Turks. The Turkic rulers, who traditionally followed shamanistic belief system with a complex hierarchy of gods and goddesses, began converting to Islam en masse. In the past, various Turkic rulers experimented with Buddhism, Manichaeism, and even eastern Christianity. This time, however, the newly adapted religious system took deeper roots not only among the Turkic aristocrats, but also among commoners. The conversion to Islam had changed the status of the Turks among the other Central Asians and Persians. They turned from being the political outsiders and the religious enemies to being political insiders and religious associates, which opened the roads to the Middle East and the Caucasus.

Many rulers around the Muslim world from Herat and Nishapur to Damascus, Baghdad, and Cairo were very impressed by Turks' military skills and bravery and rushed to hire them for their personal armies. On many occasions, they simply bought young boys, soldiers, or even whole regiments at slave bazaars or got them to serve as personal slaveguards (*gulyams*) in royal guards or palace troops. These professional troops proved to be very effective in fighting small and large military campaigns against various contenders for thrones and against the mortal enemies, such as the Byzantine Empire. Yet, they also proved to be very dangerous for their rulers in time of peace because ambitious slave-officers frequently wanted the power for themselves or for princes whom they could control and manipulate.

In the meantime, back in central Asia, the Great Seljuk Empire emerged and transformed yet again the pace of the regional and world history. This empire eventually grew powerful enough to have a notable impact on Persia, the Fertile Crescent, and the Byzantine Empire. In the late tenth century Seljuk-Bey[9] (ruled c. 990–1038), the legendary founder of the Empire, led a large confederation of Turkic clans away from the ruling Oghuz tribal group and established his stronghold in the southwestern areas of Central Asia. Gradually Seljuk-Bey and his successors became involved into the dynastic struggle in the Persian Empire and established their control over what is now the northern Iran. In 1055, Togrul-Bey (ruled c. 1038–1063) captured Baghdad forcing the Caliph, the spiritual leader of the Muslim world, to bestow a title of sultan upon him and his successors. By establishing control over Persia and part of the Caucasus, the Great Seljuks began their expansion to the west directly colliding with the Byzantine Empire over the control of Syria, Palestine, and Anatolia. Sultan Alp-Arslan (ruled 1063–1072) fought a large

and heavily armed Byzantine army at the Battle of Manzikent in 1071 and utterly defeated the Romans and even captured Emperor Romanus IV Diogenes
(1068–1071). This was one of the decisive battles in world history that led to
the ultimate demise of the Byzantine Empire and the rise of the Ottomans.
Within twenty to thirty years after the battle, the Turkic generals established
numerous principalities (called *beyliks* or *begliks*) throughout Anatolia. Many
Turkic soldiers and officers moved into the region along with their extended
families or took local wives and settled among Armenians, Greeks, and others.
Internecine quarrels and political instability undermined the Great Seljuks,
and they lost control over the Holy Land during the First Crusade (1096–
1099). Sultan Ahmed Sanjar (ruled 1118–c. 1153) was able to defeat the Second Crusade (1145–1149), but he could not prevent the disintegration of the
Empire.

Although the religious identity had been strong among all ethnic groups in
Anatolia, and the wars that Crusaders constantly waged were initiated under
the religious banner, people throughout Anatolia managed to tolerate each
other and to live in peace. Gradually, the Turks became very much a part of the
local landscape to the extent that they frequently allied themselves with either
crusaders' states or Byzantine in their feudal quarrels and wars or were called
by the crusaders or Byzantine princes (and even by the Byzantine emperors)
to help in their never-ending brawls for power against and influence over each
other.

RISE OF EARLY TURKISH KINGDOMS AND ESTABLISHMENT
OF THE OTTOMAN STATE

By the twelfth century the Seljuk Sultanate of Anatolia (also called Sultanate
of Rum Seljuks)—one of the sucessors to the Great Seljuks—became one of
the most notable kingdoms in Anatolia, although probably not the most powerful. Arturks, Danimeshmendis, Mengujegs and others contended Seljuks for
power, but Seljuk rulers proved to be the most successful in the long run.

In the meantime, their archenemy and frequent ally—the Byzantine
Empire—experienced a mortal blow from which it had never recovered. In
1204, the knights and mercenaries of the Fourth Crusade (1202–1204) seized
Constantinople and stripped it of almost all of its treasures, when the marauding knights destroyed a number of orthodox Christian churches and monasteries, killing thousands of people and looting the valuables. The crusaders
ruled for just over fifty years but during their reign the city experienced ir-
reparable decay, loosing most of its industries, skilled craftsmen, and traders
and a significant portion of its population. Constantinople had never recovered to its past glories until the Ottoman era.

The Turks also experienced their military downfall. In 1243, the Mongols led by Genghis Khan utterly destroyed the Seljuk army at the Battle of Kose Dagh, sacking and pillaging Sivas, Kaysery, and many other cities. Genghis Khan appointed his grandson Hulegu as the ruler of the area south of the Caspian and Black seas. Hulegu stormed Baghdad, capital of Abbasid Caliphate, and put to death the last Abbasid caliph. However, as Hulegu concentrated his troops on the territory of what is now Iran and Iraq, the Turks of Anatolia began reviving their fortune, strengthened by numerous Turkic refugees from Central Asia, northern Persia (Iran), and the Caucasus. The newcomers, who were much less tolerant to representatives of other ethnic and religious groups, readily confiscated the land of Christian churches and monasteries and distributed it among the refugees or the Islamic endowments (*waqf*) that supported mosques and dervish lodges.

By the beginning of the fourteenth century, Turkic rulers, particularly Osman-Bey (1258–1326) and his son Orhan-Bey Gazi (1284–1359), felt that they were strong enough to begin consolidating their powers and expanding their territories. Tradition holds that Osman was the founder of the dynasty and the Empire; thus the Turks always called the state *Osmanli Devleti* (the State of Osman). Osman-Bey, whom Ottoman historians called the "bone-breaker" for his determination and energy, defeated Byzantine forces at the Battle of Nicaea in 1301, and captured Ephesus and the important city-port Bursa in 1326. Orhan-Bey I defeated the Byzantine troops at the Battle of Pelekanon in 1329 and sent his army to capture Nicaea in 1331, Berghama and Karasi (Mysia) in 1336, and Nicomedia in 1337. Orhan-Bey became also deeply involved in the Byzantine politics and readily sent his soldiers to participate in various quarrels between different political parties and contenders to the throne. In 1347, Orhan-Bey even married the emperor's young daughter Theodora. During his reign, the Turks frequently campaigned in southern Europe, and they even established their strongholds there by conquering Trympe (Cinbi) in 1356 and Gallipoli in 1354.

Murad-Bey, who succeeded Orhan-Bey I, further expanded his power by establishing control over eastern Thrace and destroying joint Macedonian-Serbian army at the Maritsa River in 1371 and by capturing Sofia in 1385 and Salonika in 1387. He also led his army to defeat a coalition of Balkan armies at the Battle of Kosovo in 1389. By the 1390s, the Ottomans controlled most of the Balkans and even forced the Byzantine Emperor to pay them tributes. The Ottoman ruler Beyazid I the Thunderbolt (*Yıldırım*, ruled 1389–1402), successfully destroyed the Crusade of Nicopolis in 1396 and won many battles in eastern Europe. Yet, in 1402, he was taken prisoner and spent a humiliating time in the court of Tamerlain, Amir (ruler) of Samarqand.

The ruins of ancient Ephesus. Courtesy of the author, 2007.

The Era of Achievements

It took several decades for the Ottomans to recover from the defeat at the hands of Tamerlain. The Ottomans effectively fought various Anatolian feudal lords (*beys*), rulers of Balkan principalities, and Byzantine generals and princes. As their military skills grew stronger, they became ready to challenge their main adversary, the Romans, once and for all.

Sultan Mehmet II the Conqueror (*Fatih*)[10] (1432–1481), whom Turks also called Fatih Sultan Mehmet, at the age of twenty-one, led the Ottoman army in the greatest battle of all times—the siege of the city of Constantinople in 1453. The fortifications of the capital of the Byzantine Empire relied on the genius achievements of engineering thoughts of the Middle Ages and many people believed that its walls were simply insuperable to their enemies. The city was protected by thick brick walls fortified with towers and surrounded by a deep moat filled with water. From the sea, it was protected against attacks by huge iron chains that prevented ships from coming close to the city waterfront. According to the chronicles of that era, the city walls, however, suffered from many years of neglect, while its greatly diminished population had no fighting spirit due to the decades of economic stagnation, interdynastic wars, corruption, and over-taxing. The army that defended the city was underpaid for years and suf-fered from low discipline and morale. Yet, all these factors did not make the task even a grade easier and it was the military brilliance of Mehmet II and his generals, who organized an overnight bridge and orchestrated a sudden attack on the weakest walls of the city that brought the ultimate victory.

This was a symbolic victory that instantaneously turned the Ottoman state and its ruling dynasty into one of the most respected powers in Europe, as the Ottomans inherited thousands of years of the Roman Empire's glory and prestige. Some chronicles reported that to boost his legitimacy and stature, Mehmet II claimed, among other things, the title of Emperor of Rome (*Kayse-i-Rum*). In fact, he and his royal family did have close blood lineage to the Byzantine Imperial family due to numerous intermarriages during a century of close interaction. With assumption of the title, the Sultan also declared himself the protector of Eastern (Orthodox) Church in his state. He immedi-ately transferred his capital to Constantinople and soon renamed it Istanbul. He also carried out several actions to stimulate the economic recovery of the city by repopulating it not only with the Turks, but also with representatives of other subjects of the empire.

After successfully storming the capital of the Roman Empire, Mehmet II continued consolidation of his control over both Anatolia and southern Europe. In a series of battles, he subdued the separatist-minded principalities (*beyliks*) of eastern Anatolia, destroyed the Trebizond Kingdom on the Black Sea, and took on the powerful Turcoman tribal confederation of the White Sheep group (*Akkoyunlu,* also *Aq Qouynlu*).[11] In Europe, his army captured Belgrade in 1456, Orlanto in 1480, and later some other cities and territories.

Mehmet II's successors proved to be as capable leaders who strengthened and expanded the empire's territory by capturing realms in Asia Minor, de-feating armies of Persian Shi'a rulers, and expanding their influence to the Crimean Peninsular and then further to the steppe north of the Black Sea. One among the most priced possessions of the Ottoman Empire was the cap-ture of Arab Peninsular and most sacred centers of the Islamic civilization—the cities of Mecca and Medina. Thus, the Ottoman rulers became also the caliphs of the whole Muslim world.

For about three centuries, from the early 1500s to the mid 1700s, the Ottoman Empire remained one of the world's most magnificent and powerful empires. With different level of success it battled many Western European powers, and effectively controlled the entire Balkans, parts of central and southern Europe, the Middle East from Egypt all the way to the borders of Persia. The empire also regularly clashed with the Persian Shahs in the east and

Russian tsars in the north for power, influence, and control over the trade and resources. Many rulers and generals of that era trembled at a simple mention of potential battles with the Ottoman forces.

The power and influence of the Ottomans was built on the effective-for-its-era administrative, political, and military systems of the empire. The administrative and legal systems were systematized by Sultan Suleyman I the Lawgiver (*Kanuni*, ruled 1520–1566). Under his order and supervision of imperial Council (*Divan*), the state employed jurists who codified the legal foundation for functioning of all important institutions of the state. This corpus of sultans' decrees and Islamic jurists' interpretation of Islamic Law (*Shariah*) provided legal frameworks for law and order in the state by regulating and protecting the rights of the inhabitants of the empire—the nobility and the ordinary people. Like *Magna Carta* of England, these laws also established some limitations on the sultans' powers, although it was not a constitution in its modern meaning. In the center of the political system was the royal court, whose members (including women) were involved in the administration of the state affairs. The sultan was advised by the imperial *Divan*, a cabinet-like institution that directed political, judiciary, financial, and administrative functions of the government. It was led by the Grand Vizier (*Vazīr-e Azam*), who chaired the Council in the absence of the sultan and managed day-to-day duties.

In political terms, one of the most important institutions was the semiautonomous millet system. Most of the subjects of the state were divided and governed according to the religious affiliations. The caliph was a leader of all Muslims and "protector" and "enforcer" of Islamic law and Islamic teaching. Christian and Jewish communities were led by their religious and community leaders who regulated internal affairs of the communities, their relations with the Ottoman state, the development of education, and various religious duties (baptisms, weddings, funerals, etc.)

The Ottomans built a powerful standing army that included an infantry, a cavalry, and a navy. The core of the military system was the Janissaries, privileged professional-type infantry units. The Ottomans filled the ranks of the Janissaries and some ranks in the palace and provinces through a special system of an extraordinary levy on the Christian population in the Balkans called the *devsirme* (pronounced dev-shir-me). Every year, a certain number of young healthy boys were taken away from their families and sent to Anatolia to be converted to Islam, and to undergo vigorous training and education.[12] Upon graduation, they entered the state system for life (thus many Western scholars compared this system to state-endorsed slavery). The *devsirme* system intended to create a ruling class loyal exclusively to the sultan, the royal family, and the state; but it was done at the very high cost of separating children from their parents and destroying the lives of many families. Enforced by a professional corps of trained officers and a vigorous training system, the Ottoman army remained among the best in the region in terms of military discipline and organization. Nevertheless, by the early eighteenth century, its military equipment and tactics became outdated compared to the most of the Western European armies. The Ottoman navy was among the largest in the Mediterranean, but it did not venture to transatlantic voyages and, on many occasions, it was outrun by the mobile and more advanced fleets of marine powers of the region—Venice and Genoa.

FOUNDING MODERN TURKEY

The birth of the modern Turkey was a very complex process because the country had to undergo a painful political, psychological, and economic transformation, live through the shock of numerous conflicts and wars, endure the collapse of the empire, and witness the abolishment of the Royal Court and Caliphate before it reinvented itself as the modern Turkish Republic in 1923. This opened new pages in the history of the land and the people of Turkey.

The Ottoman Empire entered the nineteenth century, in the words of Tsar Nicolas I of Russia, as a "sick man of Europe,"[13] despite having one of the largest army in the European war theater, and controlling one of the largest territories and, strategically, nearly all of the most important areas in the Middle East—the Holy Land and shortest routes from the Mediterranean to the Read Sea (the Suez Canal was built in 1859). Turkey's army and navy kept loosing battle after battle in the Balkans, the Mediterranean, and the Russian Empire's southern frontiers. Its economic system was crumbling and more and more people expressed their discontent with the social conditions in the country.

There is no doubt that the Ottoman elite were fully aware of these problems. Most of the representatives of the royal family and ruling class agreed that considerable reforms should be introduced. However, they disagreed deeply on the direction of the reforms and the measures that should be taken. One group of the elite strongly believed that the old order was fine and it had just needed to be reinforced and reinvigorated by emphasizing important Islamic values, while rejecting various Western ideas and innovations. The other camp strongly believed that a new set of reforms should be initiated, and those reforms should bring new Western ideas, especially Western education and Western-style institutions in order to save the country from a downfall.

The Turkish state was not a stranger to Western influences. In 1794, Sultan Selim III (1761–1807) introduced some military and economic reforms that included the establishment of the so-called New Order Army (*nizam-i cedid*) and a "New Order" Treasury (*irad-i cedid*). The new army was built according to Western military standards and was trained by the British, German, and French officers. One of these officers was vividly described by Alexandre Dumas, Sr. in *The Count of Monte Cristo.* However, the growing importance of the new army overshadowed the influence of the traditional military units and especially the influence of the Janissaries. In the meantime, the "New Order" Treasury effectively collected taxes for the reforms, but its work negatively affected many entrenched interest groups in the Turkish society. The reforms of the army and tax system were resisted by the conservative forces to a degree that Sultan Selim III was murdered in his palace by Janissary officers.

Yet, the reformist leaders did not give up. Between 1839 and 1878, they introduced a new series of reforms. This era became known as the era of "Reorganization" (Tanzimat). These reforms began with the announcement of the so-called Rose Garden (*Gülhane*, pronounced—*Gulkhane*) Decree. This decree affirmed that all subjects of the empire are equal before the law, regardless of their religious and ethnic affiliation. It also abolished certain taxes, systematized the taxation system, and devised a new system of recruitment into the Ottoman army. During this era, many reforms were pioneered and vigorously promoted by the members of civil administration and, on many occasions, by career diplomats. The reforms included significant changes in the legal system, including introduction of new penal and commercial codes and a new civil code. At the peak of the reforms, the first Ottoman constitution was adopted in 1876, nearly thirty years ahead of the constitution of the Russian Empire. Within two or three years, however, the conservative elite staged a comeback and attacked the reforms, which abolished and revoked much of the four decades of changes. The constitution was suspended in 1878 and the newly elected parliament was dismissed permanently.

The social and interethnic relations in the empire turned toward the worse because of the rising nationalism and growing national identities, many ethnic groups throughout the state began demanding independence. The tensions ran so high that very often people turned to the sword and the rifle to settle differences, and, on some occasions, conflicts resulted in the territorial cleansings on religious or ethnic principles.

Throughout the last quarter of the nineteenth century and the first quarter of the twentieth century, the Ottomans faced a nearly perpetual series of wars with various world powers and internal conflicts with various rebellious ethnic groups. It is not surprising that the military—newly trained officers and the personnel in the war ministry—became increasingly active in the political life. Unhappy with the pace of the reforms within the country and demise in foreign affairs and military campaigns, a group of young officers came together to advance radical changes. The group leaders became known as "the

Young Turks" (*Jeunes Turques*)—the term that entered into many languages to symbolize a radical new generation of reformers. These groups gradually acquired many sympathizers in the provinces and in the capital, and in 1908 they staged a coup that ignited a revolution.

Despite the courage and determination, the young reformers were unable to reverse the fate of the empire that suffered significantly from the Balkan Wars (1908–1909 and 1913) and the humiliating defeat in the World War I (1914–1918), in which Turkey allied with Germany. In 1918–1919, the whole country was on the verge of collapse as various separatist groups split away various provinces of the empire encouraged by newly born radical nationalist leaders or foreign powers or both. At one point, the Greeks who won their independence from the Ottomans about one hundred years earlier, captured the city of Izmir in western Anatolia and moved close to Istanbul, threatening to storm it.

In this environment of great chaos, confusion, and mayhem, it took a great courage for a group of young officers led by strong-minded Mustafa Kemal Pasha (1881–1938) to consolidate the army and civilians and to reach the National Pact. From 1920 to 1923, the small remnants of the Ottoman Army, on many occasions led by the newly emerged national leaders themselves, rose against foreign occupational troops. They also defeated the Greek army both in Anatolia and Eastern Thrace and forced British, French, Italians, and Russians out of Anatolia and consequently to recognize the Turkish government. The War of Independence (1919–1923) was victorious, and its results were finalized by the Lausanne Treaty in July 1923. The country lost most of its territories in the Middle East and southern Europe, but kept control over the entire Anatolia and eastern Thrace.

After much heated debates among various political groups, the National Parliament declared Turkey a republic on October 29, 1923. The supporters of the republic established their own political organization, the People's Party, in September 1923, modeling it after Western political parties. In 1924, the People's Party was renamed the Republican People's Party (*Cumhuriyet Halk Partisi*) and remained the single ruling party for nearly thirty years. Within the next few months, the Parliament abolished the office of Caliph (leader of all Muslims)[14] and the office of *Shaykhylislam*, closed *Shariah* courts, and shut down numerous Islamic colleges (*madrasahs*) and Islamic endowments (*waqf*). A new constitution was introduced in April 1924, which declared Turkey a republic.

Under the leadership of charismatic and hard-willed Mustafa Kemal Pasha, who was bestowed the title Ataturk (farther of Turks) by the national Parliament, the country underwent a wide range of radical reforms that reshaped its political, social, cultural, and economic landscapes. The essence of Mustafa Kemal's reforms was summarized in the *Six Arrows of Kemalism* and included etatism, nationalism, populism, republicanism, revolutionism, and secularism.[15] Until his death in 1938, Ataturk vigorously promoted his vision of the republic and very often turned to harsh measures to implement his reforms.

MANY VISIONS OF MODERN TURKEY

Ataturk's successor, Ismet Inonu, led the country from 1938 to 1950. He strongly believed in the ideas of Kemalism and intended to preserve the existing political and economic system.[16] The emergency situations and dangers that Turkey faced during World War II allowed President Inonu to keep a tight state control over the national economy and political control over the society. Despite the pressure from European powers, he maintained Ankara's neutrality until February 1945, when the country joined the allies in the war against the Nazis thus strengthening Turkish positions in the international arena. With the end of the war, however, many groups in the society, even within the ranks of the ruling Republican People's Party (CHP, Turkish abbreviation), envisioned a different future for the country. They began criticizing the government and its harsh policies and demanding democratization, greater economic freedoms, and free and fair elections. Consequently, the Turkish government decided to ease some of the emergency-era policies and introduce several democratic measures and reforms allowing registration of the newly formed political organizations, including the Democrat Party (*Demokrat Partisi,* or DP) in January 1946.

The DP lost the general election to the national parliament in July 1946, winning only forty seats. However, the party led by Adnan Menderes (1899–1961) was more successful in the parliamentary elections in 1950, 1954, and 1957 winning the majority of the votes. During the decade under the Democrat Party rule, the country experienced an unprecedented economic growth combined with the significant rise in the living standards among general population. The government lifted the most restrictive measures that regulated agricultural and industrial development, opened the Turkish market for international trade, and invested significantly into the development of infrastructure—highways, railroads, hydroelectric power-stations, and large state-run industrial enterprises. This development was significantly boosted by the large-scale assistance from the United States. Among many actions that promoted the popularity of the DP was the relaxation of the restrictions over the Islamic institutions. The government allowed regular religious broadcasts, teaching the Islamic creed in public schools, and provided tacit support for opening new mosques across the country, although it came out heavily on any attempt to desecrate the images of Ataturk by some radical groups.

During this era, an important development started as a little-noticed event about 1,000 miles to the west of Turkey. In 1955, Germany, which experienced economic boom and shortage of labor, introduced a guest workers program inviting Turkish citizens to move in and pick up some jobs. Within the next two decades, almost 2 million Turks moved to Germany and then to other countries in western Europe, such as Austria, Netherlands, Belgium, and others. Often times, temporary events have a tendency to become permanent—many Turks have settled in western European countries for good. These migrants sent home significant remittances and stimulated the development of business and trade ties between Turkey and European countries by contributing to the economic stabilization of Turkey and becoming an important factor in its cultural and political development as well.

In the second half of the 1950s, however, Turkey began experiencing serious economic difficulties due to economic mismanagement, weaknesses in the financial sector, rising inflation, and a budget deficit. The Democrats responded to the criticism of their political and economic missteps by turning to undemocratic and harsh measures to silence the growing opposition among the state bureaucracy, intelligentsia, and various political groups. Although Menderes and his party won the early elections in 1957, the general public, students, and trade unions began expressing their dissatisfaction with the increasingly authoritarian and no longer popular regime through numerous mass rallies. The government responded by introducing even tougher actions and more violence against the opposition, which further destabilized the political situation in the country.

In this environment of increasing political chaos, the military decided to take initiatives into their hands and staged a military coup d'état on May 27, 1960. The coup members established the National Unity Committee (NUC) headed by General Cemal Gursel, who later became the president of the republic. Unlike military juntas in Latin America or Greece, the Turkish military decided against keeping the political power for themselves, and, within a year after stabilizing the political situation in the country, they transferred the power to the civil government. The new constitution that was introduced in July 1961 by a public referendum was so significant and revolutionary in a sense, that Turkish historians, inspired by the French revolutionary traditions, declared that it manifested the beginning of the Second Turkish Republic. The constitution brought major changes that largely deconstructed supercentralized and paternalistic political system in Turkey while it preserved the founding principles of the state. The national parliament received an additional chamber and became bicameral. The presidential term in power (elected by the parliament) was extended to seven years, but it was limited to a single term. In October 1961, the Republican People's Party led by Ismet Inonu came to power in the elections conducted under the watchful eyes of the military.

Although the military gradually withdrew from the politics, the political and economic situation, especially, still remained volatile. In the next parliamentary elections in 1965 and again in 1969, a young and ambitious former engineer Suleyman Demirel (1924–) led his Justice Party (JP) to defeat Ismet Inonu's CHP and became the country's prime minister. Despite his enormous energy and political skills, Demirel was unable to pacify the radical groups, especially young people, who were inspired by the revolutionary mood of students in France and the civil rights movements in the United States. Strikes, demonstrations, sit-ins, and antiestablishment actions, along with clashes with police and radical right-wing groups, became fashionable among the revolutionary youth in Turkey. These young people set up their own radical left-wing organizations and often took weapons into their hands. The country was again slipping into the political chaos.

On March 12, 1971, the army entered the political scene one more time and sent a memorandum to the parliament demanding radical actions and forcing Demirel to resign. As in 1960, the military turned to harsh actions by arresting hundreds of radical youth leaders and members of the radical groups and wiping out small militant groups who tried to escape to the countryside and wage a guerrilla-style campaign. The military soon withdrew from the political scene and the parliament elections brought the CHP back to power in 1973, this time led by Bulent Ecevit (1925–2006). He formed a coalition with the newly established National Salvation Party led by Necmettin Erbakan (1926–).[17] The cycle of political instability, however, repeated itself as the country began spiraling into a new tide of conflicts and political infighting. Although the June 1977 elections were conducted peacefully and the CHP won the elections, various radical political groups and militants found their ways into the streets of major Turkish cities and towns. The violence culminated in 1978–1980 when about 3,000 people were killed across the country.

In the meantime, another problem emerged in the late 1970s and early 1980s greatly affecting the Turkish political scene for the next two decades— the rise of the Kurdish nationalist movement. The Kurds, who are concentrated mainly in eastern and southeastern provinces and have small but representative communities all over the country, have always been an inseparable part of the Turkish nation. Like all citizens of Turkey, they went through the tumult of the war of liberation, and the economic and political difficulties of the early republic. Yet, since the early days, groups of Kurdish intellectuals and community leaders demanded greater political and cultural autonomy and the most radical groups demanded full autonomy and even independence.[18] The Kurdish communities periodically clashed with the Turkish authorities and by the 1980s, some radical groups consolidated into a political movement—the Kurdistan Worker's Party—known by its Turkish abbreviation as the PKK (*Partiya Karkeren Kurdistan*). The PKK, led by charismatic leaders such as Abdullah Ocalan (1948–), turned into an insurgent movement and did not stop short of including terrorist actions as part of its political arsenal. The PKK was responsible for several highly publicized actions and attacks both in and outside Turkey. Despite government efforts, the PKK remained active for decades, and only in February 1999, Ocalan was captured in Nairobi, Kenya, with assistance from U.S. intelligence services.

The military decided to step into Turkish politics again in September 1980, claiming a need for calming down the political tensions and confrontation; although this time they stayed in power longer promising to stabilize the country once and for all.[19] General Kenan Evren (1918–) became the head of the state and retired admiral Bulent Ulusu (1923–) became the prime minister. The junta introduced draconian policies in the name of saving the country from downfall. As many as 200,000 people were detained for a short period of time and up to 50,000 people found themselves in prisons for longer terms. The generals decided that in order to keep a sustainable political environment, most public institutions, such as mosques, trade unions, and universities, must be depoliticized. Many prominent politicians who played key roles in the 1970s, and some political parties, were temporarily banned from politics. As a next step, the generals introduced a new Turkish constitution in November 1982. Yet, when the newly established Motherland Party, led by a civilian, Turgut Ozal (1927–1993), won the elections in November 1983, the generals accepted the popular vote and supported Ozal's government and his policies.

The 1980s changed the economic, social, and political landscape of Turkey to the extent that it became a completely different country. Within a few years, the political situation was stabilized, and Turkey began experimenting with economic liberalization. Many Turkish experts believe that it was Turgut Ozal, the prime minister between 1983 and 1989 and president from 1989 until his death in 1993, who orchestrated the liberalization and privatization programs and presided over the economic reforms with his belief in a free market-oriented economy and private entrepreneurship. During the 1980s and 1990s, the whole country came into the movement in search of new opportunities; and the population of all major cities nearly doubled during that era. A number of small and medium enterprises mushroomed across the country and Turkey significantly increased its exports.

Turkey significantly improved its political standing in the international arena with the beginning of the first Gulf War against Iraq in 1990, and with the independence of the Turkic-speaking republics of central Asia and

Caucasus in 1991. The war brought considerable political and some economic dividends and promises from Washington, DC to increase economic assistance and investments, placing Turkey at the center of world geopolitics.[20] The independence of the central Asian republics and Caucasus states helped Turkey to "rediscover" Turkic-speaking nations, making Turkey a champion of the 200 million-strong Turkic-speaking world. Along with the moral stand, came economic opportunities as a dozen Turkish companies and conglomerates received lucrative contracts in the region and imports of Turkish goods by the newly independent countries skyrocketed. In 2006, an oil pipeline brought central Asian oil to Turkey, thus diversifying energy importing partners and generating revenue from oil transits. Along with liberalization gradually came economic prosperity. The middle class, which was very small in the early 1980s and suffered from the economic downturn in the 1990s, began growing rapidly in the early 2000s. Public and private funds were poured into new construction and infrastructure, including roads, airports, and highways.

The unexpected death of President Turgut Ozal from a heart attack in April 1993 drastically changed the political landscape in the country, although his successors officially continued his policies. Suleyman Demirel was elected president in May 1993 and in June 1993 Ms. Tansu Ciller (1946–), a U.S. educated economics professor, became the first-ever female prime minister of the Turkish Republic. Tansu Ciller, a young and charming technocrat, represented the new face in Turkish politics, but she presided over the toughest economic measures introduced in Turkey in living memory. This included a devaluation of the Turkish lira that wiped out between US$1.2 and US$1.4 billion of the national wealth in a matter of days and measures to curb inflation that exceeded 100 percent.

The structural adjustment program prescribed by the IMF improved the macroeconomic situation in the country, but ordinary citizens were forced to bear the price of the program. Inflation was running high and in some years it reached triple digits. A significant number of people lost their jobs and unemployment stayed at the 20-percent level for several years. Thousands of people who moved into urban areas did not have enough money to get housing, health care, and education and lived in slums similar to some of the poorest Third World countries. In the 1995 elections, the Welfare Party (*Refah Partisi*) won the largest share of the popular vote on the promise to fix the economy and to introduce socially responsible economic policies and a new vision of modern Islam to balance the excesses of globalization and westernization. In doing so, Necmettin Erbakan and his supporters heavily relied upon the new middle class of self-made entrepreneurs. The latter largely came from central and eastern Anatolia and began demanding a greater say in politics at the expense of the so-called White Turks of Ankara and Istanbul who had traditionally dominated politics since the establishment of the Turkish Republic. However, Erbakan's attempt to increase the presence of Islam in politics, public life, and education, his talks about turning away from integration with Europe and creating the Islamic version of the EU combined with his inability to resolve the economic difficulties, alarmed the military. In February 1997, the National Security Council (NSC) published a public statement demanding strict adherence to secularism and the secular constitution. This time, the Turkish military decided to stay in barracks pushing their vision of political development through nonmilitary means. Erbakan was forced to resign in June 1997 and the Turkish Constitutional Court ordered the dismantling of the Welfare Party in January 1998.

The political situation stabilized by 1999–2000, but the economic mismanagement of the 1980s and 1990s, consequences of the hastily arranged privatization program, and lack of fiscal discipline haunted the Turkish politicians well into the twenty-first century. In February 2001, the Turkish stock exchange collapsed, the lira lost nearly half its value, several banks failed, and millions of ordinary citizens found themselves without jobs. Many Turks have bitterly joked that they all became millionaires carrying millions of liras to make a basic purchase, as a simple cup of coffee cost 1 to 2 million Turkish lira.[21]

In this environment, the Justice and Development Party (*Adalet ve Kalkınma Partisi* or *AK Parti*) took the political arena by storm, increasing its popularity on the promise to deliver clean government, socially oriented economic policies, and defending the Turkish culture, religion, and identity against the destructive forces of globalization.[22] The party triumphed during the elections in November 2002 by winning 362 seats in the parliament (of 550 seats). It presided over the economic stabilization in the country for five straight years of high economic growth, as the government led by Recep Erdogan (1954–) was consistent in addressing economic and financial problems and in fighting corruption and mismanagement. In July 2007, the party won 341 seats in the parliament. Yet, it was deadlocked in the political struggle with the powerful military, the state bureaucracy, and Western-oriented intelligentsia over its stand regarding the broadening the presence of Islam in Turkish politics, public life, and education. This has blown up into a full-scale political confrontation: in March 2008, the Constitutional Court announced that the Party's action violated some articles in the secular Turkish Constitution, and the AKP should be banned if the violations would be proved.[23] However, in summer 2008 the case against the AKP was dismissed.[24]

Recent Trends

Turkey entered the twenty-first century as an economic success story—being able to stabilize its economy, finances, and its currency system. According to Recep Erdogan, within two years after his coming to power, the Turkish government "[has] made deep-rooted changes to our society that many countries wouldn't be able to accomplish in ten or twenty years."[25] Within the next decade or two, the Turkish economy might become one of the largest and most important economies in southern Europe, if the current annual growth rate of about 6 to 7 percent remains unchanged (as of summer 2008). The Turkish economy proved to be quite resilient during the turbulent days of the world financial crisis in the autumn of 2008, although the global credit crunch negatively affected the Turkish economy and the Turkish lira experienced several weeks of extremely volatile trading sessions in October–November 2008.[26]

The country's political system remains extremely fragile because it is being torn apart by competing visions of future Turkish political development, its identity, and cultural development. Some politicians advocate strict adherence to the secular principles of the republic. Others believe that giving a greater role to Islam in both public life and the political arena will benefit the country. A confrontation between these two groups led to the political crisis and stalemate of 2007 and 2008, and the quarrel manifested in the country's chief prosecutor's attempt to bring a case against the ruling AKP. If the attempt is successful, the Turkish court might ban Prime Minister Recep Tayyip Erdogan and 70 other AKP members from politics for five years.[27] This stalemate, which led to growing political instability in the country in 2008, revealed the urgent need for a compromise and dialogue between the competing factions and groups.

In the international arena, Turkey experienced a mixed fortune in the early 2000s. The terrorist attacks on the United States in September 2001 turned the world's attention to Ankara again, as Turkey immediately joined the U.S.-led coalition in the war against the Taliban regime in Afghanistan. Turkey played quite an important role during the decisive stages of the war against the Taliban movement from 2002 to 2008, as it contributed its troops to the NATO coalition forces and participated in various operations and humanitarian relief efforts along with the U.S. forces. Turkish General Hilmi Akin Zorlu, for example, led the International Security Assistance Force (ISAF) in Afghanistan. The ISAF, which includes soldiers from different countries, came under Turkish command in 2002 when Turkey took its turn providing leadership in the war against the Taliban.

The second Gulf War against Saddam Hussein was a different matter. As Turkey became a frontier state again after the U.S.-led coalition invaded Iraq in 2003, Turkish politicians were divided in their views about the war. In sharp contrast to the first Gulf War against Iraq in 1990–1991, many members of the Turkish parliament were very reluctant to provide full unconditional support to the United States or to send the Turkish troops to Iraq as part of the coalition. In the end, the majority of Turkish parliament members voted against granting overflight rights to the U.S. military planes in the early days of the second Gulf War. The Turkish government considers the military and political development in northern Iraq a matter of national security, and it claims that the Kurdish separatists regularly find refuge and support in the Kurds-controlled areas in Iraq.[28] The emergence of the militant Islamic groups in and the arrival of Al-Qaida fighters to the areas of Iraq neighboring Turkey also alarmed the Turkish politicians. Thus, the Turkish government authorized its Special Forces to conduct several raids and operations in northern Iraq in 2008.[29]

Nevertheless, the Turkish government declared its strong interests in stabilizing Iraq and achieving peace and economic prosperity in that country. Between 2005 and 2008, Turkish companies invested hundreds of millions of U.S. dollars in various projects in Iraq, especially in its northern provinces. These projects ranged from real estate and retail trade to telecommunications, infrastructure, and education, proving crucial to reviving the Iraqi economy and providing jobs for thousands of people in both countries.[30] Many experts believe that the growing economic cooperation between Iraq and Turkey would help re-establish the multi-billion dollar trade relations, which had existed before the first Gulf War and had mutually benefited both countries in the past.

NOTES

1. Gerald MacLean, ed. *Writing Turkey. Explorations in Turkish History, Politics, and Cultural Identity*. London: Middlesex University Press, 2006, p. xi.

2. The Turkish name for the state is the State of Osman (*Osmanlı Devleti*); "Ottoman Empire" is a term that was introduced by Western scholars.

3. Turkey also shares common maritime borders with Russia in the north.

4. See Peter Alford Andrews, ed. *Ethnic Groups in the Republic of Turkey*. With the assistance of Rüdiger Benninghaus. Wiesbaden, Germany: Reichert, 1989.

5. For scholarly discussions, see Gerard Clauson. *Studies in Turkic and Mongolic Linguistics*. London: Routledge Curzon, 2002.

6. See Martin Tamcke. *Koexistenz und Konfrontation*. Berlin: Lit-Verlag, 2003.

7. Gerald MacLean, ed. *Writing Turkey. Explorations in Turkish History, Politics, and Cultural Identity*. London: Middlesex University Press, 2006, p. x.

8. See Keith Jenkins. *Re-thinking History.* 3rd ed. London: Routledge, 2003.

9. In some sources, his name spelled as Seljuk-Beg.

10. The name also spelled Mehmed II (*Mehmed-i sani* in Ottoman Turkish).

11. For further discussions see John E. Woods. *The Aqquyunlu: Clan, Confederation, Empire: A Study in 15th/9th Century Turko-Iranian Politics.* Minneapolis: Bibliotheca Islamica, 1976.

12. Nobel Prize—winner Ivo Andric wrote his famous novel *The Bridge on the Drina,* which was based on the true story of life a Bosnian peasant's son who was taken away by a Janissary corp. Muhammed Sokollu became a Grand Vizier of the Ottoman Empire in 1565. See Ivo Andric. *The Bridge on the Drina.* New York: Harvill Press, 1994.

13. There are still scholarly debates about the origin of the phrase, but some scholars attribute it to Nicolas I of Russia.

14. The Ottoman Royal family was forced into exile.

15. Andrew Mango. *Ataturk: The Biography of the Founder of Modern Turkey.* Woodstock, NY: Overlook Press, 2000.

16. For political views of Ismet Inonu and his relations with Ataturk see Metin Heper. *İsmet İnönü: The Making of a Turkish Statesman.* Leiden and Boston, MA: Brill, 1998; John M. Vanderlippe. *The Politics of Turkish Democracy: İsmet İnönü and the Formation of the Multi-party System, 1938–1950.* Albany, NY: State University of New York Press, 2005.

17. In some publications the name is also spelled Nesmettin Erbakan.

18. For a detailed overview of the Kurdish question, see Marcus Aliza. *Blood and Belief: The PKK and the Kurdish Fight for Independence.* New York: New York University Press, 2007; Wadie Jwaideh. *The Kurdish National Movement: Its Origins and Development.* Syracuse, NY: Syracuse University Press, 2006; and Michael M. Gunter, and Mohammed M. A. Ahmed, eds. *The Kurdish Question and the 2003 Iraqi War.* Costa Mesa, CA: Mazda, 2005.

19. For different views of the role of the Turkish military in the political development in the Turkish Republic see William Hale. *Turkish Politics and the Military.* London and New York: Routledge, 1994.

20. For the discussion of controversies and Turkish economic losses from shutting down oil pipeline from Iraq see http://query.nytimes.com/gst/fullpage.html?res=9C0CE7D61438F934A3575BC0A966958260&sec=&spon=&pagewanted=all; http://www.csmonitor.com/2002/0116/p21s1-coop.html (accessed October 21, 2008).

21. The exchange rate reached 1,350,000 Turkish lira per US$1 in 1994, winning a place in the *Guinness Book of Records.* In 2005, the New Turkish Lira (*Yeni Turk Lirasi*) was introduced on an exchange rate of one new lira per 1 million old lira.

22. For an analysis of the rise of the Justice and Development Party in Turkey, see Ümit Cizre. *Secular and Islamic Politics in Turkey: The Making of the Justice and Development Party.* London: Routledge, 2007.

23. For the Justice and Development Party position, see http://eng.akparti.org.tr/english/index.html (accessed November 4, 2008).

24. http://www.turkishdailynews.com.tr/article.php?enewsid=111327 For commentaries see Svante E. Cornell. "Turkish Constitutional Court Sets Framework For Politics" http://www.silkroadstudies.org/new/inside/turkey/2008/081024A.html (accessed November 4, 2008).

25. Quoted in Chris Morris. *The New Turkey. The Quiet Revolution on the Edge of Europe.* London: Granta Books, 2005. p. 2.

26. http://www.milliyet.com.tr/Ekonomi/SonDakika.aspx?aType=SonDakika&Kategori=ekonomi&KategoriID=&ArticleID=1006035&Date=21.10.2008&b=Dolar%201,56%20YTLyi%20asti&ver=68 (accessed October 21, 2008)

27. http://www.time.com/time/world/article/0,8599,1722785,00.html.

28. In February 2008, the Turkish army even entered northern Iraq to conduct a series of operations there. See http://www.nytimes.com/2008/02/23/world/middleeast/23turkey.html?n=Top/News/World/Countries%20and%20Territories/Turkey (accessed March 29, 2008).

29. Ercan Yavuz. "Turkish Army to set up security corridor in northern Iraq after ground operation" http://www.todayszaman.com/tz-web/detaylar.do?load=detay&link=135196 (accessed October 21, 2008)

30. http://www.economist.com/world/international/displaystory.cfm?story_id=10808408.

2

Thoughts and Religions

The question of religion [always] remained in the forefront of the Turkish concerns, and played an important part both in the intellectual controversies and in the political conflicts...[1]

—Bernard Lewis

ISLAM

SINCE THE FIRST Muslims arrived in Anatolia many centuries ago, the relation between Islam and other religions and the role of Islam in society has been continuously at the center of public debates. For the past two centuries, these debates have been further complicated by much heated discussion about the relationship between religion and secularism. Turkish secularists habitually represent themselves as the forerunners of modernization and liberalization and as the guards of the country's democratic traditions. Their claim is that only secularism can bring Turkey closer to the West and make it a full and equal member of the European "family" and, more recently, of the European Union (EU). The opposing camp, often dubbed as "Islamists," includes a wide range of groups, from liberal intellectuals to hard-core conservatives, who maintain that Turkish society should keep stronger adherence to Islam and Islamic norms. According to this group, the foundation of the Turkish identity is found in Islamic traditions (and only in Islam), and its ethics and values will keep the moral and social strength of Turkish society. The frequent rigorous interactions and intense debates between the followers of these two large camps usually are closely followed by the media and are reflected in books, politics, and even in the economic activities of the country.

Muslim and non-Muslim communities in Turkey and across the Middle East pay particular attention to these debates for a simple reason: Turkey holds a very special place in modern Islamic civilization and in the historical development of Muslim intellectual thought because it is a source of inspiration, a discourse, or an example to learn. First, many Muslims consider the Turks to be the saviors of Islamic spirituality, and after the fall of Baghdad to the Mongol conquerors in 1258 and execution of the last Abbasid Caliph al-Mustasin, it was the Ottoman rulers who reclaimed the title of *Caliph* few centuries later and proclaimed their spiritual and political leadership in the Muslim world. The Turkic warriors were instrumental in invigorating the Muslim world during the Middle Ages, and they fought fiercely to expand the influence of Islamic teaching in different parts of the Old World. Second, the Islamic world also widely credits the Turkic rulers for safeguarding the intellectual continuity of Islamic thought because the Ottoman rulers provided refuge and patronage to many influential Islamic thinkers who moved in and taught in the royal courts. The Ottoman sultans have also been known,

The interior decoration of a mosque from the Ottoman era. Courtesy of the author, 2007.

throughout the Muslim world, as the welcoming hosts for many mystic broth-erhoods that flourished in this land for centuries. In fact, the influential Sufi orders of Mevlevi dervishes claim their spiritual abode in the Turkish city of Konya. Prominent Sufi orders, such as Bektashia, Nakhshbandia, and oth-ers, attained both spiritual and political influence throughout Anatolia. In the modern era, Turkish scholars were among the first in the Muslim world to champion the development of modern education, theology, and political thought. In addition, most of the Turks accepted the Sunni teaching of Is-lam, and, for many centuries, they defended their religious traditions against the Shi'a expansionism supported by the Persian Shahs. Some Sunni theo-logical tenets are significantly different than the Shi'a tenets and, on some issues, are a rival to Shi'a theological thought. Therefore, there were many battles fought in the name of religion from the Middle Ages to modern times.

In the sharp departure from the long-standing traditions, however, in the beginning of the twentieth century, the Turkish society turned to secularism, and the modern Turkish Republic was established on secular principles. In fact, the founder of the modern Turkish Republic, Mustafa Kemal Ataturk, called the Caliphate "the laughing-stock in the eyes of the civilized world,"[2] and restlessly fought for disengaging the Caliph and all individuals and insti-tutions associated with him from the political scene of the country. He and his followers seemingly won the battle against their opponents by dissolving the Caliphate, pushing Islam out of the educational system, closing hundreds of Islamic colleges (*madrasahs*) and mosques, and nationalizing Islamic endow-ments (*waqfs*). Yet, after World War II, Muslim activists began to gradually regain their influence and presence in the public space. By the end of the twen-tieth century, the Islamic groups, organizations, and parties gained influence and entered the political arena, vigorously battled the secularist politicians, and won several elections at the local and national levels. At the same time, there emerged some Muslim groups that called for a constructive dialogue be-tween religious activists and secularist, condemned fundamentalists and for dialogue between civilizations.[3]

As in other parts of the Muslim world, many individuals in Turkey are heav-ily involved in discourses about the role of their faith and religious norms in the shaping of the relationships among citizens, governments, and civilizations in the era of globalization. For the national census, the Turkish government does not record the religious affiliation of the Turkish population; however, most of the experts consider that about 98 percent of the Turkish citizens are Muslims or "belong to Muslim traditions." The "Muslim traditions" represent a whole spectrum of contemporary Islamic thought from Sunni to Shi'a, ex-clusive spiritual orders (Sufi), and other groups, such as Alevis (which will be discussed in this chapter). The absolute majority of the Turks (between 75%

and 85%) belong to the traditional Sunni school of teaching. Yet, Turkey is a religiously diverse country because representatives of almost all Abrahamic religious traditions live on this land.

Again, it is very difficult to come up with precise numbers, but most of the experts have come to a consensus that there are between 200,000 and 300,000 Christians and between 20,000 and 40,000 Jews in Turkey (as of 2008).[4] In addition, there is a small and quickly diminishing number of atheists and agnostics.

Throughout the Republican era, Muslims and non-Muslims coexisted peacefully most of the time. Nevertheless, there were periods of confrontation, and some of them were quite violent. These confrontations did not always reflect the internal political dynamics; on some occasions they were influenced by the international politics, such as the Cyprus conflict with Greece or periodic crises in the Middle East.

History and Tenets of Islam

There are many stories in popular Turkish folk traditions about a wandering and cheerful jokesmith, Nasreddin Hoca, who ridicules the views and actions of some sanctimonious liberal members of Muslim clergy and makes remarks about his own religious life and beliefs and his relations with clergy (*imams*) and judges (*qazis*). These stories are readily narrated during everyday conversations, family gatherings, at informal and even formal parties, provoking a good amount of laughter. Yet, most of the Turks take their relationship with Islamic teachings quite seriously, although with different levels of devotion. This seemingly irreconcilable contradiction between the pleasure of ridiculing the religious clergy through jokes and the piety is deeply rooted in the history of Islam in this country.

Islam emerged in the sixth century A.D. in the Arabian Peninsula, where its founder, Prophet Muhammad, was born in 570 A.D. The word "Islam" derives from an Arabic word that translates as "submission to the will of God." This is the youngest of the three major monotheistic religions, which include Judaism and Christianity. In fact, very often these three monotheistic religions are called *Abrahamic religions* because Muslims, like Jews and Christians, recognize Abraham (Ibrahim in the Quran) as one of the most important prophets. Muhammad was born and lived for a long time in the city of Mecca, a prominent trading center at the crossroads of the regional trade routes. The city hosted followers of different religious traditions from idol worshipers to Judaists and Christians.

A pious and inquisitive young Muhammad had probably heard the discussions and debates led by these quite different religious followers, but he was unsatisfied with the given answers to his questions. He frequently spent time in seclusion reflecting on the meaning of life and the relationship between the humanity and God. Muslims believe that during one such seclusion he received his first revelation, in which he learned about the oneness of God (Allah) and the sinfulness of idolatry and ignorance. He immediately accepted this revelation to be the word of God and shared the news with his wife, Khadijah, and then with a small group of friends, colleagues, and followers. Muhammad and his followers—Muslims (translated as "those who submit")—were extremely upset by the sinful immoral life in their home city; and they began to loudly denounce the polytheistic practices of the city's residents and went as far as destroying some of the idols. The hostile rival groups threatened the very existence of the early Muslim groups, and these groups were forced to escape from Mecca to the city of Medina in 622. This migration was an important event for consolidating the Muslim community—the *Ummah*—because it basically helped to expand their influence among the people. The Muslim world adopted the year 622 as the beginning of the Islamic calendar, while the Christian calendar starts with the birth of Christ.

Gradually, the power of the *Ummah* grew to such an extent that the Muslims became capable of defeating their opponents and establishing their control over Mecca. The difficult and, at times, extremely hostile environment of that time demanded full consolidation of the political and spiritual power. Since then, the concept of unanimity of the powers has become central for many Islamic political thinkers. Even today, many Islamic scholars believe that political and spiritual power is inseparable in the Islamic political thought.

When Muhammad died in 632, he left a very important spiritual heritage. The central place in this spiritual heritage is the Quran. Muslims believe that all 114 chapters (called *surahs*) are, in essence, God's revelations to Muhammad delivered through Angel Jibrail (Gabriel), and that Muhammad received the revelations orally and transmitted them orally. Every single revelation was written down and compiled in a book—known as the Quran—decades later. All Muslims believe that the Quran represents God's eternal words in the nonexchangeable form transmitted in the Arabic language. Therefore, the Quran has always remained in its original language, and all translations are considered to be only attempts to interpret the true wisdom of the Sacred Book.

The Quran demands that all Muslims follow a "pure" way of life and avoid any wrongdoing or "deviations" from the true teaching, but being relatively short, it does not spell out how to achieve this. The Muslims have learned about spiritual, moral, legal, and social examples and ways of life by observing and studying the best example—the life and deeds of Prophet Muhammad.

Many observations by the Prophet's companions were initially transmitted orally and many years later they were collected into books of Hadith (traditions). The collectors (Imam Bukhari, Muslim ibn al-Hajjaj and others) experienced significant difficulties as they tried their best to verify the authenticity of every tradition and every source. As it was often difficult to do so, the Hadithes are subdivided into several categories—the most authentic and authoritative are called *sahih* (true) Hadithes. This collection of traditions, which are called *Sunna*, became the most authoritative source in Islamic thinking after the Quran. Muslims who believe that the Hadith is an authoritative source of wisdom are called *Sunnis* (pronounced *Suu-nees*). However, not all Muslims believe that the Hadith is the ultimate authoritative source. Because of the nature of the traditions and of the Hadith's codification, some Muslims have different ideas and perceptions about the place of the Hadith in the Islamic teachings. These groups are considered to be outside the mainstream Sunni traditions, and they form separate groups, including such groups as Shi'a, Alevi, and others.

The Quran and Hadith spell out specific fundamental principles that all devoted Muslims are obliged to follow throughout their life. These principles are called the *Five Pillars of Islam*.

Creed (shahadah). All devoted Muslims must accept the oneness of God and declare, without reservation, the fundamental principle that "There is no God, but Allah, and Muhammad is the Messenger of Allah."

Prayer (solah). Devoted Muslims must pray five times a day. In their prayers, they face Kaaba, the holy place in the city of Mecca in Saudi Arabia. It is strongly encouraged that people pray in mosques or assemble together for prayer in any other suitable house or place. However, people can also pray in any other clean place, including their homes, offices, fields, and so forth. In Islam, Friday is a holy day, and this day is reserved for a special prayer at noon; thus, in many Muslim countries in the Middle East and in some other regions, people rest on Fridays, rather than on Sundays, although Turkey has chosen to have the weekend on Sunday.

Charity (zakat). Regular charity, called *zakat*, is also an obligation of devoted Muslims. All Muslims are strongly encouraged to give money or other forms of support to poor members of their communities, especially at the end of the fasting month, called *Ramazan* (also *Ramadan*). It is believed that this will keep selfishness and greed at bay.

Fasting (sawm). During one lunar month a year, Muslims are expected to fast, abstaining from food, drink, and sex for the duration of the day, from sunrise to sunset. It is expected that this will help people understand the life of the poor and hungry, while it teaches discipline and compassion. Traditionally, young children, the elderly, sick people, some women, and people in some other categories are exempt from fasting.

Pilgrimage (*Hajj*). Devoted Muslims are expected to make a pilgrimage, called the *Hajj*, to the holy city of Mecca in Saudi Arabia at least once in their lifetime. It is believed that the pilgrimage will purify a person and cleanse his or her sins.

All mainstream Muslims—regardless of their geographical location, cultural differences, and differences in social and political organization—believe in following the five pillars of Islam. Yet, every Muslim community and every Muslim country is unique and different from each other and every Muslim community has made its own contribution to the richness and diversity of the Muslim culture.

One of the most important contributions introduced in the early Islamic era, in which Turks played a particularly significant role, was *mystical asceticism*. From the earliest days of Islamic history, some groups of devoted Muslims developed various practices that emphasized the advancement of

A typical minaret in Istanbul. Courtesy of the author, 2007.

a personal spirituality, an internal comprehension of divinity, and divine love. This mystical movement in Islam is called *Sufism* (from *suf*—"wool" in Arabic) or *Tasawwuf* ("wool-dressed" in Arabic). The *Sufis* (also called *dervishes* and *fakirs*) practice and preach personal asceticism, which are special meditation techniques that brought a "genuine mystical experience,"[5] self-control, and piety; they developed a special system of symbolism and terminology, and they are widely engaged in missionary work, especially in remote areas.

Most scholars trace the beginning of Sufism to the seventh or eighth century A.D., although there is some disagreement about a more precise date. In order to pass special knowledge from teachers to students, the followers of Sufism established a number of schools and secret or semisecret societies that gradually developed into vast networks of exclusive fraternity orders known as *tariqats*. To this day, little is known about the development of the Sufi orders or the workings of their inner circles. Many influential *tariqats*, including Bektashia, Nakhshbandia, Kubrawiya, Yasawiya, and others, originated in central Asia. The *tariqats*' institutional forms and methods varied: some formed endlessly traveling groups that disseminated the "true love" and "true knowledge" of God; others settled around famous mosques and shrines of the most respected *sheikhs* or saints; and some formed secret brotherhoods, living among ordinary people and recruiting the most gifted young people as their disciples to whom their mystical knowledge would be passed on. Others formed secretive and exclusive societies, some of them no less secretive than the *Opus Dei* famously described in *The Da Vinci Code* by Dan Brown, although in the Islamic mystic orders' case, they have relentlessly worked to preserve Islamic values and treasures and worked against international intrigues of their various opponents.[6]

Many Islamic mystics mastered a type of allegorical lyric poetry about the true love and the personal emotions of the individual seeking love. They contributed greatly to the development of sophisticated poetry and literature in Persian (Farsi), Turkish, Panjabi, Pashtu, and Urdu. Those works gave inspiration to organizations of dervishes, who practiced achievement of ecstatic trances through dancing rituals, chanting, and frenzied music. The mystical poet Jalal ad-Din ar-Rumi (?–1273), for example, lived and worked in the Seljuk city of Konya and was renowned for lines such as:

The secret of my song, though near,
None can see and none can hear,
Oh, for a friend to know the sign
And mingle all his soul with mine!

'Tis the flame of Love that fired me,
'Tis the wine of Love inspired me.
Wouldst thou learn how lovers bleed,
Hearken, hearken to the reed![7]

Sufi *sheikhs* (scholars and spiritual leaders), *murids* (students), and *dervishes* (members of a Sufi fraternity) played an important role in spreading Islam in the frontier land, first in Anatolia and then in the Holy Land and ultimately in the Balkans and southeast Europe. They helped preserve spiritual values during the dark ages of perpetual wars and conflicts. On many occasions, the Sufi *sheikhs* and *dervishes* were the only knowledgeable people who lived among peasants and nomads, and often they were quite liberal in interpreting many doctrinal issues and in incorporating local rituals into their practices.

During the early years of the Turkish Republic, it was the Sufis who went underground and preserved the Islamic heritage, using their centuries-long experience in developing secret societies, clandestine relations, and hidden messages.[8] However, not all people in the Muslim world accept the Sufis and Sufi ideas without reservation.[9] Numerous critics attack the Sufi orders for various faults, including, supposedly, their attempts to conserve the traditional institutions of the society. Some Salafi Islamic scholars accuse the followers of Sufi orders of saint-worshiping, adulation of tombs and shrines, and the adoption of pre-Islamic symbols and rituals. Other critics disapprove losing touch with the contemporary politics and for secluding themselves in a world of meditation and spiritual development. In the meantime, some Western experts stated that, at present "[sometimes] the esoteric teaching and disciplines of great masters [were] reduced to distorted, illiterate echo of the original."[10]

About the same time as the rise of Sufism, Alevi communities emerged in eastern Anatolia and western Persia. The Alevis, like all Muslims, accept the oneness of God and recognize Muhammad as the prophet. However, some of their practices and interpretations of the Islamic creed make some Sunni Muslim scholars quite uncomfortable. This includes the ways the Alevi pray (men and women pray in *assembly houses* and not in mosques) and for their acceptance of some concepts of Shi'a doctrine about Imam Ali and the Twelve Imams, and so forth.[11]

It is interesting to note that the Turks first came into contact with Islam and Muslim communities while competing with the Arabs for power and influence in Central Asia and Khorasan (now northern Afghanistan, Iran, and Iraq) in the eighth and ninth centuries. For many decades, they resisted the Arab armies and fought fiercely to defend their traditional culture and belief system. The Islamization of Turks was a very long process that probably started in the mid-eighth century and continued for two or three centuries. The process of Islamization took various forms from the series of military campaigns, cultural exchanges, and royal marriages to the activities of numerous Sufi orders and individual Sufi sheikhs. Within a century or two, the Turks experienced a meteoric rise to power and prominence throughout the Muslim world due to a combination of factors. Among others, there was one factor that played a significant role—many royal courts in Muslim-dominated areas recruited young Turkic slaves into their military units, buying them in slave bazaars, capturing them during numerous military campaigns, or simply taking them forcefully from their families. These boys were then trained, converted to Islam, and sent to serve in elite royal guard units. This policy was emulated later by the Turks in their infamous *devshirme* practice.

The role that religion played in the numerous campaigns the Turks launched in Caucasus, Persia, Golden Christendom, and in Anatolia is still open to debate. It is probably safe to say that the religious motivation among Muslims was quite strong in their anti-Crusaders campaigns. The Crusaders and Muslim armies battled for years, but capricious *Fortuna* (the goddess of fortune) ultimately left the Crusaders. Not only did the Muslim armies successfully drive the Crusader armies out of the Holy Land, they also moved even further, waging attacks on the former Crusading Knights of the Templars in Malta, Hapsburg rulers in Vienna, Venice, and Genoa, and on the very symbol of Christianity—Constantinople. Like the Crusading armies, the Ottoman anti-Crusading campaigns attracted very different groups of Muslims—from the devoted Islamic warriors (*gazi*) to adventurers and entrepreneur traders, and landless (or herdless) peasants and nobles.

Religious symbolism played an important role in the Ottoman policies and practices after the Ottoman conquest of Anatolia and especially of Constantinople. This symbolism manifested itself in the renaming of the city of Constantinople to Istanbul, converting one of the world's largest churches of that era—Haghia-Sophia (the "Church of Holy Wisdom")—into Aya-Sofya Mosque, and reclaiming the title of Caliph to the Ottoman rulers. The Muslim religion played an important role in shaping the Ottoman society, political system, and Ottoman identity. For example, the Islamic judges contributed greatly to the codification of the Ottoman legal system according to the *Shariah* law. The Muslim clergy and scholars (*ulema*) also had a pivotal role in maintaining law and order in the country, mystic brotherhoods (e.g. Bektashia and Mevlevi) exercised considerable spiritual and intellectual influence, and warriors of Islam (Janissaries) exercised significant political and military weight.

The magnificent Haghia-Sophia Mosque in Istanbul. Courtesy of the author, 2007.

What worked in the Ottoman Empire for centuries, however, began crumbling when the country entered the modern era and the industrial revolution. The central position of faith in public life and public policies left little space for separation of individual and social values from the religious values in times when the separation of the public space and religion was the essence of the emerging individualism and secularism in the western Europe of that era. Like their counterparts in the Vatican of that era, none of the religious establishments in the Ottoman state were prepared to deal with the innovations of the emerging era of capitalism. Many members of the religious establishment were honest, pious, and knowledgeable people who maintained high spiritual and ethic values, but they had no knowledge of modern industry and manufacturing, railroads, or modern military tactics. They knew little about a modern education system where science and free thinking played a crucial role. Very often, members of the religious establishment represented their personal ignorance as the government's position, for example, calling steamboats and printing machines a "creation of Satan." A deep divide emerged in the Ottoman society, as the youngest and most active increasingly turned to the West and to the Western body of knowledge for answers, technologies, and new knowledge. The situation was further complicated by the fact that young modernized Turks wanted to learn from the colonizing powers that clipped out the pieces of the Ottoman territories and weakened the Empire. Thus, all together, these factors contributed to the heat of the debates between the conservative forces and the groups who called for radical changes in the empire.

It is important to understand that the arguments that were based on logic and reasoning were not necessarily the most important arguments in these debates. The political and economic power of the conservative *ulema* in pre-modern society is hard to overestimate. They controlled thousands of Islamic schools (*madrasahs*) and many universities. They were the largest landowners in the region because they controlled *waqf* (Islamic endowments)—land and properties accumulated through donations to mosques and *madrasahs* by wealthy individuals and royal family members over hundreds of years.

Throughout the eighteenth and nineteenth centuries, the Ottomans lost many battles to the relatively small expeditionary armies of major Western powers of that time. The bravery of their troops could not match the technological advances of Western weaponry. Nor did it help when many *ulemas* fiercely rejected the idea of modern schooling systems in favor of spiritually pure religious education. Their views were increasingly at odds with reality.

Responding to these new challenges, Turkish intellectual reformers, including some Islamic scholars, declared that the Muslim communities "must gather knowledge and develop commerce and . . . [must] advance and progress beyond what [they] had in the past."[12] Yet, the conservative *ulemas* condemned their reformist opponents and stubbornly exhorted the faithful to stick to the letter of the old interpretations. This confrontation grew even more intense and reached the climax after the defeat in World War I and the War of Independence (1919–1923).

As the battle between conservative forces and the modernists heated up, both sides became increasingly polarized and hostile to each other. For the modernists, the collapse of the Ottoman Empire and defeat in the Balkan wars and World War I, and the loss of nearly three-quarters of the state's territory was largely the responsibility of the Ottoman dynasty and the conservative forces. This perception and desire to leap forward making the Turkish Republic a modern developed and westernized state led to introduction of very harsh measures toward the Islamic establishment and the Islamic institutions, which were introduced by Mustafa Kemal Pasha.

Very soon after the end of the War of Independence, the Turkish government abolished all *waqf* holdings by confiscating all land and properties and closing thousands of *madrasahs* and mosques. During the peak of the secularization campaigns in the late 1920s and early 1930s, hundreds of mosques and *madrasahs* were converted into public institutions such as libraries and secular schools or were closed all together. In a symbolic step, the government converted the Aya-Sofya Mosque into a museum in 1935.

The government revised its policies toward Islam only after the death of the founder of the republic in 1938. The Turkish authorities slowly liberalized their policy toward Islamic practices, lifting some restrictions and allowing a limited number of mosques and Islamic universities. The changes of that era established a cornerstone for government policies for many years: people were allowed to practice Islam as long as their practice was kept a private matter and as long as practicing Muslims did not openly criticize the secular principles of the republic, did not participate in politics, and did not organize any groups, movements, or parties based on religious values. Practically all family traditions—childbirth, naming, boys' circumcisions, weddings, funerals, and so forth—have been performed according to Islamic traditions and with Islamic authorities, such as *imams*, present.

The government also initiated the establishment of the Directorate of Religious Affairs (*Diyanet*), which directly reports to the prime minister's office. This directorate is in charge of religious education and of all appointments of *imams* and religious authorities in about 77,500 officially registered mosques.[13] In addition, it controls educational programs, pilgrimages to Mecca (*Hajj*), and the issuing of all *fatwas*.

The most important changes arrived in the early 1980s with political liberalization in the country, as the government significantly relaxed over the religious development and public discourses on the place of Islam in contemporary Turkey and on the legacies of the past. Many people—both secularists and Islamic intellectuals—have been drawn into these debates with traditional Turkish passion and enthusiasm, spilling their ideas to the pages of all major press outlets, radio, and television and regularly taking their supporters to the streets of Istanbul and Ankara. Since the early 1990s, this competition of ideas has become a focal point of the local and national elections. The secularists believe that their main objective should be to prevent their opponents from entering the national political scene. In the meantime, the competing camp of the Islamic activists, ranging from nationalists and moderates to radicals and devoted conservatives, claim that their main objective is to prove that their political views are viable and workable in the era of globalization.

As for the general public, it received an opportunity to observe vivacious debates and have a free choice among abundant shades of political views. Many people supported the Turkish constitution of 1982 that institutionalized compulsory religious instruction in all primary and secondary schools in the country. These classes provide knowledge about moral values, Islam, and major world religions.[14] Though society still remains divided over the various issues related to the religion, as are the societies of most Western nations, the majority of the people in Turkey consider these debates and political competitions as part of the healthy democratic process and a significant step toward liberalizing the country.

NON-MUSLIM COMMUNITIES

Anatolia occupies a very special place in the history of Judaism and Christianity as well. In fact, many places in Turkey have been very important for the history of Judaism and have been intimately linked to the birth and development of Christianity and the Christian creed. For example, archeologists have excavated the remains of ancient synagogues and Jewish settlements in Sardis, the Aegean and Black Sea coasts that are believed to be among the oldest in the world. Some scholars believe that St. John accompanied the Virgin Mary to Ephesus after the Crucifixion, and that she spent her last days in a small secluded house on Mount Koressos. Several prominent apostles, like St. Paul, St. John, and St. Philip, lived and preached in Anatolia. In addition, the first Christian church—Grotto of St. Peter—was carved in Antioch. Even St. Nicholas—kids' beloved Santa Claus—is believed to have been born in Patara and worked in the city of Myra (Demre).

The Ottoman rulers declared themselves custodians of all inhabitants of the Empire, regardless of their religious affiliation, and the Ottoman state was home to large non-Muslim communities. Their status and relations with the state were greatly affected by past historical experiences, international relations, and the Islamic theological views on relations between Muslims on the one hand and the Christians and Jews (the "People of the Book" in the Quran) on the other.

After 1453, Sultan Mehmed II the Conqueror (Fatih) even invited Christian communities to settle in Istanbul in the effort to repopulate the city and its suburbs. A number of Jews also sought and found refuge in the Ottoman land, when they faced prosecution and difficulties in Europe. In fact, the Ottoman Sultan Bayazid II formally invited about 50,000 Jews of Spain to settle within the state when the Spanish inquisition launched attacks on them, which threatened the very existence of the community. The Ottoman authorities regulated their relations with the religious minorities through the system of the so-called millets (a system that gives a certain degree of autonomy to various groups of the population according to their religious affiliations) that allowed maintaining relatively peaceful relations between Muslims and other religious communities for centuries.

The situation changed radically with the surge of modern nationalism in the Balkans and throughout the state in the nineteenth and early twentieth centuries. Yet, the Ottoman rulers looked at the growing grievances and conflicts as essentially religious confrontation between the world of Islam and the world of Christianity. As the prominent scholar on Islam, Bernard Lewis, put it: "The first reaction by Muslim thinkers to the facts of the decline and relative weakness of Islam were, in this sense, religious, not national..."[15] Thus, many devastating conflicts and campaigns were carried out in the name of religion, including territorial cleansings in some parts of the Empire. The conflicts and clashes in eastern Anatolia that left tens of thousands of Armenians, Kurds, and Turks displaced or killed between 1915 and 1923 are still hotly debated by scholars in Turkey and in the West. With the establishment of the Turkish Republic, one of the most tragic pages in history happened as Turkey and Greece approved population swaps. In the early 1920s, hundreds of thousands of Christian Greeks and others left their centuries-long homes in Anatolia and Constantinople, and hundreds of thousands of Turks left their centuries-long homes in southeastern Europe. In 1955, and in 1964 during the height of conflict over Cyprus between Turkey and Greece, the Orthodox Christian communities again experienced turmoil and problems. Between the 1940s and 1960s, thousands of Christians and Jews left Turkey for Europe, the Americas, and Australia, thus further reducing the size of Christian and Jewish communities within the state. By the early 2000s, there were probably between 200,000 and 300,000 Christians and between 20,000 and 40,000 Jews in Turkey. The huge discrepancy can be explained by the fact that the Turkish census does not record the religious or ethnic backgrounds of Turkish citizens.

Christianity

The Turkish government recognizes three major religious communities—the Greek Orthodox Christians, Armenian Orthodox Christians, and Jews, although small communities of Catholics, Protestants, Mennonite Christians, Jehovah's Witnesses, and Georgian and Syrian Orthodox Christians also exist in the country. The status of the Christian communities and their relations with the Turkish government underwent significant changes in the twentieth century and has been further transformed in the early twenty-first century when Turkey began harmonization of Turkish laws with the legal norms of the EU.

The Greek Orthodox Christians represent the largest Christian community in modern Turkey; they maintain a relatively high profile and work closely with the head of the Patriarchate. It is one of the three major branches of Christianity, along with the Catholic Church and the Protestant Church, and traditionally, Istanbul is its historic, religious, and cultural center. The Orthodox Christians recognize the autocephalous (autonomous) status of its churches headed by their own *bishops* (patriarchs or metropolitans) and recognize Episcopal *synods* (councils), but not the Pope, as the highest doctrinal and administrative authority. The Orthodox Church came into conflict with the Roman Catholic Church over some doctrinal and political issues in the Middle Ages and this conflict culminated in the Great Schism in 1054; although, in the aftermath, both churches made several attempts at reconciliation.

The Greek Orthodox Church claims about 70,000 to 85,000 followers in Turkey. The Ecumenical Patriarchate of Constantinople is the central church authority for the Greek Orthodox Christians, not only in Turkey, but also in Europe (outside Greece), the United States, Canada, Central and South America, Australia, and New Zealand.[16]

The Armenian Church is one of the oldest branches of Christianity. It traces its roots to the work of St. Gregory the Illuminator who came to Armenia and introduced Armenian King Tiridates III and members of his court to Christianity. The special status of the Armenian Church has been strengthened further by the translation of the Bible into the Armenian language by monk and scholar, St. Mashtos, and by the refusal of the Armenian Christians to accept the decisions of the Council of Chalcedon that ultimately led to the formation of a separate church. The Armenian Christian community in Turkey is led by the Armenian patriarch of Jerusalem and Istanbul (residing in Istanbul). Various sources estimate that there are between 50,000 and 70,000 Armenian Orthodox Christians living in Turkey (as of 2008).[17]

The Protestant and Catholic Christian communities existed in Turkey for quite a while, and they increased their size in the late nineteenth and early twentieth centuries with the temporary and permanent immigration of Germans, Hungarians, Poles, and some others to the Ottoman land. According to various estimates there were between 10,000 and 20,000 Protestant and Catholic Christians in Turkey in the early 2000s.

Judaism

Some ancient Jewish texts claim that during the reign of King David, in the tenth century B.C., Jews already lived in the cities and towns of Anatolia. In fact, some sources claim that Jewish communities had their synagogues in Icononium (present-day Konya), Ephesus, Sardis, and some other cities in Anatolia as early as the fourth to third centuries B.C. Since then, Jews have lived in Anatolia engaging in trade, financial transactions, and so forth. There is, in fact, evidence that they have been a continuous presence in the territory of Turkey for nearly 2,000 years.

During the Ottoman era, the Jewish communities were spread throughout several cities of the region, but the most prominent one was in Istanbul.[18] By the late nineteenth century, these communities reached up to 400,000 to

500,000—people living all over the territory of the Ottoman Empire. After partition of the Ottoman Empire, many Jews found themselves within the boundaries of newly created political entities. In the time of the political turmoil during the republican era, however, there was a significant outflow of Jews from many Turkish provinces, especially in the 1920s and again in the 1940s and 1950s, because many were sent into exile or voluntarily moved out of the country. By the early twenty-first century, between 20,000 and 30,000 Jews lived in the country, maintained synagogues in Istanbul, Bursa, and some other cities, and successfully ran various businesses. Turkey was among the first predominantly Muslim countries that established and maintained diplomatic, economic, and military relations with the state of Israel.

ISLAM IN TURKEY AFTER 9/11

Since 2001, the religion has begun playing an increasingly important role in both the Turkish domestic and international politics. Turkey has found itself on the frontline of the war on international terrorism and of the conflict in neighboring Iraq. It has been soundly affected by the development in the neighboring Middle Eastern countries and, probably, very few Turks can remain indifferent to the events and intellectual discourses among the Muslim intellectuals in the region with which the nation has been linked by the myriad of historical, cultural, and political ties.

Witnessing the rise of militant Islamic groups in the Middle East, Afghanistan, and Pakistan, various Muslim political groups in Turkey declared that they have a viable and peaceful alternative to the confrontational rhetoric of the militants. In this regard, the Justice and Development Party (*Adalet ve Kalkınma Partisi* or *AKP*, see Chapter 1) attracted the wide support of Muslim intellectuals and businesses in Turkey by declaring that Islamic teaching conforms to the liberal democratic values and the dialog of civilizations.

Yet, the domestic political dynamics and increasing presence of the religious vocabulary in the political debates in Turkey since the early 2000s have galvanized a wide range of political activists whom Turkish mass media has often dubbed *secularists*. These political groups have strongly disagreed with the political views of the AKP, criticizing it for bringing an Islamic component into its political platform. The secularists have claimed that the AKP and Islamic organizations have undermined the founding principles of the Turkish Republic and have gone against ideas set up by Mustafa Kemal Ataturk.[19] The secularist commentators went so far as to claim that the AKP might have a hidden agenda of "trying to turn the country into an Islamic state."[20] The political debates became so heated that, on several occasions, they nearly paralyzed the political life in the country.[21] This was especially true in April 2007 when the Turkish army voiced a strong "concern" about attempts to revise the secular principles of the republic.[22] On another occasion, in spring and summer 2008, Turkey's Constitutional Court moved against the AKP, questioning the legitimacy of the parliamentary and presidential elections of 2007.[23]

The AKP and their supporters repaid the secularists in kind. Some commentators went so far as to accuse their opponents of waging a "secular Jihad" against the AKP.[24] The AKP announced that it supports Islamic values and the reestablishment of the moral principles and honest politics that were lost during the decades of secular rule.[25] It also claimed that it fully supported the founding principles of the Turkish Republic and Turkey's bid to join the EU. At the same time, the AKP announced that it would have liked to abolish some harsh measures introduced by the secular governments in the past. In this environment, some issues, such as wearing head scarves in public buildings, became one of the most hotly discussed topics distracting the attention of politicians from the important state affairs.

By and large, Turkish society remains deeply divided on the role of religion in its social life. Some people support the existing status quo and the secular nature of their country, believing that religion should remain a private matter and that religious organizations should not participate in the political lives of its citizens. There are groups and individuals who demand a greater role for Islam in public and political life. In between, there is a large segment of the younger generation, which is busy searching for jobs and which has more concerns about everyday life than about political debates on the role of the religion.

In the meantime, on the grassroots level, a new trend has emerged that has captured the support and attention of a sizable part of Turkish society—the *Gulen* movement. The conservative *Economist* of London even called the movement, "a global force" as "the *Gulen* message is well received in the West [and in the East]."[26] What made the movement so different from all other political groups and parties in Turkey is its emphasis on education, "belief in science, inter-faith dialogue and multi-party democracy,"[27] and its nonintervention into Turkish political life.

During recent decades, Islam has regained some of its position in everyday life; yet the religious landscape in Turkey still differs significantly from that of the Middle East. In general, most people still prefer liberal Western dress and are open-minded about forms of socialization and behavior. A number of prominent politicians, scholars, and intellectuals have been involved in debates on the meaning of the changes in the region's religious life and the interaction between doctrinal Islam and popular Islamic practices. Islamic activists have attempted to take their personal beliefs and religious views into the public domain, thereby stirring heated public debates about the role of the religion in political life and the relationship between religion and the state.

The official Islamic clergy tends to continue the practice of nonintervention into the politics of the state, although they work actively among the general population. There are small but rapidly growing groups of Islamic activists, usually religiously trained young people, however, who demand stricter observance of Islamic traditions and greater involvement of religion in political life.[28]

NOTES

1. Bernard Lewis. *The Middle East and the West*. New York: Harper Torchbooks, 1964, p. 106.

2. Mustapha Kemal. "Mustapha Kemal ('Ataturk') Outlines His Vision of the Recent Nationalist Past of Turkey and the Future of the Country, 1927," in Akram Fouad Khater. *Sources in the History of the Modern Middle East*. Boston: Houghton Mifflin Company, 2004, p. 145.

3. For scholarly assessments of the debates between secularists and Islamic activists, see Marvine Howe. *Turkey Today: A Nation Divided over Islam's Revival*. Boulder, CO: Westview Press, 2000 and Muammer Kaylan. *The Kemalists: Islamic Revival and the Fate of Secular Turkey*. New York: Prometheus Books, 2005.

4. This number excludes large communities of expatriates.

5. Arthur John Arberry. *Sufism, an Account of the Mystics of Islam*. London: Allen & Unwin, 1963, p. 64.

6. The secret order of assassins in the Middle Ages is one of the most publicized examples of such secret orders in the Muslim world. Under the order of their clandestine leaders, they carried out thousands of political assassinations terrorizing rulers from the Mediterranean to India for about 300 years before they were destroyed. See Bernard Lewis. *The Assassins: A Radical Sect in Islam*. New York: Basic Books, 2003.

7. Arberry. *Sufism*, p. 111.

8. For a discussion about the place of Sufis in contemporary Turkey, see Ande Hammarlund. *Sufism, Music and Society in Turkey and the Middle East*. London: Routledge Curzon, 2001.

9. For a comprehensive history of Sufism, see Spencer Trimingham. *The Sufi Orders in Islam*. 2nd ed. Oxford: Oxford University Press, 1998.

10. Shirin Akiner. "Islam, the State, and Ethnicity in Central Asia in Historical Perspective," *Religion, State, and Society* (1996), 24(2/3) 91–132.

11. For an example of recent scholarly assessment of the life and beliefs of the Alevi communities, see David Shankland. *The Alevis in Turkey: The Emergence of a Secular Islamic Tradition*. London: Routledge, 2007 and Martin Soekefeld. *Struggling for Recognition: The Alevi Movement in Germany and in Transnational Space*. New York: Berghahn Books, 2008.

12. "An Ottoman Government Decree defines the Official Notion of the 'Modern' Citizen, June 19, 1870," in Akram Fouad Khater. *Sources in the History of the Modern Middle East*. Boston: Houghton Mifflin Company, 2004, p. 19.

13. The number is provided by the U.S. Department of State at http://www.state.gov/g/drl/rls/irf/2007/90204.htm (accessed March 29, 2008).

14. In general, people have the choice to send their kids to schools that incorporate the study of the Islamic creed into their curricula or to schools that offer secular curriculum. For a discussion of Islamic education, see Robert W. Hefner and Muhammad Qasim Zaman. *Schooling Islam: Modern Muslim Education.* Princeton, NJ: Princeton University Press, 2006 and Nevval Sevindi, Ibrahim M. Abu-rabi', and Abdullh T. Antepli. *Contemporary Islamic Conversations: M. Fethullah Gulen on Turkey, Islam, and the West.* New York: State University of New York Press, 2008.

15. Bernard Lewis. *The Middle East and the West.* New York: Harper Torchbooks, 1964, p. 96.

16. For further information, visit the Patriarchate's website at http://www.ecupatriarchate.org/.

17. For further information, visit the Armenian Orthodox Patriarchate of Jerusalem website at http://www.armenian-patriarchate.org/.

18. See Steven B. Bowman. *The Jews of Byzantium 1204–1453.* New York: Bloch Publishing Co., 2001.

19. For example, see Amir Taheri. "A Very Turkish Coup? It May Already Be under Way," available at http://www.timesonline.co.uk/tol/comment/columnists/guest_contributors/article2127654.ece (accessed October 21, 2008).

20. "AKP Installs Shariah by Using Democracy, Prosecutor Says." See http://www.turkishdailynews.com.tr/article.php?enewsid=99170 (accessed October 21, 2008).

21. "Turkey's Political Battle: Secularism versus Democracy." http://www.cfr.org/publication/13666/ (accessed April 2, 2008).

22. http://edition.cnn.com/2007/WORLD/europe/04/30/turkey.election/ (accessed April 2, 2008).

23. For discussions, see http://www.turkishdailynews.com.tr/article.php?enewsid=100783 (accessed April 2, 2008) and http://www.turkishdailynews.com.tr/article.php?enewsid=99536 (accessed April 2, 2008).

24. http://online.wsj.com/article/SB120648058852163507.html (accessed April 2, 2008).

25. The confrontation between the two political forces took a bizarre twist when a group of political activists and intellectuals was accused in "plotting an armed uprising" an attempt to overthrow incumbent Turkish government, see Murad Sezer "Chaos Mars Trial of 86 Accused in Turkey Coup Plot." http://www.usatoday.com/news/world/2008-10-20-4002274729_x.htm.

26. http://www.economist.com/world/international/displaystory.cfm?story_id=10808408&CFID=692105&CFTOKEN=76905417 (accessed April 2, 2008).

27. Ibid.

28. For a detailed evaluation, see U.S. Department of State Reports on International Religious Freedom in Turkey. http://www.state.gov/g/drl/rls/irf/2007/90204.htm (accessed March 29, 2008).

3

Folklore and Literature

> ...to translate [Turkish poetry] is like endeavoring to copy a miniature in chalk.
> —E. J. W. Gibb

MANY PEOPLE WHO walk the streets of Beyoglu in Istanbul, or visit the numerous bookstores (*kitap-dukkani*) in the major urban centers, would probably agree with Ottomanist Walter G. Andrew, who stated that "[in Turkey] almost everyone, from ruler to the peasant, from the religious scholar to the rake and drunkard, aspired to be a poet."[1] The lives and souls of the Turks are filled with poetry and literary works. An educated urbanite is likely to add to his speech here and there quotes from famous writers or columnists as he chats with friends, colleagues, or foreign guests. Many politicians will sprinkle their public speeches with philosophical thoughts or clever phrases, or cite great orators of ancient Rome, famous poets, and statements from Turkish history, or they may simply spice up their speeches with a few humorous lines about the enduring comic Nasreddin Hoca. Anatolian peasants are as likely to begin their conversation with a Turkish proverb that, along with the lively Turkish wit, represents the wisdom of the people. They would certainly not forget to recount a folk tale or short jocular folk story to lighten a long day or give cheer to their companions over Turkish tea or coffee. In the meantime, it seems every grandmother is an inexhaustible source of so many children's tales and fairy tales, legends, stories of superstitions and supernatural powers, and stories of such richness and intrigue, which make even monumental works, such as the *Lord of the Rings*, look like a relatively modest narrative.

A traditional bookstore in Konya. Courtesy of the author, 2007.

A number of medieval Turkish folk stories, love lyrics, and classical-era heroes and heroines have much in common with those of the Arab Middle East, Iran, and central Asia. Indeed, Turkish literature and folklore, from their earliest days to the present, were largely formed as a fusion of many influences, taking in the heroic folk epics of the great Turkic warriors of the Eurasian Steppe, the subtle and sophisticated lyrics of Persian bards and poets, the deep spiritual wisdom and ideas of the Arab world, and the sophisticated culture of satirical Aesop-style fables of the ancient Greek civilization. During the classical Ottoman era, the magnificent royal courts of the Ottoman sultans and their *atabegs* in Konya, Izmir, and Istanbul welcomed hundreds of wandering *asyks* (pronounced ashy-ks) and *ozans* (wandering bards—distant cousins of the European minstrels), accomplished and well-known poets, and secretive mystic Sufi teachers (*sheikhs*) who regularly arrived from the elegant courts of the Mogul Emperor in India, from the palaces of the *Shah-n-Shahs* in Iran, and from the Spartan woolen tents of the ruthless khans of the Central Asian khanates.

Many of those bards found patrons in the caravanserais and bustling tea-houses along the numerous trade routes, or—if they were lucky—even in the palaces of the sultans. Yet, as in the Europe of the Middle Ages, "high" culture and "low" culture each evolved in a separate universe with its own standards, expressions, and circles of followers. These two cultures rarely mixed and were often expressed through different languages. Turkish folklore was customarily created and caringly passed on, generation to generation, in Turkish or various dialects of the Turkic languages; while the language of the royal courts and "high" poetry and literature was often deeply influenced by the highly refined Persian (Farsi) language.

An inventory of today's popular bookstores in Istanbul, Izmir, or Antalya, however, would probably shock many foreign travelers. A bibliophile would struggle to find early Turkish epics, folklore, or classic literature. These days, many of the bookstores would be little different from those in New York, Chicago, or London—full of Turkish translations or remakes of contemporary foreign bestsellers, romance novels, and endless rows of self-indulgent autobiographies of politicians and artists and gossipy biographies of pop stars and Hollywood actors.[2] The Turkish cousins of such literature are steadily increasing their presence, and they, too, are often written in kitsch style and colloquial language and are marketed under eye-catching covers. The bibliophile in such *kitap-dukkani* may encounter a grumbling, elderly patron who willingly strikes up a conversation, complaining that this inflow of pop culture and foreign-inspired trends is quite a recent phenomenon that started somewhere in the 1980s and 1990s. Prior to that, he might claim, a bookstore was a "palace of wisdom" (*akillilik saray*) and people read "real" and serious books, but now, "the sacred fires that burned in the depth of their souls were forgotten."[3] This kind of patron is always eager to lead a reader to the corners of the bookstore where some classical-era literature, poetry, and folklore still live in their own universe.

This new, emerging trend is a great paradox that reflects dynamic changes in Turkish culture, the impact of globalization and the birth of global pop culture. How do the Turks perceive globalization and cultural changes, including changes in literary tastes and creative expression? Will distinctively Turkish writing survive this massive intrusion, or will it become an inseparable and indistinguishable part of the trend?

FOLKLORE AND ORAL TRADITIONS

A Turkish tale claims that since the time "when the flea was a porter and the camel a barber, [and] a *padishah* ... was very, very quick tempered," the Turkic-speaking subjects of the Ottoman state have patronized folklore and oral traditions. In the words of Barbara K. Walker, an expert on Turkish folk literature, "the tales served as more than percept vehicles, moral guides. ... Each time a given tale was told, [the whole] cultural baggage was transmitted with it."[4] The Turks initially arrived in Anatolia from areas in distant Central Asia, northern Persia, and the Caucasus in great and lesser waves as early as the eleventh to the thirteenth centuries. As newcomers, they encountered the cultures, languages, and literary legacies of the settled population of Anatolia and surrounding areas. It was the Turkic oral traditions, however, that helped them preserve their distinct culture, languages, and modes of artistic expression. Folklore kept the Turks from cultural assimilation in the Persian-, Arab-, and Greek-speaking areas, even though they remained in the minority for a considerable time. And yet, the Turks were open to cultural interchanges and embraced or creatively interpreted the themes and ideas of the locals.

The popular folklore has taken various forms and shapes and has been so rich that it is quite difficult to classify it within the rigorous parameters of terminology and theme. By and large, most experts distinguish four major genres in Turkish folk literature: traditional heroic epics, legends, and tales; popular humor and short fables; popular folk poetry; and religious folk stories.[5] Of course, as with artistic genres everywhere, demarcation among these four forms was rarely clear-cut; for example, allegoric religious themes may be found in some popular folk poetry, while certain fable elements are discernable in some of the traditional epics and legends.

Epics and Tales

Turkish epics reflect an attempt to express Turkic identity, interpretation of history, and perception of common ethics and philosophy. For centuries, these epics formed part of the oral tradition and were carefully preserved, refined, and enhanced by nameless bards and epic singers; only a few were written down throughout the Middle Ages. Most of the epics were developed in poetic form, very often in a free-poetic rhythm, making them easier to recite to small and large groups of patrons in caravanserais, at village gatherings, or during overnight stops in military campaigns and expeditions. The fact that these epics were part of the oral heritage has led to the preservation of a number of variations reflecting local histories, cultural and tribal differences, or simply the creative improvisations of individual bards.[6]

There were probably hundreds of mostly heroic epics in the early era, although many of them disappeared without a trace during the years of calamities and wars, and still others may remain hidden from a wider audience in archives or libraries. Some of the stories were probably consolidated into the larger heroic epics and became inseparable parts of them. There are a number of well-known and extensively studied epics readily identified by most Turks.

Geroglu (Also Goroglu, Gor-Ugli)[7]

This is the chronicle of the life and deeds of a Turkic knight—Geroglu—and the history of Turkic people who experienced spectacular victories and stunning downfalls.[8] Geroglu, whose name means "son of the grave," is born after his mother's death in an accident. He grows up with the help of a divine spirit. Together with forty knights, Geroglu founds an ideal city-kingdom, Chambel, and becomes its ideal ruler, showing unfailing generosity to his people and leading numerous campaigns for justice and freedom for his nation. His life is full of numerous adventures and travels as he defends the ordinary people and his fatherland from cruel foreign invaders and sorcerers with supernatural powers.

Korkut (Also Gorkut, Dede Korkut, Korkut-Ata)

This epic is a collection of stories of the life of "Korkut Ata . . . wise man of the Oghuz people . . . [who was] divinely inspired."[9] It comprises twelve long stories that narrate major events in the history of the Turkic people and the lives of heroes who played a central role in those affairs. Korkut lived for many years and provided advice and help to his people. Even as he finally departed from worldly life, his soul traveled endlessly about his fatherland, protecting the souls of the Turkic people. The Korkut stories have a number of variations in their geographical settings (from central Asia to Anatolia) and historical periods (between the eleventh and fourteenth centuries), were edited over time by bards and poets, and were systematized only in the sixteenth century, in a book titled *Kitebi Dede Korkut* (*The Book of My Grandfather Korkut*).

Oguznama (Also Oguz-nama, Literally "Epic About Oguz")

This is one of the most acclaimed epics among the Turks of central Asia, the Caucasus, and Anatolia. *Oguznama* narrates the heroic actions, war, and battles of Oguz Khan and his sons, and tells about the establishment of the early Turkic states in the western parts of central Asia and Asia Minor. Most scholars trace the epic's origin to the Middle Ages, dating it between the eleventh and thirteenth centuries.[10]

Tales were a highly popular genre in Anatolia among the ordinary people, and many famous Ottoman poets and writers turned frequently to the well-liked themes and poetically introduced them into the palaces and mansions of the Ottoman nobility. Numerous Turkish fairy tales share popular themes with those of the Middle East, south Asia, and central Asia, although many have evolved around distinctively local themes and heroes. These fairy tales traditionally depict the lives and deeds of noble princes, viziers, and knights who bravely fight powerful enemies with spiritual strength and help from saints and clever advisers.[11] Another theme includes allegories featuring animals—camels, donkeys, foxes, nightingales, snakes, wolves, and others— whose magical powers aid good people, families, or tribes; and there is a large body of children's allegoric tales in which animals are used to satirize human deficiencies such as greed, arrogance, and so on. In addition, there is a large body of tales about magic, witchcraft, and spirits, including *jinns, padishahs* of the fairies, *divs,* and *peris.* Yet, the most popular theme is the lives of ordinary dervishes, caravan drivers, farmers, hunters, shepherds, traders, and craftsmen, whose many adventures and fights for their *kismet* (fate) ultimately win each the love of a beautiful *hanim* (lady) and a wedding that always lasts for "forty days and forty nights," followed by happy lives together—ever after.

Popular Humorous Stories and Short Fables

Like Middle Eastern literature, Turkish folk literature is extremely rich in humorous stories and fables that have been loved by the common people since the early Middle Ages. The protagonists of these stories and fables are amusing personalities set in comical situations, and they express the wisdom and wit of the common people in short and compelling punch lines. In some cases, the humor in these stories carries masked social or political messages that re-flect popular discontent with the social injustice or corrupt actions of certain wealthy members of society, government officials, or clergy.

One of the most popular and best-loved personalities in such comedies is Nasreddin Hoca (Hoja) or Effendi. Nasreddin is the Turkish equivalent of the American "average Joe," a man who lives in a conservative neighborhood on a very modest income and uses his wits and inexhaustible optimism to bring joy to his life and lives of his family, friends, and neighbors. Nasreddin regularly fails in various comic situations but always tries to remain buoyant, even when facing the most difficult problems in his life. Although many other countries in central Asia and the Middle East believe that Nasreddin Hoca lived in their area, the Turks claim that he was a truly Turkish hero who initially lived in the small Turkish city of Aksehir and later in Konya. They even identify the era when he lived there—the thirteenth century, although new jokes about him have been regularly appearing all the way to the twenty-first century.[12]

There are many "miniseries" of anecdotes about the adventures of Nasred-din Hoca, from pithy jokes and stories related to his family life, relations with neighbors, and so on, to fables that have him ridiculing the swaggering behav-ior of wealthy members of society, the intelligentsia, or backward clergy. Some of these stories teach wisdom to both children and adults, others remind them of the true value of human life. One very old Turkish story about Nasreddin goes as follows:

Nasreddin used to get up very early every morning and go to a local mosque for prayer. His neighbors always joined him. One morning he got up as usual, but only one neighbor came along, as all the others were still asleep. The neighbor exclaimed: "Look! What a shame! All our neighbors are sleeping, and not even one of them raised his head for devotion!" "Well!" Nasreddin replied: "Were you asleep too, you would not have seen their faults and failings!"[13]

Viewed superficially, Nasreddin Hoca and similar comic personalities are simple, even stupidly ignorant, citizens; but beneath this facade, the sensitive listener or reader finds a special wisdom. Some scholars who study the Nasreddin stories believe that many of the jokes have multiple layers of meaning, and that they were used in the past by Sufi teachers to deliver hidden mystical messages to their devotees or to illustrate, in simpler terms, a philosophical deconstruction of everyday life in order to expose eternal spiritual values.

Popular Folk Poetry

Folk poetry was another genre cherished among the people of Anatolia. It was developed by the *asyks*, who were wandering bards similar to western minstrels. The *asyks* (also called *ozans*) traveled around the countryside reciting poems, and sharing the legends, stories, and tales they knew by heart with the common folk at the bazaars, caravanserais, and coffeehouses. They often accompanied their performances with musical instruments, in particular the *baglama*. Many *asyks* created their own works or improvised on various existing topics and themes.

In this era, when most of the population was illiterate and "high" culture was confined to palaces and the castles of the nobility, the wandering bards preserved the old Turkic folk poetry, and they also popularized the best poets and writers of their time.

The *asyks* passed on their skills and knowledge to their students in the traditional manner, probably up to the sixteenth and seventeenth centuries. Neither their works nor their repertoire was ever written down, and they remained anonymous. Only after the seventeenth and eighteenth centuries, and especially in the nineteenth and twentieth centuries, was the folk heritage gathered and studied more systematically. Some of the most acclaimed stories and poems were collected and recorded. These included the works of the famous poet Karacaoglan (c. 1610–c. 1690), who created his works in the common Turkic language. By the nineteenth and twentieth centuries, a great deal of Turkish folklore had been written down, and scholars of that period put a lot of effort into studying this heritage in a more systematic way, thereby preserving the last jewels of the great Turkish tradition that had begun disappearing with the changing lifestyle and social structure of Turkish society.

Popular Religious Folklore

Many scholars believe that in the Middle Ages (probably after the thirteenth century) the *asyks* began to come increasingly under the influence of various Sufi orders, and that many of them became dervishes (members of secretive Sufi orders) themselves. This trend gave rise to explicitly religious folklore that evolved around various spiritual and ethnic themes.

Ultimately, this trend crystallized in the so-called *tekke* folklore, clearly linked to various Sufi lounges. Most of the work in this genre was created for formal and informal meetings of the dervishes during their continuous travels around the Ottoman Empire and in the lounges of the established dervish orders. Unlike the oral epic and *asyk* poetry, most of the *tekke* literature was preserved, as it was written down by the followers of the various Sufi brotherhoods.

LITERATURE OF THE CLASSICAL PERIOD

As in western Europe, the literature of the classical Ottoman period—from the thirteenth to the eighteenth centuries—was largely represented by court (*divan*) poetry, lyrics, and heroic and religious works. Although most writers initially drew their inspiration from everyday Turkic poetry, over time they fell significantly under the influence of the classical Persian and Arabic cultures. Themes, plots, symbols, and even personalities from Persian and Arab classical literature, highly novel to Turkish audiences, came to permeate the world of Turkic literature. These new cultures also introduced extensive use of allegoric symbolism and a focus on refined wording and mellifluous rhythms. Poetry became so dominant in both high and popular cultures that Ottomanist Charles Wells wrote in the early twentieth century: "they [the Turks] have always had the greatest respect for learning and admiration for literature, and in no country, perhaps, in the world have literary men been so favoured."[14]

In addition, classical Ottoman literature introduced very strict conventions of form, style, and genre. The *dastan*, for example, is a grand epic poem that honors real historical personalities of the past or legendary, popular folk heroes in fantastic, romantic, or heroic forms. The *ghazel* is a short lyrical poem consisting of several verses devoted to a single topic, usually centered on love and passion. The *qasyda* is a collection of verses that elegantly explores various topics and ends with a panegyric to a ruler, a patron, or a saint. A *rubai* ("four" from Arabic) is a four-line verse (quatrain), which rhymes the first, second, and fourth lines (aaca, bbxb, etc.); these individual *rubai* are beautifully knitted together to form extended (usually romantic) poems. The *qitah* is a short poem that features popular themes, jokes, word puzzles, or symbols; it is recited at public events or gatherings. The *maqamah* is a poem devoted to a single theme and written in a very high style. The *masnavi* (translated "two by two") is a poem written in rhymed couplets (aa, bb, etc.) that can consist of many verses gathered together.[15]

From a very early stage, classical literature made a huge impact on the language of "high society" and of the royal court. The Ottoman language absorbed a large number of Persian (Farsi) and Arabic words, to the extent that it became unintelligible to the "peasants" of Anatolia. Use of a foreign language at the royal courts and in high society was quite common in Europe, as was, for example, the extensive use of French in the Russian Imperial court and among the Polish nobility to distinguish themselves from the commoners. What made the Ottoman linguistic experience different was the very high level of penetration of the Persian language into the literary heritage and language of the country's ruling class. Many artists, members of the Ottoman nobility, and dynastic personages mastered the Persian language to perfection and used it for everyday communication, administration, and artistic expression.

Another important influence on Turkish religious poetry came from mystic (Sufi) philosophy. Many poetic works were created as purely religious poems; others were superficially love poems but incorporated symbolism and layers of hidden meanings and messages. Typically, in such works, love and affectionate feelings are depicted in symbols such as, for instance, a rose in a garden, which could mean love for a human being but could equally often symbolize love of the universe or love of its Creator. Such symbolism, allegories, and the profound influence of Sufism diffused the boundaries between lyrics, court poetry, and religious verse.

During the classical Ottoman era, many talented and prolific poets emerged to create a number of influential religious works. Among the most respected, and traditionally highlighted by experts, are Jelal ad-Din Rumi (1207–1273) (see Chapter 2); Yunus Emre (c. 1240–c. 1320); Imaduddin Nesimi (?–c. 1404); Suleyman Celebi (?–1422); Kaygusuz Abdal (1397–?); and Pir Sultan Abdal (?–1560).

Yunus Emre (c. 1240–c. 1320)

Poet, mystic, and scholar, Yunus Emre was considered one of the most influential mystic poets of his era, along with Jalal ad-Din Rumi. In his poetry, he used the popular folk themes of *tekerleme* and composed in the Turkic language of the ordinary people. He was a prolific writer (scholars attribute between 5,000 and 6,000 couplets to him);[16] his *masnavis* and *ghazels* tell stories of love and depict the feelings of people in love, but, at the same time, have deeper mystical meanings in allegorically celebrating divine love, human destiny, and the discontented experience of life in a world that humans cannot control.

Among the classics of *divan* poetry, the most famous and influential poets included Sheyhi (c. 1371–1431); Nizami (?–1417); Fuzuli (c. 1483–1556);[17] Ahmed Pasha (?–1496); Lami-i (1472–1532); Baki (1526–1600); Nefi (c. 1570–1635); Nedim (c. 1681–1730); Sheyh Galib (1757–1799); and many others.

Fuzuli (c. 1483–1556)

Fuzuli was a poet who rose to fame as one of the most acclaimed lyricists, writing in an elegant Turkic style (he wrote mainly in Azeri, but was equally skillful in Arabic and Persian), and using formalized classical themes and rhymes. His poems glorified love that transcended earthly trammels to fuel metaphoric relationships with the divine. For example, according to his reinterpretation of the classic Persian love story *Dastan-i Leyla ve Mejnun* (*Poem about Leyla and Mejnun*), the love between Leyla and her beloved Mejnun ("the person who became mad" in Persian) turns into an exposition of the love of an earthly human (Mejnun) for an eternal divine beauty (Leyla). This love leads to the painful separation of the young couple that once more allegorically illustrates the chasm between desire and everyday reality:

To earth within her ward my tears in torrents rolled apace;
The accent of her ruby lips my soul crazed by their grace,
My heart was taken in the snare her musky locks did trace,
That very moment when my eyes fell on her curls and face.
"Doth Scorpio the bright Moon's House contain?" I said;
said she:
"Fear! Threatening this Conjunction dread, thy part; aye, truly thine!"[18]

Nefi (c. 1570–1635)

Poet and mystic, Nefi became one of the most celebrated classics of Ottoman poetry for his elegant poems and odes. He infused his works with a measure of humor and was known for numerous satirical verses. His literary heritage comprises a gracefully written collection of *qasidas* (odes), which refined the poetic styles of the Ottoman literature and influenced many poets for decades.

Sheyh Galib (1757–1799)

Poet and mystic, Galib is considered one of the last and best examples of classical Ottoman poetry. He meticulously followed the formalized norms for structure, used greatly symbolic "high" language, and depicted love in exceptionally complex wordplay. His literary heritage includes a *divan* of fine allegoric Sufi love poetry (Galib himself was a grand-master at the Mevlevi Sufi lounge) and a romantic poem about the love of young people—*Beauty and Love.*

Turkish literature was not exclusively the domain of men. A number of female poets and writers achieved fame and recognition, despite the long-standing Ottoman custom of secluding women from public life. Among them, several achieved particular respect for their beautiful poetry, including Zeinab Hatun (?–1474), Mihri Hatun (?–c. 1513), Fitnat Hanum (?–1780), and others.

Not all of the writers of that era worked exclusively in the poetic genre. The needs of the royal court and state institutions and educators stimulated a significant interest in history, including general history and biographies of prominent historical figures, geography, especially travelogs, and political admonitions.[19] Most of these works were written in prose and were commissioned by the major Ottoman libraries, colleges, or individual statesmen.

MODERN LITERATURE

Nineteenth- and Early Twentieth-Century Literature

The classical-era poets left an impressive literary legacy of outstanding and elegant pieces, but eventually both the *divan* and religious poetry grew over-formalized and inflexible, with the genres' strict rules creating rigid boundaries and norms. Most of the literary themes and allegoric and ritualized symbols were repeated time and again. The language of high poetry, which remained under strong Persian language influence, became overly distant from and alien to the language of the street and ordinary people. Thus, by the nineteenth century, many artists had begun rebelling against "formalism," demanding changes and reforms, and taking the first steps in experimenting with new literary styles.

An increasing number of scholars and artists felt the need to return to the roots—to authentic Turkish language and authentic Turkish themes. This trend, in turn, provoked high interest in both the language of the ordinary Turkic people of Anatolia and in the study of Turkish folklore.

Ziya Pasha (1829–1880)

Publicist, translator, statesman, and poet, Ziya Pasha was among the first of the leading intellectuals of Turkey to advocate freedom of thought, nationalism, and constitutionalism. He was a founder of the influential intellectual journal, *Picture of Ideas* (*Tasvir-i Efkar*). He advanced the wider use of the Turkish language in intellectual and artistic works, arguing against "polluting" the language with loan words, especially from the Persian language.

Some writers went even further in criticizing the Procrustean bed of classical literature as the era of the past. They called for a whole new literature in a new (Western) style. Their criticism stimulated a divisive philosophical debate between the modernizers and the traditionalists. For many centuries, the ideological and philosophical worldview of the Ottoman society had been built around religious values and was relatively straightforward: the West represented the immoral "infidels" against whom brave, enlightened Ottomans had successfully fought. Suddenly, however, the world was turned upside down, and the Sublime Porte began losing battle after battle. Even the social institutions of the Ottoman state lost their strength and demonstrated signs of decay and breakdown, while Western society seemingly displayed a successful order and dynamic growth.[20] In this situation, one group of intellectuals began promoting such Western values as enlightenment, free thinking, democratization, and constitutionalism. This group strongly believed that the achievements of the modernized nations were the examples to follow. They admired the Western press, planned cities, open intellectual debates and critical thinking, and the high educational standards of the Western world. Many other Ottoman intellectuals, however, rejected such foreign values, seeing Western lifestyles, social institutions, education, and political systems—everything, without exception—as ultimately corrupt and alien. They called for a return to "true" values, which often meant strict Islamic norms and values. These writers and poets tried to escape into a utopian world of the "golden past" or into a lyrical nonpolitical literature. The two groups evinced highly disparate propensities, with the conservatives demonstrating strong anti-Western sentiments and the reformers (*jadids*) calling for change and progress.[21]

The literary world at this time was even more complex because it comprised not only members of both extreme camps, but also of many groups and individuals who agonized over which side to support. Inspired by the Tanzimat reforms and the rise of the Turkish media, some journalists, writers, scholars, diplomats, and poets started experimenting in the new "Western" genres and styles.

Ibrahim Sinasi Efendi (1826–1871)

Poet, journalist, translator, and playwright, Sinasi was among the founding members of the westernization movement in Turkish literature. Fluent in French, he compiled and translated an anthology of French poetry in 1853. For a decade, he contributed to various Turkish newspapers, including one he founded in 1862. He advocated the use of the "pure Turkish" language in literature. Sinasi is best remembered for his play, *The Poet's Marriage* (*Sair Evlenmesi*), which is considered one of the first modern Turkish dramas.

Semsettin Sami (1850–1904)

Writer, journalist, translator, and accomplished scholar, Sami made a significant contribution to the development of modern Turkish literature. Fluent in several languages including French and Italian, he studied and translated a number of international classics, including *Les Miserables* and *Robinson Crusoe,* and prepared several monumental Turkish research dictionaries and encyclopedias. His main contributions were in literature and journalism, as he wrote for various Turkish newspapers. Sami's *Love of Tal'at and Fitnat* (*Taassuk-i Tal'at ve Fitnat*) is widely considered to be one of the first Turkish novels.

Namik Kemal (1840–1888)

Poet, journalist, and statesman, Kemal actively supported nationalism and liberalism in his writing. He regularly contributed to many Turkish newspapers, translated articles into the Turkish, and commented on the works of Victor Hugo, Jean-Jacques Rousseau, and Charles Montesquieu. He made a considerable contribution to the development of Turkish nationalist intellectual debates, influencing the Young Turks and inspiring Mustafa Kemal. Among his most famous works are *Fatherland or Silistria* (*Vatan Yahnut Silistre*), *Awakening* (*Intibah*), *The Dream* (*Ruya*), *Sezmi,* and others.

As Ottoman society became increasingly polarized and fragmented on the eve of the twentieth century, so too did the Ottoman literary world. Proponents of the rival new and traditional literary trends, individual writers, poets, and journalists began organizing themselves into literary societies that manifested their respective political and artistic credos.

The New Literature Movement

In 1891, a group of young writers came together and founded the literary journal *Scientific Wealth* (*Servert-i Funum*). This helped them, very quickly, to consolidate their support base into the New Literature Movement. The movement's members, who were largely influenced by nineteenth-century French prose literature, especially French science fiction, declared their support for the creation and promotion of a Western-type "high literature" in Turkey. The numerous discussions and debates organized by this society shaped intellectual debate among young artists for many years, though the movement remained more a club of like-minded comrades than a truly consolidated artistic or political organization.

The Dawn of the Future Movement

This movement was established in 1909 by a group of young writers, with the publication of their literary manifesto in *Scientific Wealth*. In it, they declared their opposition to a blanket acceptance of Western culture, and to the politicization of literature. They emphasized the importance of compromise, highlighting Turkish artistic achievements and the aesthetic value of literature.

The National Literary Movement

This movement emerged in 1891 around the newly established literary journal, *Young Pens* (*Gench Kalemler*). Members of this group were inspired by the Young Turks political movement and emphasized the distinctiveness of Turkish identity, culture, and language. They rejected Ottomanism as a multicultural, multiethnic, and multireligious concept of the state, and called for an exploration of "pure Turkishness."

THE LITERATURE OF THE REPUBLICAN PERIOD

The literature of the early Turkish Republic developed around three major themes: the lives of ordinary people who represented the "true values" and "true virtues" of Turkish society; social change, such as the breakdown of family values and the endless conflict between traditionalist groups and those who advocated modernity; and the social problems and issues of rural or "Anatolian village" life. These themes were expanded upon against a background of the dramatic collapse of the social and political institutions of the Ottoman Empire, losses in the War of Independence, and the new policy of the Cultural Revolution. One of the most important events in this revolution, and one that directly affected the literary world, was the abandonment, in 1928, of Arabic script and the introduction of the Latin-based alphabet. Along with reforms in the writing system, the government and ruling elite advocated profound changes in and purification of the Turkish language, calling for the elimination of Arabic and Persian words and "reintroducing" true Turkic words.

The republic was based on the utter rejection of its predecessor—the Ottoman Empire and everything related to its refined "high" culture. The classical, highly abstract, and rigidly formulated *gazels* and *qasydas*, which were based on classical Persian and Arabic poetry, went out of fashion and were largely abandoned. New poetic forms and themes took their place promoting an energetic, if not a revolutionary, message of change. One of the most vivid and extreme examples of this trend is the life and works of Nazim Hikmet Ran (1902–1963), who achieved international fame in his lifetime and won the affection of several generations of readers not only in Turkey but throughout the world. Many contemporaries called Nazim Hikmet, who was a poet, novelist, and playwright, "the romantic revolutionary" for his powerful lyrics and energizing poetic style. He traveled to Moscow as a romantic nineteen-year-old, and was inspired by revolutionary Soviet poet Vladimir Mayakovski to battle against "the dark fanatical forces."[22] From his first books—*835 Lines* (*835 Satır*, 1929) and *The City that Lost its Voice* (*Sesini Kaybeden Srehir*, 1931)— he moved away from the time-honored metric style to free verses, which he carefully harmonized with the peculiarities of the Turkish language, winning nationwide recognition and acclaim. Like many authors of his generation, he also looked at folklore for inspiration, especially in writing his *The Epic of Sheikh Bedreddin* (*Seikh Bedrettin Destani*, 1936). He experimented not only with forms of verse but also with new symbolism and themes, ranging from patriotism and social justice (*Human Landscapes* [*Memleketimden İnsan Manzaraları*, 1942]) to depictions of the lives of ordinary people in the villages and cities. Although Hikmet's talents were often compared to those of Garcia Lorca and Pablo Neruda, he spent many years imprisoned in Turkey for his political views and was forced to leave the country in 1950. He died in exile in Moscow in 1963.

The events of the twentieth century dramatically affected Turkish society, but it was often the ordinary people who were destined to live through and navigate the crises and turmoil, unable to influence those changes. The fate of ordinary Turks who preserved their ideals and optimism in the most difficult situations was romanticized and exhaustively portrayed by many novelists who turned to social realism as the ideal vehicle to narrate the inner beauty of the simple life of villagers in Anatolia. Like many other novelists of his republican-era generation, Yashar Kemal (1922–) grew up witnessing and experiencing the political and social turmoil of Turkey during and after World War II. Like many other Turkish writers, Kemal began his career writing poems. From his earliest days he became highly respected for his carefully crafted stories and novels of newly discovered "village life." His first book, *Ballads* (*Agitlar*, 1943), was noted by the country's book reviewers. In 1951, he moved to Istanbul, where he worked as a journalist for the influential *Cumhurieyet* newspaper. In 1952, he published a collection of short stories, *Yellow Heat* (*Sari Sicak*, 1952). He wrote many novels, including *The Wind from the Plain* (*Ortadirek*, 1960), *Iron Earth, Copper Sky* (*Yer Demir, Gok Baker*, 1963), *The Eternal Grass* (*Olmez Utu*, 1968), *To Crush the Snake* (*Yilani Oldurseler*, 1976), and *Look, the Firat River is Flowing with Blood* (*Firat Suyu Kan Aktyoyr Baksana*, 1997), but he first received real fame for his beautiful novel, *Thin Memed* (*Ince Memed*, 1955), which was translated into English as *Memed, My Hawk* (1961).[23] *Memed, My Hawk* recounts the life of Memed, a young boy growing up in the tough and intensely hierarchical environment of Dayirmenoluk village in Anatolia.

He experiences injustice and cruelty from his parents and from the village head, Abdi Aga. Memed finds freedom by escaping his community and taking justice into his own hands.

In periods of difficulties, political turmoil, and censorship, many writers in Turkey turned to humor, satire, and Aesopian-style allegoric language to criticize both their political opponents and government figures. Aziz Nesin (1915–1995) was probably one of the best-known and most prolific representatives of this genre in Turkey. He began his career as a military officer, but in the 1940s became a journalist, contributed to major newspapers, and built a following for his sarcastic style and willingness to criticize domestic policies. His views, however, met with the disapproval of government officials; in 1946, he landed a prison term and was barred from journalism for several years. His early collection of stories *Dog's Tale* (*It Kuyrugu*, 1955) won him national recognition. He frequently used traditional folk heroes and plots from folk stories, especially from the stories about Nasreddin Hoca, and he often personalized the views of "ordinary citizens" to ridicule politicians, editors, public figures, conservatives, censors, and so on. In addition, he wrote and published several dozen books. He also became an active public figure, establishing the Nesin Foundation in 1972, which was devoted to providing support for the education of children from poor families and to leading intellectual debate on free speech and human rights in the country.

RECENT TRENDS

Political and economic liberalization in Turkey in the 1980s and 1990s set an important milestone in the development of its literature. Many restrictions that had been imposed by the government quite suddenly disappeared. Many topics (although not all) previously considered politically incorrect became open for public discussion. As the confrontations over the country's future and intellectual influence intensified, once more a debate heated up between traditionalists, including Islamic activists, and a Western-oriented secular intelligentsia, which focused on such issues as national identity, Turkish history, politics, human rights, and freedoms.

While intellectuals were busy reevaluating the achievements and faults of their national literature, and ways in which to respond to the changing world, the world itself arrived at their doorsteps in the form of crises that struck at literary circles on many fronts. The government withdrew or significantly cut their previously generous subsidies to publishing houses, writers' unions, book clubs, and individual authors. It was now up to the market or rich philanthropists to decide which authors could publish and survive in this highly unstable environment. At the same time, the reading audience was shrinking at a catastrophic rate, with economic recessions and a marginalization of the book industry. Because of high inflation in the 1990s, many people, even professionals—teachers, researchers, doctors, lawyers—could no longer afford to buy books.

The life and works of Orhan Pamuk (1952–) most revealingly illustrate the controversies and extremes of recent developments in the literary world of Turkey. Pamuk represents a new generation of Turkish writers who feel free of any social or political limitations and often use their literary talents to deconstruct political conflicts between Islamic and secular values, between past and present, and to stir up debate on these controversial issues. Almost every book written by Pamuk has explored new territory. His first novel, *Darkness and Light* (*Karanlık ve Isık*, 1974), depicts the country's changing social landscape and rapidly transforming world and moral values through the life of a wealthy family in Istanbul. The book was a great success, earning him the Milliyet Press Novel Contest prize. Subsequent books *The Silent House* (*Sessiz Ev*, 1984) and *The White Castle* (*Beyaz Kale*, 1985) were promptly translated into English and brought him international recognition. But it was his unconventional *The Black Book* (*Kara Kitap*, 1990) and *New Life* (*Yeni hayat*, 1995), which became national bestsellers that won him the most recognition. His novel *My Name is Red* (*Benim Adım Kırmızı*, 2000) returns readers to his beloved Istanbul of the sixteenth century, where mystery collides with romance and religious conflicts. His book *Snow* (*Kar*, 2002) explores the conflicts between time-honored and modern values, and clashes between different groups in Turkish society personified through a mixture of mysticism and naturalistic depiction of suicidal moods in the small Turkish town of Kars. The English translation of the book was named by the *New York Times* as one of the best books of 2004. Pamuk's novel *Istanbul: Memories and the City* (*İstanbul: Hatıralar ve Sehir*, 2003) became an unofficial literary guide to the capital.

Despite his success, however, and perhaps because of his high public profile, some of the statements in his books brought him into conflict with the Turkish authorities, and attracted open hostility from certain other groups in the country. His suggestion that there was a need to recognize and discuss the killing of Armenians during the conflicts in the early twentieth century brought legal charges against him in 2005.[24] Although he was never prosecuted, this conflict found its way into the international headlines and received public attention around the world.[25] In 2006, Orhan Pamuk became the first Turkish writer to win the Nobel Prize in literature, stirring a mixture of pride and rebuff in his native country.

It would not be an exaggeration to say that Turkish literature has been at a crossroads ever since the 1980s and 1990s, as new literary trends started gaining ground. One of the most important contributing factors to this change was the diminishing role of the government in regulating the artistic world, as it reduced (but did not eliminate entirely) censorship and political interference in the writers' creative work. The government also significantly relaxed its restrictive regulation of the import of printed products; it now allows major international companies and franchises to operate in the Turkish market. In addition, several local printing houses were established in the country, contributing to greater competition and a free-market environment. Commercial TV and the Internet have also made huge inroads in Turkey, especially since the late 1990s, and their content has challenged book readership. The government abandoned or significantly reduced direct and indirect subsidies to Turkish publishers and writers. Finally, the winds of globalization that brought U.S.-style consumerism and pop culture have also become decisive in forming new trends in Turkish literature.

The first and most important trend is the shrinking or stagnating readership, especially among the young generations, as they increasingly turn to the TV, Internet, and other forms of entertainment at the expense of serious and leisure reading. A further factor is the high inflation of the 1990s and 2000s, which has forced many families and individuals to cut down on buying serious books.

The second trend is the increased commercialization of the writing profession. The literary world has begun transforming into a Western-style and Western-product-dominated literary market, in which Turkish writers often lose ground due to the influx of Western literature and media, especially television. For publishers, it is often much cheaper and more commercially viable to publish translations of already established Western bestsellers, such as *Memoirs of a Geisha* or *The Da Vinci Code*, than to nurture local talent. And it is more profitable to publish popular fiction, such as adventure novels, detective stories, plus celebrity biographies, and so on, than to deal with writers of high literature who reach a very small audience.[26] This trend has made a particularly strong negative impact on poetry, which, in the past, held a very strong position in the country; there are fewer people who appreciate poetry in Turkey and fewer people who write serious poems.

The third important trend is the fragmentation and polarization of society. There are dozens, if not hundreds, of literary societies that fiercely compete with each other over differences in political, social, and religious views and over personal rivalries and clashes of ambition. Add to this a growing gap between the secular intelligentsia and the religiously oriented intelligentsia, along with significant differences in values and lifestyles between the country's rural and urban populations.

The fourth trend is a surge of public interest in religious and spiritual literature that represents the views and ideas of Islamic thinkers of the distant past, such as Yunus Emre, and of the nineteenth- and twentieth-century Islamic intellectuals, such as Said Nursi (1878–1960), and poets Mehmet Akif Ersoy (1873–1936), and Ismet Ozel (1944–).

The fifth recent trend is the reemergence of popular humor. There are many examples of oral humor and satirical traditions, and thousands of jokes have been created around different people or social groups. Typical among them is the body of so-called *Laz* jokes, which are very popular among Turks. *Laz* jokes focus on a small regional group of people in the northeastern region of the Black Sea coast in Turkey, and are very similar to the ethnicity-based humor encountered in the United States or the United Kingdom. In the 1980s and 1990s, a new type of joke—political anecdotes—became very popular in Turkey, often satirically targeting individual politicians for their clumsy usage of the language (in similar fashion to American humorists' treatment of Donald Rumsfeld's "known unknowns") and ridiculing their behavior or style of public appearance.[27]

NOTES

1. Walter Andrews et al., eds. *Ottoman Lyric Poetry: An Anthology (Publications on the Near East)*. Austin, TX: University of Texas Press, 1997, p. 4.

2. Personal observation in Istanbul book shops in 2007.

3. Mehmed Fuad Koprulu. *Early Mystics in the Turkish Literature*. London and New York: Routledge, 2006. p. iii.

4. Barbara Walker. *The Art of the Turkish Tale*. Vol. 1. Lubbock, TX: Texas Tech University Press, 1990, pp. xxii, 200.

5. Kamal Silay. *An Anthology of Turkish Literature*. Bloomington, IN: Indiana University Turkish Studies, 1996.

6. See Karl Reichl. *Turkic Epic Poetry: Traditions, Forms, Poetic Structure*. New York and London: Garland Publishing, 1992.

7. There are several versions of this epic, which varied among the Kazakhs, Uzbeks, Tajiks, and Turkmens. For an example of the Turkmen version, see N. Ashirov, ed. *Geroglu, Tartibe Salan Ata Govshud Geroglu*. Ashgabat: Ylym. 1958.

8. See Zhirmunskii and Zaripov. *Uzbekskii narodnyi geroicheskii epos* [Uzbek People Heroic Epic]. Moscow: OGIZ, 1947, pp. 184–210.

9. Faruk Sümer, Ahmet E. Uysal, and Warren S. Walker, trans. and eds. *The Book of Dede Korkut. A Turkish Epic*. Austin, TX: University of Texas Press, 1972, p. 3.

10. Karl Reichl. *Turkic Oral Epic Poetry*, pp. 33–39.

11. See, for example, "History of Forty Viziers," in *Turkish Literature. Comprising Fables, Belles-letters, and Sacred Traditions*. Introduction by Epiphanius Wilson. New York: Books for Libraries Press, 1901, reprint 1990, pp. 361–460.

12. See, for example, *The Khoja: Tales of Nasr-ed-Din*. Translated from the Turkish text by Henry D. Barnham, C.M.G., with a foreword by Sir Valentine Chirol. New York: A. L & J. C. Fawcett, 1998.

13. Author's own translation.

14. Charles Wells. *The Literature of the Turks: A Turkish Chrestomathy. The Near East.* London: Bernard Quaritch, 1891, p. xi.

15. Bernard Lewis, trans. *Music of a Distant Drum: Classical Arabic, Persian, Turkish, and Hebrew Poems.* Princeton, NJ: Princeton University Press, 2001.

16. Mehmed Fuad Koprulu, p. 304.

17. Poets Nuzami and Fuzuli are highly acclaimed in Azerbaijan because they wrote in a Turkic language close to the language spoken in present-day Azerbaijan. Yet, their poetry made a great impact on the Ottoman divan literature.

18. *Turkish Literature. Comprising Fables, Belles-letters, and Sacred Traditions.* Introduction by Epiphanius Wilson. New York: Books for Libraries Press, 1901. reprint 1990, p. 101.

19. See, for example, Evliya Çelebi. *Evliya Çelebi's Book of Travels: Land and People of the Ottoman Empire in the Seventeenth Century: A Corpus of Partial Editions.* Edited by Klaus Kreiser. Vols. 1–5. Leiden; New York: E. J. Brill, 1988–1998.

20. Bernard Lewis. *The Middle East and the West.* New York: Harper and Row, 1964.

21. For discussion of the heated debate between the conservatives and reformers, see Bernard Lewis. *The Emergence of Modern Turkey.* New York: Oxford University Press, 2001.

22. This was the title of one of Hikmet's early poems (1921). See Nazim Hikmet. *Beyond the Walls. Selected Poems.* London: Anvil Press Poetry, 2002, p. 246.

23. See Yashar Kemal. *Memed, My Hawk.* New York: New York Review Books, 2005.

24. For Pamuk's position, see Maureen Freely. "I stand by my words. And even more, I stand by my right to say them ..." http://www.guardian.co.uk/world/2005/oct/23/books.turkey (accessed October 22, 2008).

25. http://news.bbc.co.uk/2/hi/europe/4205708.stm (accessed October 22, 2008).

26. for the list of the most popular commercial books in Turkey see: http://www.pandora.com.tr/coksatan.aspx (accessed October 22, 2008).

27. Several collections of such jokes have been published in Turkey since the 1990s. See, for example, Can Ozan. *Demirelinonu. Koalisyon Fıkraları* [Demirel and Inonu. Facts about the Coalition]. Istanbul: Arkadas Yayinlari, 1995; Can Ozan. *Cikin Ciller Fikralari* [Facts about Tansu Ciller]. Istanbul: Kora Yayin, 1998; and Ercan Deva. *Bir Basbakan Varmis, Bir Basbakan Yokmus.* Adana: Umit Yayincilik, 2000.

4

Media and Cinema

—What is a visontele?
—A vizontele is a radio with moving pictures, which would bring us news from
[the center of the world] Ankara without delays....
                                        —A dialogue from Vizontele (2001)

THE DIVERSITY OF Turkey's political, cultural, and social spectrum of opinions may be best seen by a foreigner under the magnifying glass of the Turkish
media. Journalism as a profession still carries high social prestige and influence, for journalists and commentators of all calibers from CNN-Turk to the
smallest provincial newspaper in Cappadoccia or eastern Anatolia. Politicians,
tycoons, parliamentarians, and scholars like to rub shoulders with journalists,
listen to their opinions, read their commentaries, and hotly discuss their op-
eds. During times of political turmoil in the country, the journalists have traditionally been the ones with the courage to run into the middle of events to
report and comment; and, too, they have always been first to be arrested or
dragged in to the detention centers.

This influence is built on decades of past experience. In Turkey, the mass
media was established and developed on principles different from those of
many other countries. While in the United States, for instance, the media
developed with the dual purpose of entertaining the public and reporting
the news without bias, in Turkey, it was established to educate the public and propagate the ideas and ideals of modernization and change. Many

Modern Turkish media offers a variety of choices.
Courtesy of the author, 2007.

generations of Turkish journalists were brought up with, educated toward, and constantly reminded of this mission in society.

Another distinctive aspect of the Turkish media is the high level of trust it commands among Turks, as, for example, 72 percent of respondents in a media survey in summer 2008 indicated that they believe that "truth" and "objectivity" are "very important" in their selection of newspapers for purchase.[1] Turkish history contains numerous instances of the government or the military trying to impose various forms of control and censorship over the national press and television. Most Turkish journalists defied these pressures.

Significant changes in the 1990s, when Turkish markets became open to domestic and international competition, did not leave the media world unaffected.[2] Commentators and readers have noted a rapid commercialization and polarization among newspapers, magazines, and radio and television stations. The number of newspapers and glossy magazines increased sharply, especially those that focused on gossip-oriented news, entertainment, and lifestyle issues. Paparazzi appeared on the scene, hunting for spicy pictures of celebrities, love triangles, or scandals, and at the same time the number of pages devoted to all kinds of salacious and unsavory news skyrocketed. Even serious newspapers began to periodically place photos of scantily dressed singers with "malfunctioned wardrobe"[3] and actors from around the world on their front pages. Despite this, however, quality journalism remains alive and well in Turkey, as do the mechanisms of government scrutiny that regularly remind journalists of the restrictions and censorship placed on their profession, and the legal actions and fines used to enforce those constraints.

THE PRESS

The newsstands in major urban centers, such as Ankara, Istanbul, or Izmir, are colorful and extremely diverse. They present a broad range of newspapers and magazines, from light and entertaining to ultraconservative, representing a full palette of political and social opinion and deep political, cultural, and generational divides within the country. The stands are often dominated by racy periodicals and tabloid newspapers that tend to capture the youth readership, yet the more conservative papers, sporting the far less cheerful faces of politicians on their front pages are also there. In the small cities and towns, however, a distinctly different picture emerges; fewer newspapers reach these local audiences; and many villagers probably do not read them at all—current statistics indicate that up to 30 percent of the population of rural Turkey remains illiterate or semi-illiterate.

This divide has survived since the Ottoman era. The beginnings of the press in Turkey illustrate the peculiarities of the country's media development over the past 200 years. The first newspaper, *Takvim-i Vekayi* (*Agenda of Events*), was published in 1831, although various periodicals in foreign languages (Persian [Farsi], Greek, Hebrew, and some others) preceded it, probably in the early 1800s. The *Takvim-i Vekayi* was founded by government officials to propagate the official government agenda—promotion of reforms and modernization of the military, state institutions, and the legal environment. It took about a decade for a second newspaper to be founded: *Ceride-i Havadis* (*News Letter*) was launched in 1840, and it focused on the economic and financial sectors. Importantly, *Ceride-i Havadis* was founded as a private enterprise; it was edited by a foreigner and provided considerable coverage of international affairs. Another newspaper that stood as a milestone in the history of the Turkish press was *Tercuman-i Ahval* (*Interpreter of Events*), which was founded in 1860 and gave birth to independent professional journalism. This paper also focused on reform, enlightenment, and education by soliciting contributions from leading intellectuals whose views appeared regularly in its pages, creating and contributing to public debate, and expressing diverse opinions.

In the late nineteenth century, the development of the press gained momentum and the number of periodicals, including various literary journals and papers, reached about a hundred. Some had very small circulations and were short-lived. Others managed to navigate through difficult times to establish their readership, a market niche, and commercially successful models. Not all newspapers supported the government and its policies. The Ottoman administration reacted by imposing the Press Regulation Act in the 1860s and censorship in the 1870s. These actions, however, did not deter the journalists who actively participated in the political process and public debates. The number of newspapers and magazines continued to multiply and by 1908 had reached 350, each with a circulation ranging from few hundred to several thousand.

The establishment of the Turkish Republic also significantly affected the development of the country's press. After becoming the president, Mustafa Kemal envisioned, supported, and actively stimulated the development of all types of media, seeing the media as a key instrument in promoting government policies, the reform agenda, modernization, and literacy among the people. This approach had a huge impact on the media because newspapers were closely watched by government officials and printing and distribution were subsidized from the state budget. Several popular newspapers, such as *Cumhuriyet*, were established during that era.

In the time of the military coups in the 1960s, 1970s, and 1980s, the national press came under especially heavy control. The censorship regime proactively screened the publications of those journalists who took a position critical of the policies of the government and individual politicians. One of the most striking records of that era is the newspapers that were published with blank spaces as the censors removed certain articles just before the papers went to press.

Political rivalry between different groups in Turkey has also hit journalists hard, with many suffering intimidation or even imprisonment for publishing articles and material critical of the government and government policies. Some have lost their lives. Journalists also have been targeted by ultraradical political groups and organizations. One of the latest victims was Hrant Dink, the editor of the bilingual Turkish-Armenian newspaper *Agos*, who was killed in 2007 by a young gunman who apparently disagreed with his published point of view.[4]

The free-market-oriented reforms of the mid-1980s opened new doors of opportunity for many media outlets. The press progressively turned to increased advertising as a source of revenue and significantly benefited from the resulting sharp rise in income. The economic changes led to increased competition between companies, and they began directing more resources into advertising and marketing, which in turn contributed to further prosperity.

The market-oriented reforms combined with some relaxation of state-imposed controls allowed the appearance of new media outlets. The respective histories of the newspapers *Zaman* and *Radikal* are exemplary, even though they represent very different segments of the print market.

Zaman had a relatively modest start in Istanbul in 1986. Within a few years, it had won a large audience in the country and overseas, with the support of the Fethullah Gulen movement. The newspaper positioned itself as a centrist publication and this strategy propelled it into the ranks of the top five papers in Turkey within two decades, and it is one of the most read newspapers among Turkish communities overseas as it is published in fourteen countries.[5] According to press statistics, *Zaman* became the number one newspaper by total circulation (as of March 2008), outselling its nearest competitors, *Posta* and *Hurriyet*, by a solid 15 to 18 percent.[6]

Radikal began in 1996 with backing from the powerful Dogan Media Group. It positions itself as a liberal left-of-center publication that aims to be unaffiliated with any political group. Within a decade it had become one of the most influential newspapers in the country, especially renowned for its top-drawer columnists and its coverage of intellectual debates. Nevertheless, its circulation numbers remain sluggish, and it struggles in twenty-fourth place in the periodical rankings for 2008.[7]

Growing competition among newspapers and the sharp increase in media outlets led to a gradual segmentation of the media market, with several distinct groups of newspapers arising. The first group consists of newspapers, such as the *Hurriyet* and *Cumhuriyet*, which are Turkish equivalents of the *New York Times* or the *Washington Post*, or perhaps the *Guardian* in the United Kingdom. These newspapers cover political issues and international affairs with depth and sophistication and are oriented toward educated urbanites.

The second group comprises several tabloid-style newspapers, such as the *Posta* and the *Star*, which are similar to the New York *Daily News* or the *Star* and *Mirror* of London. They target wider audiences, including women and youth, by watering down the political and economic news with a substantial ration of gossip, entertainment, and extensive coverage of local issues.

A new trend in Turkey is the rise of English-language newspapers and other periodicals. One of the official channels communicating news in English has traditionally been the official news agency—the *Anadolu* Press Association. The *Turkish Daily News* has also been an important source of information in English since 1961. In addition, *Zaman* began publishing an English edition, *Today's Zaman*, in January 2007.[8] One of the country's flagships in the international media market is *Zaman USA*, also established in 2007. Another reliable English-language source is *The New Anatolian*,[9] whose "Cross-Reader" section provides useful summaries of major publications from the most prominent Turkish newspapers. As the number of Turks in western Europe and the Organization for Security and Cooperation in Europe countries increased by several hundred percent over the last three or four decades, the Turkish media began to service a speedily expanding overseas diaspora.

Changing lifestyles and the country's rapidly growing prosperity led to enlarged readerships of various magazines focusing on a range of interests from political and economic issues to home decoration, music, and theater. Specialized men's and women's magazines have also enjoyed this boom. According to official statistics, the number of magazines jumped from about 20 in 1990 to around 140 in 2008, with total circulation exceeding 2.5 million copies. Many newspapers also began regularly publishing weekly or monthly inserts and magazines that cover various interests from books to home design. For example, Cumhuriyet's *Kitap* (Book) is an interesting book review insert that is comparable to the weekly book review section of *The New York Times* in the United States.[10]

Like many of their counterparts in the West, a large number of Turkish newspapers have invested heavily in building web portals and shifting their contents onto the Internet. Today most of the leading Turkish newspapers can be found on the World Wide Web, with many of them maintaining a small presence in foreign languages, primarily English and German. Other technological advances have also made huge inroads in the country's media. Computer technology arrived in Turkish newsrooms relatively late compared with those of the United States, the United Kingdom, or Australia. Old-fashioned typewriters were still quite common in the 1980s and happily clattered on the desks of editors and journalists well into the 1990s. In the early 2000s, staff of many of the leading newspapers experienced a huge leap forward when they received the latest state-of-the-art technology, right there on their desks, bypassing in the process some of the intermediate technological developments with which their Western counterparts had experimented for some time.

One of the factors contributing to the rapid changes in the Turkish press and its adoption of new technologies is a peculiarity of media ownership in the country. Most of the largest newspapers and magazines belong to several large holding companies, such as the Dogan Media Group, Milliyet, Bilgin Media Group, and a few others. These holding companies, having deep financial pockets, have been able to successfully navigate the rapidly changing reader-ship tastes, technological innovations and the turmoil of the media market, and to increase their market share in the 1990s and early 2000s.

The new developments in the media market led to significant changes in journalism as a profession. In the past, many journalists had also written se-rious fiction, nonfiction, and poetry, and often built on their prestige and in-fluence by publishing novels, poems, and short stories. The new generation of journalists, who joined the profession after the hectic era of market-oriented reforms in the late 1980s and 1990s, tend to be dynamic and articulate and to work with a tincture of the "cowboy" in their style. Thus, the deliberate, elegant presentation of news and commentary is being replaced by a more brash, rapid-fire, American-style coverage.

Another recent change in journalism is that whereas in the past the profes-sion was overwhelmingly dominated by men, there are now increasing num-bers of women in the field, especially in the cultural, entertainment, lifestyle, and youth areas, and, of course, women's publications.[11] However, some jour-nalists claim that women's presence at the managerial level has been lagging behind.

The Turkish press entered the twenty-first century as one of the most dy-namic and rapidly growing media in Europe. Despite the growing popularity of the Internet and the shift of youth audiences to television and personal computers, the press experienced healthy annual growth between 2000 and 2008, surpassing the psychologically important circulation benchmark of six million weekend newspapers in February 2007.[12] This represents a very size-able increase of 59 percent. If the current trend continues, total circulation for weekend editions would double by 2014–2015.

Yet, despite the growth and expansion of the press, journalists still en-counter difficulties in fulfilling their professional duties. Long gone are the days when critical or unorthodox writing could land a journalist in a prison cell with perhaps a heavy beating by the police. However, some restrictions remain in place and many Turkish journalists claim that the government is adept at finding ways to reach out and silence such critics. Journalists still exercise a degree of self-censorship and restraint by avoiding certain topics and issues. In its 2007 Annual Survey of Press Freedoms, the Freedom House ranked Turkey 105 out of 195, behind Mexico and Argentina but ahead of Albania, Madagascar, Ukraine, and Russia.[13]

RADIO AND TELEVISION

Radio remains exceedingly popular among all generations in Turkey. It is relatively easy and inexpensive to access the airwaves, to set up new stations and to tailor programs to the tastes of highly diverse audiences. Radio relay stations effortlessly cover the whole country, reaching even the most remote mountainous areas in the east, where people live in small, poor villages without access to other modes of communication. Even illiterate peasants can operate a radio with ease or call the local station to request a favorite song or comment on community events. The accessibility and popularity of the medium is clearly illustrated by the statistics for radio ownership: Turkey is 33rd out of 221 in the world, ahead of Malaysia, Uzbekistan, and Venezuela, with the total number of radio receivers in the country exceeding 11.3 million.[14]

Radio broadcasting began in Turkey in 1927—quite late compared with western Europe or the Americas. The first broadcasting stations were established by the republican government under the initiative of Mustafa Kemal, who passionately promoted radio as the most powerful mode of popularizing the ideas of modernization, nationalism, and *kemalism*. Within a decade, the medium was reaching all the major urban areas, but it was around three decades before more than half the country could claim coverage. In 1964, the main regulating and controlling organization—the Turkish Radio and Television Corporation (TRTC)—was established, with a brief to direct investment into expanding the number of radio stations and to control the licensing process for new stations. It was not until 1987 that the whole of Turkey had radio coverage, and in the 1990s the radio market experienced double-digit annual growth.

The radio market has benefited from liberalization and the private-sector initiatives of the late 1980s and 1990s, with most stations abandoning the formal, official style of presenting information and introducing more entertaining content, such as talk-shows, music programs, and so on. As a result, the number of radio stations has rocketed to about 1,200 (as of 2008).[15]

The TRTC manages several state-subsidized radio channels. Radio 1, for example, provides coverage of the domestic and international news, Radio 3 broadcasts mainly classical music and news in English, French, and German, TRT FM specializes in Turkish classical music, and FM 91.4 specializes in Turkish folk music. One of the TRTC's flagship channels is the Voice of Turkey, which broadcasts in twenty-six languages, targeting an international audience.[16]

Among the most popular private radio stations are *Alem* FM, Best FM, Number One FM, Power FM, Radio D, Slow Radio, and Super FM. Many private radio stations develop their own niche audiences and maintain groups of devoted listeners as they broadcast popular Turkish pop and folk music, Western (mainly U.S.) pop and rock, and so on. They also increasingly cover sports, especially soccer, and devote more time to talk shows on family values, spiritual issues and social development. Regulations dictate that the private radio stations must allocate some air time for educational and cultural pro-grams.

In a recent trend, most radio stations, both public and private, have estab-lished their presence on the World Wide Web and have begun broadcasting over the Internet.[17]

CINEMA

Turkish cinema is probably one of the most under-appreciated and little-known phenomena of world cinema.[18] The rich and lengthy history of the Turkish film industry reached its zenith in the 1970s, when Turkey was pro-ducing between 200 and 250 movies a year, rivaling both Hollywood and Bollywood in sheer numbers. There may well have been a total of between three and four thousand movies made in Turkey during the twentieth century. Of course, the quality of the movies emerging from such a mass-production "conveyor belt" process was very uneven. Turkish movies have been widely screened in the developing countries, especially in the Middle East and south Asia, but unfortunately they have struggled to find their way onto Western screens. The *mirabile visu* of the Turkish cinema is hidden in a small Cin-ema Television Museum that remains "Turkey's first and sole museum of cinema."[19]

Turkish cinema is best known for its melodramas, naturalistic, in-depth depictions of the lives of ordinary people in rural environments and realistic portrayals of the social and personal lives of people in the "jungles" of large ur-ban centers. Turkish producers have also experimented in other popular genres of contemporary cinema, from westerns and science fiction to musicals, ad-venture, and erotica. They could never match Western productions in terms of finances and special effects; but these shortcomings were well-compensated for by their mastery in depiction of rich cultural backgrounds and psycholog-ical intrigues of people living in complex social and family relations.

Like many national film industries in southern and eastern Europe, Turkish cinema had its beginnings very early, but took several decades before it could flower and begin producing significant works. The very first film screening in the Ottoman Empire was arranged in 1897. Within a few years, the cinemato-graph had quite a large audience, and entrepreneurs were opening movie the-aters in all the major cities within the Empire. During the first decade, all films were imported from western Europe, and no attempt was made to develop lo-cal production. Yet, many young people were fascinated by the medium and the opportunities it presented, so they eagerly learned from foreign theater managers who worked in Istanbul and they traveled to Europe to grasp every-thing they could from their European partners.

The glory of the past: movie posters from the 1960s. Courtesy of the author, 2007.

The first attempts to produce films locally were made just before and during World War I. Turkish cinema historians generally cite 1914 as an important benchmark. That year Fuat Uzkinay, an Ottoman Army officer, produced the very first documentary—*The Demolition of the Russian Monument at St. Stephan* (*Ayos Stefanos'taki Rus Abidensinin Yikilisi*). There are also claims that several years earlier the Ottoman royal family's life was filmed on several occasions. During this period, General Enver Pasha, Minister of War and Commander of the Ottoman Army, turned his attention to the cinema and gave his support to the establishment of the Army Film Center (AFC). The AFC commissioned several documentaries and motion pictures. The events of the war and subsequent political turbulence prevented the completion of many films, but local producers managed to finish two major projects—*The Spy* (*Casus,* 1917) and *The Claw* (*Pence,* 1917). These films laid the foundation of the early Turkish cinema.

Despite the industry's increasing experience and the rise of local talent, cinema production was put on hold for some years due to the War of Independence and the economic difficulties of the postwar period. Yet, this did not hinder the popular interest in cinema. The number of movie theaters continued to grow throughout the country.

In 1922, the Seded brothers established their first production studio and company, Kemal Film, which produced several motion pictures, including *A Love Tragedy in Istanbul* (*Istanbul'da Bir Facia-i Ask*, 1922), *The Mystery on the Bosporus* (*Bogazici Esrari*, 1922), and *The Shirt on Fire* (*Atesten Gomlek*, 1923). This studio contributed to the development of Turkish cinema in several ways. First was the establishment of an artistic and managerial approach to movie production: the studio founders invited theater actors and actresses and directors to take part in their motion pictures. Second, the producers often adapted existing popular dramas from the Istanbul theaters, with minor modifications and editing. For various reasons, however, Kemal Film closed down within two years.

It took another five years before a new movie studio, Ipek Film, was established. This time it was a commercial enterprise backed by the deep pockets of the Ipekci brothers, who owned a network of movie theaters across the country. The movies they were screening were traditionally imported from France, Germany, and Italy. The brothers felt, however, that there was a market for local movie production. Their control over the distribution and marketing network enabled them to carefully manage the distribution of locally produced films, making them financially viable. The Ipekcis hired producer Muhsin Ertugrul (1892–1979), who had previously worked for the Kemal Film. Ertugrul retained his signature approach to producing movies, inviting theater performers to play in his films and adapting successful plays from Istanbul's theatrical repertoires. Ipek Film produced about twenty movies, including *The Streets of Istanbul* (*Istanbul Sokaklarında*, 1931), *A Nation Awakens* (*Bir Millet Uyanıyor*, 1932), *The Million Hunters* (*Milyon Avcıları*, 1934), *The Victims of Lust* (*Şehvet Kurbanı*, 1940), and others. Ertugrul was very familiar with trends in European cinematography, and European influences may be seen in many of his works. Yet, he made a significant contribution to the development of a distinctive Turkish cinema by introducing authentic Turkish themes and by experimenting with distinctly Turkish cultural elements. Ertugrul extended himself into a variety of genres, from elegant and sensitive dramas to social-realism-style depictions of the life of his native Istanbul, and monumental historical epics about Turkey's national awakening and the War of Independence.

The 1920s and 1930s were also crucial for the industry as its entrepreneurs built up a nationwide distribution network. Although some government officials considered the cinema to be merely part of the government's propaganda machine, for most of the people, it was one of their major forms of entertainment, being easily accessible regardless of their social or economic background. By the end of the 1930s, there were movie theaters in practically every city and town across the country; their numbers had mushroomed from about one hundred in the early 1920s to several hundred by the early 1940s.

Throughout this period, the cinema market continued to be dominated by films imported from western European countries and the United States. From the mid-1930s the distribution companies invested significantly into dubbing. Thus, many films were screened in the Turkish language, and hence gained huge popularity as young affluent urbanites began dressing, acting, and talking like their favorite screen actors and actresses.

Turkish cinema went through significant changes in the 1940s. New producers entered the field with different ideas and approaches. A new production company, Ha-Ka Film, emerged and attracted new blood and new talent.[20] As a result, a number of new directors, such as Baha Gelenbevi (1907–1984), Samil Ayanoglu (1913–1971), Lufti Akad (1916–), Aydin Arakon (1918–1992), and others entered the would of the Turkish cinema.[21] They tried to position themselves differently from the approach established by the towering architect of Turkish cinema, Muhsin Ertugrul, and to develop their own distinctive styles and methods in directing motion pictures. One of the most important developments was an attempt to break ties with the theatre and to work exclusively with cinema scripts and cinema actors.

One of the most celebrated films of this era was Lufti Akad's *Strike the Whore* (*Vurun Kahpeye*, 1949), which many movie critics consider "a landmark in Turkish cinema."[22] It tells a simple story, a personal drama of a young woman caught in a web of conservative social and archaic family traditions. These types of stories were quite common in Turkey. What made this work markedly different and almost revolutionary in Turkish cinema was a radical departure from theatrical traditions both in terms of the way scenes were shot and in changing the ways the actors interacted with each other. To achieve realism in conversations and action Akad rejected the idea of a tightly constructed sequence of moves and dialogues and encouraged the actors to act and speak naturally and even to improvise.

The commercial success of Turkish movies in the late 1940s, combined with the appearance of new companies and a milieu of greater intellectual freedoms and discourses about culture and society, fired enthusiasm for movies made in-country. A number of individuals began seeking fame and glory by joining the industry as actors, producers, directors, screenwriters, technicians, and so on. They established their very own "Hollywood," with a number of movie actors and impresarios moving to a location of choice—Green Pine Street (*Yesilcan*) in Istanbul. The era of classic Turkish cinema, often referred to as the "Yesilcan era," had begun.

The 1950s and 1960s became the golden age of the national film industry. Young Turkish producers worked with boundless energy on numerous

projects to meet the demand from a growing middle class, while, in the process, contributing to intellectual discourse within the country. They experimented with genres and deeper exploration of various themes. One of these
was the so-called village theme, which became hugely popular because many
Turkish producers at some stage or another of their creative work came to
admire the beautiful simplicity of small Anatolian village life and the quan-
daries and everyday dramas of the ordinary people. This theme had first been
explored by Muhsin Ertugrul in his *Aysel, the Girl from the Marshy Village*
(*Batakli Damin Kizi Aysel*, 1935), and for decades it continued to attract
producers.

Another category of movies addressed issues of social justice, especially the
fate of "little people" struggling to find their identity and achieve their dreams
in a rapidly changing social environment. Atif Yilmaz produced notable films,
such as *The Secret Diary of a Chauffer* (*Bir Soforun Gizli Defteri*, 1958) and
The Children of This Country (*Bu Vatanin Cocuklari*, 1959); Metin Erksan
released *The Lord of the Nine Mountains* (*Dokuz Dagin Efesi*, 1958); Memduh
Un produced *The Three Comrades* (*Uc Arkadas*, 1958); and Ertem Gorec made
The Angry Young Man (*Kizgin Delikanli*, 1964) and *Those Awakening in the
Darkness* (*Karanlikta Uyanarlar*, 1964).

Many producers were also especially fascinated with the dual themes of the
changing position of women in Turkish society and passionate, all-consuming
love. This combination was particularly controversial and difficult to deal with
as Turkey remained a very conservative country with strong Islamic traditions.
In this regard, producer Hallil Refig became known for his *Forbidden Love*
(*Yasak Ask*, 1961), *Birds in Exile* (*Gurbet Kuslari*, 1964), and *I Loved a Turk*
(*Bir Turke Gonul Verdim*, 1969); Duygu Sagiroglu produced *My Death is My
Birth* (*Ben Oldukce Yasarim*, 1966); and Metin Erksan created *The Revenge of
the Snakes* (*Yilanlarin Ocu*, 1962), *Waterless Summer* (*Susuz Yaz*, 1963), and
The Well (*Kuyu*, 1968). In a remarkable coup for the Turkish industry, Metin
Erksan's *Waterless Summer* (*Susuz Yaz*) won the Golden Bear Award at the
Berlin Film Festival in 1964.

History and spirituality also became popular themes in Turkish cinema, as
Atif Yilmaz produced *Poet Karacaoglan's Hopeless Love* (*Karacaoglan'in Kara
Sevdasi*, 1959), *The Legend of Ali of Kesan* (*Kesanli Ali Destani*, 1964), and *The
Song of Murat* (*Murad'in Turkusu*, 1965); these were followed by Lufti Akad's
The Legend of the Black Sheep of Kizil Irmak (*Kizilirmak-Karakoyun*, 1967).

During this period, Yilmaz Guney (1937–1984)—one of Turkey's most
controversial actors and movie directors—entered the industry, eventually
achieving a near-cult status in western Europe. After attaining a significant
success and recognition as a movie actor, he turned to screenwriting and
directing. His Kurdish background, left-leaning political views and sharp,

realist-style interpretation of personal and social dramas brought him into conflict with the Turkish authorities, but won him support among the intelligentsia and movie critics. His early *Umut* (*Hope*, 1970), *Umutsuzlar* (*The Hopeless*, 1971), and *Aci* (*Pain*, 1971) artfully narrated the social and political tensions of his times, while in *Suru* (*The Herd*, 1978) and *Dushman* (*Enemy*, 1979) he turned his attention to the lives of the Kurdish minority. In 1982, he completed his masterpiece *Yol* (*The Road*, 1982), which powerfully depicted the harsh realities of life in the highly complex environment of eastern Anatolia; this work brought him international fame and the Cannes Film Festival's award in 1982.

It was, however, the popular film genres—simple melodramas, musicals, detective stories, science fiction, westerns, and historic epics—that continued to win the hearts and wallets of mass audiences. The typical straightforward plot usually involved a love story and intrigues of evil rivals, or stifling social norms and archaic rules. These plots were blended with national music, sometimes with folk dancing, and were generally shot against backgrounds of beautiful landscapes or in affluent mansions. These films won millions of viewers and proved commercial success in the domestic and overseas markets. During the industry's peak years, in the late 1960s and early 1970s, about 2,500 movie theaters across Turkey attracted around 250 million viewers a year. The studios beat one record after another, producing around 220 films in 1970 and setting an absolute record of 300 in 1972.

The popular cinema genres created "superstars" with enormous numbers of followers. The mere mention of names such as Kemal Sunal, Kadir Inanir, Turkan Soray, and Sener Sen sent the pulse rates of many teenagers, and even their parents, soaring.

By the 1970s, Turkey's commercial cinema was faced with difficulties. The producers were overexploiting the existing plots and themes and running out of ideas. In their attempts to bring audiences back into the theaters they increasingly turned to "hot" topics, exploring sexuality and discussing topics that were too "racy" for the prudish Turkish society, and even adding gratuitous erotic scenes that gradually expanded into genres of their own, in the form of "soft" and "hard" erotic cinema. Such movies as *Raziye, Suclular Aramizda, Mum Kokuklu Kadinlar, Donjuan 72, Yumusak Ten, BayE, C-Block, Nihavent Mucize*, and many others found the way onto the screen. Many Turkish producers tried to use eroticism to explore social issues and conflicts, to reinterpret sexuality, and to discuss falling family values. And yet, many others ventured into eroticism and depictions of sexuality with a simple goal of achieving commercial success.[23]

Despite various efforts the Turkish film industry had to retreat on many fronts: especially due to increasing competition from television and its invention, the television movie series, people's changing habits of entertainment, and due to political and economic downturns. The first signs of a decline in the national cinema appeared in the mid-1970s, and the downturn became particularly severe in the 1980s. In spite of the commercial success of Cetin Inanc's *The Man Who Saves the World* (*Dunyayi Kurtaran Adam*, 1982), which was often called the "Turkish Star Wars," the slump became worse than ever, until, by the early 1990s, the Turkish studios had reduced their output to a dozen or so movies a year. Even so, some directors continued working on major projects, and their films continued winning international awards; however, these masterpieces were rarely a commercial success and could not alone rescue the industry. In order to survive, many actors and directors moved to television, which became the favorite entertainment avenue for ordinary people and was financially successful due to the deregulation of the media and the appearance of private television channels.

Although the boom years are over, Turkish cinema has survived, and there are still directors who continue working on new releases in an attempt to restore the industry's past glory. For example, Yilmaz Erdogan's *Vizontele* (2001) and *Vizontele Tuuba* (2004), comic recountings of the adventures of a small town's inhabitants with the arrival of the "new" device—television, were well received nationally and attracted the attention of both the general public and the critics. Omer Faruk Sorak's comedy *Sinav* (*The Exam*, 2006) was developed as a distant cousin of Jackie Chan's *Rush Hour*, and revolves around the adventures of students attempting to steal national exam papers. *Sinav* was an instant hit. In the meantime, Serdar Akar's Rambo-style exploitation of the gruesome war in Iraq, the *Valley of the Wolves Iraq* (*Kurtlar Vadisi Irak*, 2006), was a huge commercial success and stirred up a lot of controversy within and outside the country.[24] In the meantime, Abdullah Oguz's tragic novel *Bliss* (*Mutluluk*, 2007) won a wide international recognition and many international awards.[25] In the words of Turkish movie producer Umut Unal "Since the early 2000s, the Turkish cinema experienced a kind of revival in festival circuits and art house cinema, but if the key actors of the industry, i.e., producers, managers, distributors, and sale people would think more internationally, and be as brave and open as independent directors, the Turkish cinema would win hearts of many more international viewers, and would take the respectable position in the world cinema."[26]

THE INTERNET

The Internet arrived in Turkey quite early, but due to cost constraints and the underdevelopment of the nation's communication system it did not win mass appeal until the mid and late 1990s. Yet, with the deregulation of the media sector, improving communication systems, and especially the growing demand from expatriate Turkish communities in western Europe and the

Americas, the Turkish-language Internet quickly improved in quality, accessibility, and sophistication, offering a wide range of content.

Government agencies and large businesses took the lead in establishing well-designed websites, making documents and significant information available online. Although there was a debate about controlling and regulating access to the World Wide Web, by and large, the government refrained from censoring, restricting, or banning access to the Internet content.

As in many other countries, the younger generation immediately jumped at the opportunities that the Internet provided. Many people, especially teenagers and students, began to chat, search for friends and dates, exchange music, seek personal advice, discuss politics, play games, network, and so on. Together with the radio stations, the Internet's dating, chat, and hobby portals have facilitated the shaping of a new kind of youth subculture in every major metropolitan area in the country, each with its own values, interests, customs, and lifestyles. As in the West, in the latest trend YouTube, Facebook, and other similar Internet sharing portals caught the minds of millions of young Turks.[27]

From the very early days of the Internet in Turkey, the mass media—television, radio, and newspapers—have established searchable websites that, in most cases, provide free access to all users. Almost every media outlet runs its own comprehensive and user-friendly website, often with searchable archives containing a wealth of information on cultural, political, social, and economic issues; these websites can easily compete, in the quality of their presentation of news and reports, with many established media outlets in western Europe and the United States. However, in the remote areas the cost of access and the rudimentary infrastructure hinder the Internet's spread and availability. Although it is relatively easy to access the Internet in the capital and other major urban centers, most of Turkey's rural population is still excluded from the cyberworld. This is probably the chief reason the country lags behind many other countries in terms of per capita Internet users. According to the World Bank's World Development Indicators, out of 167 countries surveyed regarding Internet use, Turkey occupies sixty-fourth place (22.2 per 100,000 people, as of 2008),[28] just behind the Czech Republic, Poland and Costa Rica. By comparison, the United States is in fifteenth place and France holds the thirty-sixth spot.[29]

NOTES

1. "Readers dissatisfied with Turkish newspapers, latest survey shows." http://www.todayszaman.com/tz-web/detaylar.do?load=detay&link=155844 (accessed on October 22, 2008).

2. Personal interview with Abdulhamit Bilici, deputy editor in chief, at the *Zaman* newspaper on June 13, 2007.

3. Here, I refer to the episode with Janet Jackson, whose "wardrobe" seriously "malfunctioned" and exposed some of her body during her performance at the Super Bowl halftime show in 2006.

4. For media coverage of the event, see http://www.iht.com/articles/ap/2007/01/19/europe/EU-GEN-Turkey-Journalist-Killed.php (accessed on March 4, 2008).

5. Author's personal interview with Mukremin Gunaydin at the *Zaman* newspaper on May 30, 2007.

6. For ranking, see http://www.medyatava.com/tiraj.asp (accessed on March 11, 2008).

7. Ibid.

8. For access to content and information about the newspaper, see http://www.todayszaman.com (accessed on March 1, 2008).

9. For access to content and information about the newspaper, see http://www.thenewanatolian.com (accessed on March 11, 2008).

10. See http://www.cumhuriyet.com.tr/.

11. For example, according to Mukremin Gunaydin about 30 percent of journalists at the *Zaman* newspaper are women. Author's personal interview with Mukremin Gunaydin at the *Zaman* newspaper on May 30, 2007.

12. *Turkish Daily News*, February 13, 2007.

13. Annual Survey Freedom of the Press Freedoms. See http://www.freedomhouse.org/template.cfm?page=362 (accessed on March 11, 2008).

14. Some radio channels can be reached over the Internet: Listen to Radio 1 on http://www.trt.net.tr/wwwtrt/rdakis.aspx?kanal=1; TRT FM Radio onhttp://www.trt.net.tr/wwwtrt/RdAkis.aspx?gunler=1&kanal=4&akistur=1&tdgun=1; and Radio 3 on http://www.trt.net.tr/wwwtrt/RdAkis.aspx?gunler=1&kanal=2&akistur=1&tdgun=1 (accessed on November 15, 2008).

15. Official statistics, see http://www.byegm.gov.tr/references/radyo-tv2002.htm; http://www.tbsjournal.com/Archives/Spring03/catalbas.html. For a list of selected radio station, see http://radiostationworld.com/locations/turkey/radio_websites.asp.

16. Listen for the Voice of Turkey on http://www.trt.net.tr/voiceofturkey/vot.htm (accessed on November 15, 2008).

17. For the list of private channels available on the Internet, see http://www.creatonic.com/tronline/i_real.htm (accessed March 1, 2008).

18. Interview with Prof. David Cuthell, executive director of the Institute of Turkish Studies, Washington, D.C., March 31, 2008.

19. For more information, see http://turvak.com/english/inside/muze/index.htm.

20. Ha Ka (short for Halil Kamil) Film studio was founded in 1934.

21. For the bios of the most renown Turkish producers and actors, see Agah Ozguc. *Turk Film Yonetmenleri Sozlugu.* Istanbul: Agora Kitapligi, 2003.

22. Christine Woodhead, ed. *Turkish Cinema. An Introduction.* London: Turkish Area Study Group Publication, University of London, 1989, p. 25.

23. For an overview of sexuality in Turkish cinema, see Agah Ozgun. *Turk Sinemasinda Cinselligin Tarihi.* Istanbul: Parantez, 2000.

24. For plot and movie trailers, see the official webpage of the movie at http://www.valleyofthewolvesiraq.com/.

25. For more information see *The 10th New York Turkish Film Festival. October 3–11, 2008.* New York, New York Turkish Film Festival, 2008.

26. Author's personal interview with Umut Unal on October 10, 2008.

27. For example, the Turkish Eurovision entry generated hundreds of comments and views. See http://youtube.com/watch?v=vjEkjprpTZA.

28. See http://www.nationmaster.com/graph-T/int_use_cap (accessed on November 15, 2008).

29. United Nations Development Programme. *Human Development Report 2005: International Cooperation at a Crossroad.* New York: United Nations Development Programme, 2005, pp. 262–263.

5

Performing Arts

The concept of the "national" dance is an intriguing business in Turkey. It concerns a variety of dance genres, ranging from folk dancing to national ballet, and from belly dancing to modern dance.

—Arzu Ozturkmen, Turkish scholar[1]

WHEN THE DOGUS Kids Symphony Orchestra took the stage at the Thirty-Sixth International Istanbul Music Festival in the summer 2008, it caused a sensation. The two-year-old orchestra, consisting of school-age children from various art schools across Turkey, evinced incredible professionalism through a high-quality performance of classical music. It was symbolic that they chose such a widely popular event to reach out to the international audience because the festival has been hosting the best world musicians since 1973 by offering a rich selection of classical music, ballet and opera, and traditional folk performances. The young musicians were among hundreds of artists performing for their faithful fans. Tens of thousands of viewers, often with friends, colleagues, and entire families, come to enjoy the elegant dances of ballet stars, the virtuoso pianists, violin players, and the beautiful voices of famous opera singers. At the same time, both the performers and viewers have a unique opportunity to listen to some traditional guitar players, children, and college choruses from different parts of Europe and the Ottoman court music.

The festival does not usually end with formal concerts and performances. It spills over into the streets and informal stages at music clubs, bars, and restaurants. The locals often joke that a musicologist or music lover would find no fewer than 1,001 music styles at 1,001 places in Istanbul's Taksim and Beyoglu areas in a single evening. Indeed, during the festival, thousands of amateur and professional solo and group singers and performers come out to the streets and various public spaces of Istanbul and most of the Turkish cities and towns to entertain their friends, guests, and even strangers without asking for pay or a reward.

Contemporary Turkish performing arts are cosmopolitan and multifaceted indeed, woven from many cultural traditions. At the core, there is an ancient Turkic culture of nomads and settlers preserved through centuries of travel and interaction. Around this core, there are some elements of ancient Persian traditions that became inseparable from the rich cultures of the Caucasus and Anatolia. The classic Ottoman music represented by the original *makams* (traditional musical compositions consisting of different musical modes) and *usuls* (classic Ottoman music compositions consisting of complex rhythmic patterns) are the best examples. These traditions have been further enriched by the Middle Eastern (especially Arabic) and European influences, Islamic and secular inputs, and musical and performing traditions of the modern times.[2] The Western musical styles were further facilitated by the policy of the Cultural Revolution promoted by the young Turkish Republican government throughout the 1920s and 1930s.

TRADITIONAL MUSIC

Musicological travel into the soul of Turkish music should probably begin in central and eastern Anatolia. Many villagers have carefully preserved traditional instruments, songs, and family epics and legends about distant ancestral homes in central Asia and the Caucasus. Since ancient times, the musical instruments have been made by self-taught masters and their students who used natural materials, often observing and learning from great masters and bards traveling along the Great Silk Road. Their musical instruments, although authentic to the Turkic nomadic traditions and rhythms, distantly resemble those from the Middle East, south Asia, Persia, the Caucasus, and the Balkans.[3]

The musical traditions have been developed and preserved by traveling bards—*ozans* and *asyks* (pronounced *ashy-ks*), who recited ancient and medieval legends and epics, singing about heroes and great ancestors, distant lands and homes, and long military marches and campaigns. A bard usually traveled and performed solo, playing on a simple and light instrument or was accompanied by a student or two who helped him during a difficult journey and learned the secrets of ancient legends and improvisations on various musical instruments. When the time was right, these students themselves became bards and eternal troubadours.

A traditional Janissary band performs before the public. Courtesy of the author, 2007.

It is important to note that as in Persia and western Europe of the Middle Ages, there was a clear distinction between popular or "low" music of the streets and "high" music of the royal court and nobility. For centuries, the courts of Seljuk and Ottoman rulers were profoundly influenced by the Persian and Middle Eastern musical traditions, and often performances in the royal courts were done in the Persian (Farsi) language. In contrast, the bards used the Turkic language of the street, which could be understood by both seminomadic tribesmen and settled peasants.[4]

Like their European counterparts, the nineteenth-century Ottomans experienced the rise of national identity and interest in truly "national" culture, roots, and traditions. Increasingly wealthy Ottoman nobles turned into philanthropists by supporting the bards and poets who sang in the Turkic language. Thus, *ozans* began performing not only in coffeehouses and caravanserais, but also in the homes of influential intellectuals, artists, and politicians around the empire and especially in Istanbul.

The process of identifying and rethinking the truly Turkish "imaginary community" (a term coined by an influential scholar Benedict Anderson)[5] and its boundaries accelerated in the twentieth century. Like governments in central Asia, Russia, and Ukraine, the Turkish Republican government sponsored a large-scale program of collecting, recording, and archiving

Turkish folklore. This program lasted almost thirty years between 1924 and 1953, and, in the end, Turkish musicologists collected tens of thousands of folk songs and laments, and descriptions of many traditional Anatolian music instruments. In addition, the government funded studies and publications of this incredible folk heritage and a campaign to collect various musical instruments for museums and universities. It also supported the establishment of various folk bands that performed folk music for a wide audience. Between 1932 and 1951, numerous People's Houses (*halkevi*, plural—*halkevleri,* a sort of a cultural club) were founded in almost every city, large town, and village supporting local talents, including folk singers, dancers, and folk-instrument players.

These efforts systematized, codified, and preserved the best folklore traditions of Anatolia.[6] Even today, many traditional musical instruments are widely used by both ordinary villagers, who preserved their folk traditions, and professional folk players, who study and disseminate these traditions among the general public.

The government's support, hard work of music devotees and scholars, and efforts of the ordinary musicians culminated in the wide popularity of the Turkish musical heritage among the population. Today, it is easy to come

A folk singer performs before the public. Courtesy of the author, 2007.

across excellent examples of traditional folk music both in major urban centers and in remote rural areas. Bands and music groups perform the folk music pieces during family events, such as weddings, boys' circumcision celebrations, and other various family gatherings, whether they take place at home, in numerous restaurants, cafés, and coffeehouses; or simply on the streets. Folk songs (*turku*), epics (*destans*), laments (*agits*), and others usually deal with timeless issues important for people regardless of age, social status, or interests, and with the emotional aspects of love, anguish for a hometown; or they simply express the festive moods of people who had a long, hard day or season, and who came together to celebrate various festivals.

One of the most recognizable and important of Turkish instruments is the *saz* that distantly resembles a lute. Traditional *saz* is about 4 or 5 feet (about 120–150 centimeters) in length. This is a stringed instrument with a pear-shaped body (*tekne*) that is usually made of wood, such as juniper, spruce, or walnut; its flat sounding board (*gogush*) is often made of spruce; and the 2-foot-long (about 60 centimeters) neck (*sap*) is also made of wood, such as juniper. The *saz* usually has three strings, but sometimes these strings are doubled. The instrument is mainly used to play traditional folk-music pieces and is still popular among the Turks who live in Central Asia, the Caucasus, and Anatolia. It is traditionally played in a finger-picking style or with a plectrum (*tezene*). Over time, the *saz* makers experimented with different sizes, materials, and number of strings, creating a whole family of stringed instruments known as *baglama*.[7] For example, the *divani-saz* (court *saz*) is the largest instrument in the family (varying between 5 and 6 feet in length or 150–210 centimeters); while the *cura* is the smallest member of this family (between 3 and 4 feet in length or 90–120 centimeters). In the late twentieth century, some musicians even created electric *baglamas* and added more strings.

The *tar* is another popular folk music instrument of Persian or central Asian origin, a distant cousin of the Turkmen *dutar* and Persian *setar*. This is a stringed instrument with a double-pear-shaped body and a long neck. Conventionally, its body is made of mulberry wood and is covered with a stretched leather membrane (usually made of lambskin) that serves as a flat sounding board. The classic *tar* has five strings, although some musicians and craftsmen experimented by adding a sixth and sometimes even a seventh string. The *tar* was popular among different ethnic groups and in the royal courts in central Asia, Azerbaijan, and the Persian and Ottoman empires for many centuries, especially for performing complex music compositions called *maqams*. Historical chronicles and miniature paintings captured images of musicians (sometimes women) playing the *tar* as early as the fifteenth and seventeenth centuries.

The *kemenche* is a popular bowed string folk instrument, a distant cousin of the central Asian *kobuz*. The *kemenche* has a long, bottle-shaped body and a short neck (both made of wood), and is played with a bow (called *doksar*). When played, this instrument is held vertically, placed on a knee, although it also can be held in front of the musician on the chest. Its body shape varies from a long half-sliced bottle to a half-sliced pear. It is a small instrument that is usually between 1.5 and 2 feet in length (40–50 centimeters). The *kemenche* is a member of quite a large family of musical instruments that have been popular among different ethnic groups since the Middle Ages in the Caucasus, along the Black Sea shores and in the Balkans. The shape and the playing and tuning techniques differ in various places for the diversity of the local musical traditions.

The *zurna* is a traditional woodwind folk instrument with either five or seven finger holes and is a straight pipe that widens into a conical end; it is a distant cousin of the central Asian *surnay* or the Arabic *mizmar*. In the past, this instrument was traditionally made of wood, although over time *zurna* makers used various materials or combination of materials. This instrument also varies in length between 1.5 and 2 feet (45–60 centimeters) or even longer. It produces a sustained loud and deep tone, and, therefore, was widely used in the Ottoman military bands.[8] In Anatolia, it is still commonly used during outdoor public events such as weddings or community festivals, often accompanied by another *zurna* or by a drum player.

The Turkish *ney* (also *nay*) is a straight end-blown flute that comes in different lengths (between 2 and 3 feet or 60–100 centimeters). It is a close cousin of the Persian *ney* and the Arab *nay*. In the distant past, it was made of wood and bone (for a mouthpiece), although the modern *ney* is usually made of metal (brass); and it usually has five or six finger holes. Since the Middle Ages, the *ney* has been particularly popular among the Sufis, especially the Mevlevi dervishes of Anatolia. This instrument can be found in different variations in terms of length and tones among the various ethnic groups in the Middle East, Iran, the Caucasus, and the Balkans.

The *davul* is a traditional large, double-headed drum. It ranges between 2 and 3 feet in diameter (60–90 centimeters), though sometimes it might be larger. The *davul* consists of a drum shell made of hardwood that has been bent into a cylindrical shape and fastened by leather or metal straps. The heads are usually made of cow or bull skin, although sometimes goatskin, sheepskin, and even donkey skin is used, because the heads of different thickness and strength produce different tones. A player usually uses a thick stick to play it. The *davul* probably originated in central Asia, and, since the Ottoman era, has been widely used in performing Ottoman military marches (*mehter*). In modern Turkey, it accompanies public events and is a part of military marches and *mehter* music concerts. In addition to the *davul*, there are different types of drums in Turkey, including the *nagara*—a smaller cousin of the *davul* that is played by hands rather than sticks, the *tef* (Turkish *tambourine*), and some others.

The *berdir* is a traditional frame drum that is also widely used in Central Asia and the Middle East. It is between 1 and 1.5 feet (30–50 centimeters) in diameter and consists of a drum shell made of hardwood (such as walnut), that has been bent into a cylindrical shape, and a single head (membrane) made of sheepskin. A player usually uses his or her fingers to produce different rhythmic tones. The instrument is popular among Sufi order members who use these drums for various religious ceremonies. It is also played by women, for example, belly dancers, to create fast passionate rhythms.

DANCE

The most acclaimed and appreciated Turkish contribution to the world's dancing traditions is the mystic dances of the whirling dervishes and the sensual and moving performances of belly dancers. Yet, the dancing traditions in contemporary Turkey are much richer,[9] because they incorporate the dancing styles of various ethnic and regional groups. They also embrace many modern Western elements and genres, as in the Ankara, Antalya, and Istanbul theaters stage performances of both the classic European and modern Turkish ballets. Dance clubs and discothèques in all major cities around the country could easily be mistaken for similar places in Germany, the United Kingdom, or the United States.

The early dancing traditions of Turks probably had their roots in distant parts of nomadic central Asia and were enriched by Persian, Caucasian, and ancient Anatolian elements. As in many parts of the modern world, the early traditions in individual and group movements under a musical accompaniment were probably related to ancient spiritual and meditating rituals. Travelers who visited the Turkic-speaking world in the Middle Ages reported various rituals where people performed different dances.

The arrival of Islam has radically changed the musical and performing traditions among the Turks in various geographic locations. Like their contemporaries in the Christian world, the early Islamic scholars introduced their own interpretation of the code of public conduct, as they demanded strict sexual segregation in the Muslim communities, anathematized alcohol, and any public activities that would negatively affect the "moral stand of the society." This included ostracizing the public and community entertainments where the music or the performers' movements were suggestive, "immoral," or related to pre-Islamic rituals and beliefs. Yet, music and dance were not totally

Mystic dances of the whirling dervishes. Courtesy of the author, 2007.

banned and existed in diminished and segregated ways. There were always all-women bands and groups of individuals who performed in the women's living quarters or harems. Although the boundaries were probably quite fuzzy, the masters of the harems would probably have had little restraint in attending musical events arranged for their female family members.[10] There also were all-male bands and groups who performed for men, especially members of the upper classes of the society.[11]

By and large, dance survived all restrictions and regulations throughout the Seljuk and Ottoman eras. In one way, paradoxically, the survival was facilitated by the Islamic religious traditions themselves. For example, the Mevlevi Sufi order, founded by Jalal Ad-din Rumi in the thirteenth century, used the whirling movements with the accompaniment of various musical instruments for performing *zikr* (meditation) and for establishing ecstatic relations with the divine and mystic spirituality. At the same time, music and dancing traditions of non-Muslim minorities faced fewer restrictions because the Ottomans greatly tolerated the cultural and religious differences of their subjects. The non-Muslim population of the Empire celebrated their festivals and community and family events in coffeehouses or taverns, where they were often joined by Turkic travelers, adventurers, or simply by music lovers.

Yet, as in Victorian England, not all members of the society approved of public entertainment. For example, the conservative public in puritanical Ottoman communities in the seventeenth and eighteenth and even in the nineteenth centuries often accused and persecuted the professional female dancers and their male counterparts for "immoral" behavior and for breaking the social boundaries and norms. Across the country, all Muslim women were still obliged to cover their bodies and faces and not to appear in public without being accompanied by male relatives.

It is not very clear how, in this environment, belly dancing existed in the public scene and became quite popular among various strata of the Ottoman society. There are conflicting views on this phenomenon among the art historians. Some scholars claim that the belly dancing took its roots in ethnic folk dancing and survived within extended families and in the close-knit community context because it was a part of social and family life. The other scholars suggest precisely the opposite—historically the belly dancing was a part of the entertainment business in the Middle East and Persia and, thus, has survived through history solely for this reason. They point out that both pre-Islamic- and Islamic-era miniature paintings depicted images of dancers entertaining the royal courts and members of the nobility. In the nineteenth century, the sexuality of belly dancers was popularized and romanticized by the orientalist painters (see Chapter 6) who firmly associated them with the harem life throughout the Muslim world. The experience of watching a belly-dancing performance was probably at the top of the to-do lists of many Western dignitaries, adventurers, and travelers who visited Istanbul during that era. The fascination with belly dancing was so high that in the late nineteenth century, these performances were arranged at world fairs in western Europe and the United States to a huge outcry by the Western media, the religious establishment, and the conservative groups of the societies.

This was not, however, a one-way fascination with the dancing art. The Ottoman society was equally attracted to something that was popular in the West—ballet. Many members of the Ottoman elite became acquainted with ballet during their extended visits to western Europe and through performances of Italian groups in Istanbul in the nineteenth and early twentieth centuries. Yet, it took decades before the first ballet school was established on Istanbul soil, overcoming prejudice and suspicion of the conservative members of the society. In 1917, a ballet instructor, Krassa Arzumanova, arrived in Istanbul, escaping the chaos of the collapsing Russian Empire and of the Bolshevik Revolution. Within the next few years, she established her own ballet studio and recruited the first students to be trained as ballet dancers. A decade later, the graduates of the studio staged their first performances in Istanbul's and Ankara's *halkevis*, although this experiment remained quite limited and modest. The next attempt to establish a Turkish national ballet school was made on a much grander scale. In January 1948, Dame Ninette de Valois (1898–2001) of the United Kingdom, who came to Turkey at the invitation of the Turkish government, established the very first national ballet school in Istanbul—the Yeshilkoy Ballet School. Dame Ninette de Valois or "Madame," as she became known in Turkey, had extensive dancing, teaching, and managerial experience in the United Kingdom and in other European countries, and she maintained close relationships with major performing art dignitaries across the world. Her efforts and personal contacts with world-class ballet experts and influential cultural figures mobilized substantial support for her project, raised the profile of her school, and attracted several world-class performers and instructors to Istanbul to teach at the school. In 1950, the school moved to Ankara and became part of the Turkish State Conservatory. Within a few years, the ballet students performed in one of the first Turkish pieces, *Keloglan,* composed by Ulvi Cemal Erkin. In 1961, the graduates of the school presented their very own interpretation of *Coppelia*[12] to the public and, in 1965, they presented *At the Fountain's Head* (*Ceshmebashi*). They also starred in the first Turkish ballet composed by Ferit Tuzun based on Turkish folklore and folklore music.[13]

With time, the graduates of the ballet school began working on a very complex repertoire, performing such classic plays as *Giselle, Don Quixote, Sleeping Beauty, Swan Lake, The Nutcracker, Beauty and the Beast, Orpheus, The Fountain of Bakhchisarai, Legend of Love* (the latter composed by a guest Azerbaijani composer), and many others.[14] At the same time, the Turkish choreographers and composers continued searching for indigenous materials and works to produce "national" Turkish ballet pieces.[15] Among such indigenous works are *The Lady with the Dagger* (*Hancherli Hanum*), *A Woman Called Rosy* (*Pembe Kadin*), *Vicious Circle* (*Yoz Dongu*), *Ode to Beauty* (*Guzelleme*), and others.[16]

THEATER

The contemporary Turkish theatrical traditions have been formed by two very distinct theatrical schools. One was a popular shadow theater of the Turkic world—the *Karagoz*—that has survived among various Turkic-speaking people for many centuries and has traced its chronicled history all the way to the establishment of the Seljuk principalities (*begliks*) in Anatolia in the eleventh and twelfth centuries.[17] The influence of the other school—the Western theatrical tradition—is quite a recent phenomenon that probably started in the mid- and late eighteenth century with occasional performances staged for diplomats and Ottoman dignitaries in foreign embassies.[18]

The Turkish Shadow Theatre *Karagoz* (literally, black eye) is one of the most interesting and original theaters in the world and is distantly similar to the shadow theater in east and southeast Asia. During earlier eras, the *Karagoz* was exclusively the entertainment of working-class people of the street, caravanserais, and bazaars. It is not very clear if, during the early eras, the *Karagoz* followed the present-day uniform format with similar plots and sets of characters because almost no written description of the repertoire has survived from that time.[19] The existing literature, however, confirms that by the sixteenth and seventeenth centuries, certain classic plots, rules, and sets of characters were established. The performers were expected to follow these rules. A classic *Karagoz* show consists of four parts: (1) an introduction (*mukaddine*), (2) a dialogue (*muhavere*), (3) a main act (*fasil*), and (4) a conclusion (*bitish*).[20] Mr. Karagoz, an uneducated but trustworthy and comical "ordinary Joe," and his companion, Mr. Hacivad, an educated but slow-thinking and impractical handyman, are the main two characters in the play. They often find themselves in comical situations dealing with their friends, neighbors, and local or central authorities. However, they always come out of the most difficult situations, outplaying local bullies, jealous wives, corrupt authorities, and even magical *jins*, monsters, and witches, because of their wit, common sense, and bravery. The *Karagoz* remained the theater of the ordinary people for quite a long time, and it was not welcomed in the palaces of the rich and powerful due to the antiestablishment nature of many plays. However, there are historical reports and miniature paintings that documented the occasional *Karagoz* performances in the palaces of the Ottoman rulers in the sixteenth and seventeenth centuries. The *Karagoz* was closely linked to the puppet shows (*korchak*) that were traditionally oriented to the younger audience and to parents with children.

The *Karagoz* has a distant cousin—*meddah*—the one-man show in which a storyteller narrates recent or past events by impersonalizing all partakers. The *meddah* was often an improvisation on a topic suggested by viewers or by the performer himself (the performers were always men) often mixing poetry and prose, reality and fiction.[21]

The traditional theater remained popular among the ordinary people until the modern era, but it failed to attract the patronage and sponsorship of the Ottoman court and Ottoman philanthropists. Only in the nineteenth century did Ottoman enthusiasts and some members of the intelligentsia display great interest in these shows and consider them to be an important part of the newly redefined "national culture" and "national identity."

By this time, however, new theatrical traditions began captivating the imagination of the general public and of the royal court—the Western-style theater. Many members of the upper class were aware of and fascinated by playwrights of France, Italy, and the United Kingdom. Some chronicles report that Sultan Selim III (1761–1808) himself invited foreign groups to perform in the Topkapi Palace in 1797–1798. His successor, Sultan Mahmud II (1784–1839), invited Italian director Guiseppe Donizetti (Donizetti-Pasha) to advise him on the establishment of the "Musika-i Humayun" in the Ottoman Court. These efforts, however, were usually limited to foreigners performing in Istanbul and did not bring to life a permanent public theater in Istanbul. The conservative members of society and die-hard *ulemas* have strongly opposed theatrical plays, especially for public appearances or representation of women,[22] citing the need to maintain public morality and to follow religious traditions.

With the proclamation of the Tanzimat reforms in 1839, not only did Sultan Abdulcemid I and his supporters introduce a wide range of political and economic reforms, they also attempted to introduce some changes into the cultural life of the state. During the reign of Sultan Abdulcemid I, the Western theater companies (mainly Italian and French) were regularly invited to perform in Istanbul, and some actions were taken toward developing indigenous theatrical traditions. In 1840, a new building specifically designed for theatrical performances was completed in Istanbul and hosted the first opera performance translated into Turkish. Between 1840 and 1877, more than a dozen different plays and operas were staged in Istanbul, with comedies becoming the most popular genre. In fact, the first Turkish play—Ibrahim Sinasi's single-act *The Poet's Marriage* (*Sair Evlenmesi*, 1860) was a comedy. With the end of Tanzimat, however, the theater experienced significant difficulties due to both the declining revenue and the opposition of the conservative elements in the government.

A new attempt at establishing the professional theater was made in 1913–1914 when influential Cemil Topuzlu (1868–1958), then the head of the Istanbul municipality, supported the establishment of the *Darulbedayi Osmani*—the institution that became the Istanbul Municipal Theatre in 1931. In 1921, Ertugrul Muhsin (1892–1979), widely regarded as the father of modern Turkish theater, became the director of the *Darulbedayi*. He was a key figure in enriching the theater's repertoire. He also energetically pushed for a new system of actor training emphasizing professionalism and creativity. The theater based its repertoire on the classic Western and Russian plays, such as Shakespeare's *Hamlet,* Chekhov's *Three Sisters,* and plays of Henrik Ibsen, Luigi Pirandello, Maxim Gorki, and popular Turkish romantic and historic plays.

The Turkish government continued the Cultural Revolution in line with the Kemalist vision of modern performing art making theater "an influential, efficient and disciplined artistic institution"[23] and a tool for promoting modernization. According to this concept, Ankara supported staging theater performances at the People's Houses (*halkevis*) across Turkey. Between 1932 and 1951, the Turkish theater companies toured even the most remote *halkevis* contributing greatly to the popularization of Western-style entertainment, including theater, often focusing on the social dramas of that era. This included Yakup Karaosmanoglu's *The Unemployed* (*Issizler*, 1924), Nazim Hikmet's *The Skull* (*Kafatasi*, 1932), Cevdet Kudret's *The Wolves* (*Kurtlar*, 1933), Necip Fasil Kisakurek's *Money* (*Para*, 1942), and others. In fact, most of the theatrical, ballet, and opera performances in the 1930s and 1940s were performed in the *halkevis*.

In 1949, the Turkish government took another step in supporting the national theater by issuing the law on the Establishment of the State Theater and Opera. Within a few years, several theaters in Ankara and Istanbul and some other places received the status of the state theaters and with this came the state funding and support. The theatrical traditions received a further boost with the opening of new theaters in major provincial centers in the 1960s and 1970s. The Turkish theater still experiences considerable growth because the Ministry of Culture supports the opening of new theaters. For example, in 1999, the newest theatrical company was added with the opening of the Antalya State Opera and Ballet. At the same time, several theaters remained outside of the state theater system subsidized by various municipalities, forming the second group of theaters in the country. In the meantime, some theaters have chosen to go private, surviving on ticket sales and philanthropic support.

The repertoires of the Turkish theaters today include a combination of Western classic and modern Turkish plays (usually performed in Turkish). The Turkish directors pay significant attention to indigenous repertoire including such works as Odnan Saygun's opera *Tashbebek*, Havit Kodalli's ballet *Harrem Sultan*, Turan Oflazoglu's *Murat IV* (*IV Murat*, 1970), Gungor Dilmen's *The Knot of Midas* (*Midas'in kordugumu*, 1975), Turgut Ozakman's *The Girl of the Republic* (*Cumhuriyet Kizi*, 1990), and others. During the 2007–2008 theatrical season, the Istanbul Opera and Ballet Company staged Yalcin's *Folklorama*, Puccini's *La Rondine*, Mercan Dede's *Guldestan*, and a dozen other plays.[24]

CONTEMPORARY MUSIC

The development of contemporary Turkish music is a constantly evolving and complex process of experimenting with various genres and styles. Born from the interplay between Turkish folk and classic music with Western music traditions, the unique Turkish folk-rock has captured the attention of local audiences. There are also musicians, composers, and singers who remain devoted to the Turkish rhythms, language, and genres; as well as those who enthusiastically embrace Western popular music trends and freely import them to Turkish music scenes.

For many decades, small towns and villages happily ignored the cosmopolitan tastes of their cultural capital and remained loyal to the folk traditions of their ancestors. The situation changed radically in the second half of the twentieth century due to the large migration from rural areas to major urban centers. Initially, the newcomers maintained a "wall of rejection" of the entertainment tastes of their affluent urban neighbors, while the urbanites chaffed about the "backward" tastes of their newly arrived cousins. Eventually, however, with the development of modern modes of mass communication, the wall became thinner, although it has not completely disappeared. The younger generation, even in the remote areas of the country, was moved by new trends and musical experiments, while the urbanite cousins began experimenting with mixing folk and pop and rock music or trying out traditional religious music in the new modern context.

The growth of the entertainment industry changed how the public had previously viewed it. In the past, it was common that entertainers—singers, dancers, and actors—although hugely popular among their fans and admirers, would get loud disapproval from overzealous opinion makers and mass-media commentators who would associate them with loose morals and alien culture. Over time, these zealous grumblers have been largely silenced and have retreated from the frontlines and mainstream media outlets, although they have still managed to keep their influence over various segments of the society.

The younger generation took another assault of the bastions of the old traditions and tastes in the 1970s and 1980s. Often it was an old falling-apart guitar complemented by second-hand, hundreds-of-times-repaired equipment that were enthusiastically used by young, long-haired guys to produce various tunes and amateur scenes in Istanbul, Ankara, and other Anatolian cities and towns. With the rise of prosperity and stakes in the entertaining industry in the 1990s and early 2000s, the equipment became more sophisticated and bands became more professional. Their ambitions have not been limited to the scenes of the "Large Four" (Istanbul, Ankara, Izmir, and Antalya) but have extended to winning the audiences in London, Paris, Vienna, Munich, and even in such far away places as New York or Chicago.

Istanbul has always been an undisputed cultural center of the country that benefits from its multicultural, multilingual, and, to a large degree, cosmopolitan environment and from being the main gateway to the outside world. Its affluent population enthusiastically embraces all new and bold experiments in musical performances and supports young aspiring artists and groups. Today, all styles—from rock and roll to hip hop and heavy metal and rap usually performed in the Turkish language—find their ardent fans in cafés, pubs, music halls, and clubs.

One of the captivating genres that emerged in Turkey in the 1960s was the Arabesque music. It emerged by mixing contemporary Middle Eastern and Turkish rhythms produced on some traditional Turkish, Middle Eastern, and modern musical instruments (such as the synthesizer). Most of the songs in this popular genre have traditionally been in the native language or Arabic and rarely in English or German (there are large Turkish migrant communities settled in the United Kingdom, United States, Germany, and Austria). The genre was traditionally dominated by male singers, but with the rise of video industry, many singers have been accompanied by male and female dancers. Among the most-recognized names are Orhan Gengebay, Muslum Gurses, Ferdi Tayfur, and Ibrahim Tatlises.

The rise of rock bands in the West, such as the Beatles, the Rolling Stones, and Led Zeppelin, was met with great enthusiasm among the Turkish youth in the late 1960s and early 1970s. The rebellious young people exploited rock music as much as they could as an antiestablishment statement to the dismay of their parents and even some politicians, who at one stage demanded banning this "corrupting" and "pernicious" music. As in the Western countries, these politicians did not succeed. Moreover, it was a matter of time before a number of local rock bands emerged representing the so-called Anatolian rock. Such bands as *Apashlar, Kadashlar, Kurtalan Express*, and *Mogollar,* and singers Erkin Koray, Baris Manco, Murat Ses, and others bravely and impressively mixed the Turkish lyrics with various styles from classic rock to heavy metal.

Pop music made its first cautious steps in Turkey in the 1970s and only in the 1980s and 1990s did it become a momentous success on radio, television, and with a mass audience. As with other music genres, the rhythms and compositions of Western pop music blended with traditional Turkish motifs. Female pop singers quickly gained popularity in the country and among numerous Turkish guest workers in western Europe. The singing talents of Sezen Aksu and Aida Pekkan, for example, held an unyielding power over several generations of fans.

One of the peculiarities of the Turkish popular music scene is the growth of the *Ilahi* genre—a mixture of religious motifs and lyrics with contemporary Western-style music compositions. This genre has its roots in the medieval Sufi religious and folk musical traditions that were invigorated during recent decades with modern musical accompaniment. The *Ilahi*, sung solo or by a group of singers and even child singers, are hugely popular among some categories of listeners. Performed in religious recitation style, these songs are now accompanied by soft-rock, country-style, or energetic modern Middle Eastern music.

The Turkish popular music industry captured television as the main tool of entertaining the public relatively later than in most Western countries, firmly establishing itself through specialized musical channels only in the 1990s and early 2000s. Since then, however, there has been a rapid growth and diversification of music production that has revolutionized the whole industry and popular culture. One of the outcomes was the skyrocketing increase of women in the entertainment industry in all areas from soloists and all-female bands to numerous dancing groups that customarily accompany musical performances and became nearly a must in all video clips, including belly dancing. The first appearances of belly-dancer Nesrin Topkapi on Turkish television provoked a huge public outcry, but gradually belly dancing became a norm even though the costumes of the belly dancers have become shinier and more revealing, and the dances have become more erotic and temperamental.

RECENT TRENDS

Liberalization and commercialization of the popular music entertainment industry went hand in hand and radically changed the popular performing arts. One of the most important outcomes has been segmentation of the performing arts. In today's Turkey, performing-art lovers can find every single genre and style possible for all tastes and interests. As in many countries in western Europe and the United States, the classic theater, ballet, and opera found themselves in defense and in need of discovering new ways to attract audiences, especially young people, to their performances. International festivals, such as the annual International Istanbul Music Festival, International Istanbul Jazz Festival, Aspendos International Opera and Ballet Festival, and many others are organized to attract the general public, especially young people, to the classic music and theater.

Another trend is the rise of Turkish pop superstars, who achieved significant international recognition, such as Sertab Erener,[25] Mustafa Sandal, and Tarkan (Tarkan Tevetoglu).[26] These three artists managed to win audiences in eastern and western Europe, the Middle East, Latin America, and the United States by creatively mixing temperamental modern music with some elements of exotic orientalism and oriental charm combined with top-notch marketing and proposition strategies. Tarkan's single *Simarih* and Mustafa Sandal's *Isyankar*, for example, remained top hits both in Europe

A typical music store in Antalya. Courtesy of the author, 2007.

and Latin America throughout 2005. Sertab Erener won the prestigious Eurovision song contest in 2003 for her *Everyway That I Can.* The song also reached twentieth place among the world's top-forty singles in the same year.

As in many other countries, some Turkish artists, their fans, and producers began using the Internet as a new channel of communication and entertainment in the early 2000s. With it emerged the popularity of the Internet ranking of the pop star singles and their albums. For example, in June 2008, the Internet music portal http://www.turkcemuzik.com listed as the top five albums Ibrahim Tatlises's *Turkuler,* Ismail Yk's *Bombabomba.com,* Ibrahim Tatlises's *Bulamadım,* Baris Akarsu's *Islak Islak*, and *Düşmeden Bulutlarda Koşmam Gerek.*

U.S. style music competitions—similar to *American Idol* and *Dancing with the Stars*—have also become widely popular in Turkey winning especially huge television audiences, who filled numerous Internet chat and discussion rooms with hot gossip and bets. Various music award ceremonies and festivals, sponsored by some media outlets, became hugely popular with the aspiring Turkish artists, local fans, and international tourists.

NOTES

1. Arzu Ozturkmen. "Politics of National Dance in Turkey: A Historical Reappraisal," in *Yearbook of Traditional Music* 33(2001): 139.

2. Theodore Levin. *The Hundred Thousand Fools of God. Musical Travel in Central Asia.* Bloomington, IN: Indiana University Press, 1996 and Bernard Lewis. *Music of a Distant Drum: Classical Arabic, Persian, Turkish, and Hebrew Poems.* Princeton, NJ: Princeton University Press, 2001.

3. Laurence Piken. *Folk Musical Instruments of Turkey.* London: Oxford University Press, 1975 and Walter Kaufmann, *Musical Notations of the Orient: Notational Systems of Continental East, South and Central Asia.* Bloomington, IN: Indiana University Press, 1988.

4. Suraiya Faroghi. *Subjects of the Sultan. Culture and Daily Life in the Ottoman Empire.* London and New York: I. B. Tauris Publishers, 1995 and Yilmaz Oztuna, ed. *Turk Musikisi Ansiklopedisi* [An Encyclopedia of Turkish Music]. 2 vols. Istanbul: Milli Egitim Basimevi, 1969–1976.

5. Benedict Anderson. *Imagined Communities: Reflections on the Origin and Spread of Nationalism.* London: Verso, 1983.

6. For an academic research on Turkish folklore, see Bela Bartok. *The Turkish Folk Music from Asia Minor.* Princeton, NJ: Princeton University Press, 1976.

7. The words *saz* and *baglama* are sometimes used as synonyms.

8. Walter Feldman. *Music of the Ottoman Court: Makam, Composition, and the Early Ottoman Instrumental Repertoire.* Berlin: Verlag, 1996.

9. For examples of Turkish dancing traditions, see the *Best of Turkish Dances* (VHS), Arabian Video Entertainment, 1982. For an academic review of the contemporary Turkish dancing traditions, see Metin And. *A Pictorial History of Turkish Dancing from Folk Dancing to Whirling Dervishes—Belly Dancing to Ballet.* Ankara: Dost Yayinlari, 1976.

10. There are several novels that in some ways capture life in the harems. See Colin Falconer. *The Sultan's Harem.* New York: Three Rivers Press, 2005.

11. Metin And. *A Pictorial History of Turkish Dancing from Folk Dancing to Whirling Dervishes—Belly Dancing to Ballet*, pp. 135–138.

12. According to Dr. Metin And, it was the first full-scale ballet performance conducted by the Ballet School graduates. Metin And. *A Pictorial History of Turkish Dancing from Folk Dancing to Whirling Dervishes—Belly Dancing to Ballet*, p. 167.

13. Ibid., p. 168.

14. It is interesting to note that in order to support the emerging ballet talents the prime minister and president of the Turkish Republic personally attended the ballet performances. Metin And. *A Pictorial History of Turkish Dancing from Folk Dancing to Whirling Dervishes—Belly Dancing to Ballet*, pp. 170–171.

15. For a discussion of this aspect of the development of the Turkish performing arts, see Arzu Ozturkmen, "Politics of National Dance in Turkey: A Historical Reappraisal," in *Yearbook of Traditional Music* 33(2001): 139–143.

16. Evin İlyasoglu, *Cagdas Turk bestecileri* [Contemporary Turkish Composers]. Istanbul: Pan Yayıncılık, 1998.

17. For a historical review, see Mevlut Ozan, ed. *Traditional Turkish Theater.* Ankara: Ministry of Culture, 1999.

18. Metin And. *A History of Theatre and Popular Entertainment in Turkey.* Ankara: Forum Yayinlari, 1964.

19. Metin And. "Traditional Performances in Turkey," in Mevlut Ozan, ed. *Traditional Turkish Theater*, pp. 39–40.

20. Metin And gives slightly different description of the classic *Karagoz* arrangement. See Metin And. "Traditional Performances in Turkey," pp. 44–46.

21. For a discussion of other traditional theatrical genres, see Ismail Ekmekcioglu et al. *Turk Halk Oyunlari.* Istanbul: Esin Yayinevi, 2001.

22. Sometimes the women characters were played by men.

23. For a review of the development of the Turkish theater in the 1920s and 1930s, see Ozdemir Nutku. "A Panorama of the Turkish Theatre under the Leadership of Ataturk," in Gunsel Renda and Max Kortepeter eds., *The Transformation of Turkish Culture. Ataturk Legacy.* Princeton, NJ: Kingston Press, 1986, p. 166.

24. For repertoire see http://www.idobale.com/.

25. For her fan's website, see http://sertab.org/ (accessed on November 28, 2008).

26. There are even several websites devoted to Tarkan, for example, see http://www.tarkan-music.de/_en/_index_ie.php; blogs, for example, see http://tarkandeluxe.blogspot.com/ (accessed on June 16, 2008).

6

Visual Arts

Drawing and painting, calligraphy and gilding
Achieve beauty and grace in Istanbul.[1]
                    —Nabi, seventeenth-century Ottoman poet

THERE IS ONE element that, in the eyes of both foreigners and the Turks, clearly shapes and defines the distinctive "Turkishness"—Turkish art. For centuries, the elegance and simple sophistication of the artifacts created by skilled Ottoman artisans hypnotized thousands and thousands of art enthusiasts who could not resist falling in love time and again with the masterpieces. Indeed, miniature painting, ceramics, carpets, jewelry, and hand-painted tiles in the bazaar quarters of Istanbul or in any major artistic center around Turkey exude the authentic ambiance of the Turkish artistic world. Nonetheless, more than ever, even the most knowledgeable experts would struggle to identify a clear line that could separate the truly Turkish elements from Middle Eastern, central Asian, or western European elements in these works of art. A simple question: "What makes the Turkish art?"—would probably seem to be a Gordian knot to many of them, and there would be as many bitterly disagreeing with each other's answers as there are experts.

Answering that puzzling question requires a good knowledge of history and geography. For centuries, the Ottomans controlled vast territories that became a cultural and trading bridge between the north and south, the east and west. Not only did numerous caravans carry precious goods from as far away as China, Korea, and even Indo-China to western and eastern Europe, but they also brought in the cultural influences and ideas from those remote places. Curious artisans from Calcutta and Bengal, Kashgar and Samarqand, Venetia, Genoa, and Rotterdam ventured to the bazaars and handicraft quarters of numerous Ottoman cities and trade posts. Many of them were eager to share their creative works and ideas with the local artisans and were eager to learn something new and exciting from them. Some of them were able to find a rich patron who sponsored their artistic inspirations thus opening opportunities for foreign artisans to stay there longer, to create their masterpieces, to absorb ideas from the locals, and to share with them their own artistic secrets. This interchange created a unique input into the Ottoman art making it truly universal in its appeal. The interchange did not stop even during the most difficult years for the country in the twentieth century, during which the art took different forms and directions adjusting to the demands of the time.

The newly born Turkish Republic and its leaders decided to take a proactive position in promoting cultural changes in the country. In a desire to distance themselves from the Ottoman imperial era, the leaders no longer supported

A young girl demonstrates the ancient methods of silk making. Courtesy of the author, 2007.

the artistic forms, concepts, and ideas, which had roots in and links to the Islamic and Middle Eastern traditions. The Turkish government under President Mustafa Kemal strongly emphasized and promoted modern culture, art, and education that was largely associated with the western European artistic universe. The government also enthusiastically supported what it perceived to be the authentic Turkish art, which included traditional handicraft associated with small villages and towns of central and eastern Anatolia.

On the eve of the twenty-first century, the powerful forces of globalization and a market-oriented economy began forging new and profound developments in Turkish art. Notably, the state and government stopped intervening into or determining the artistic development. Strengthening of the philanthropy supported by the rise in the wealth of the country and of the middle class upheld hundreds of artistic foundations and groups. The country and its culture became a central point of interest to foreigners as art collectors around the world began discovering and appreciating Turkish and Ottoman art. This interest fueled the rise of international tourism, which made Turkey one of the world's top destinations among art lovers.

CARPETS

There are many Turkish proverbs and metaphors that express the importance of carpets in their life, which also signify Turkish national identity and Turkish history. The Turks trace their origin to the area of what is now Mongolia, western Siberia, eastern Turkistan, and central Asia, which in time immemorial were roamed by ancient Turkic tribes engaged in animal husbandry. These tribes maintained a nomadic or seminomadic lifestyle, moving around with their animals in the severe extremes of the continental climate of the great Eurasian Steppe. Animals, especially sheep and goats, provided them with a practically endless supply of wool for clothing, horse blankets, bags and pillows, and, of course, carpets to adorn the walls and floors of their dwellings.

In fact, the carpets have become one of the most widely known and distinguished forms of nomadic art. From the early days, the carpets were the souls and treasures of nomads. The carpets always carried special messages that are still understandable only to those who can read the secret language of carpet inscription. Specific patterns and motifs identified either the tribal affiliations of carpet owners, their tribal history, patterns of weather of past decades, symbolic totems of tribal groups, or their spiritual protectors. It was through the carpets that individual weavers could express their views on nature and the world around them and express their happiness or grief over losing their loved ones or manifest the birth of a new life in their simple woolen tent.

Unfortunately, very few ancient and medieval carpets have survived to the modern day. Therefore, it is very difficult to tell the history and trace the evolution of carpet creation. The nomads probably began producing simple carpets in very early days and perfected their skills through centuries of experiments and artistic imagination. The oldest surviving carpet, dating from the fifth to the third centuries B.C., was discovered in the burial place of a nomadic (probably Scythian) prince in a place called Pazyryk in the Altai Mountains. To the great surprise of the archaeologists led by Professor Sergey Rudenko, the item was quite a sophisticated example of a piled carpet woven with a double knot that has often been associated with Turkic carpet-making traditions.[2]

From Mongolia and western Siberia, the early Turks brought their technique, culture, and love of carpets to central Asia, Persia, the Indian Peninsula, and finally to Anatolia. The latter became one of the world's most celebrated and studied centers of carpet making.

Contemporary experts identify three major groups of carpets according to the weaving technique. Flat-woven carpets were traditionally made on simple

A master restores an old carpet. Courtesy of the author, 2007.

homemade looms with preset vertical warp stands and horizontal threads of different colors and length run through the warp stands. These carpets have always been inexpensive and affordable to many commoners and ordinary tribesmen. People used them for all purposes from throwing them onto the ground as floor mats, decorating walls and entrances of their tents, to sewing material for bags, saddle-bags, talisman items, and, since the middle ages, prayer rugs. Knotted-pile carpets were also traditionally made on homemade vertical looms, and the wool was two-plied with S-twists and Z-spins. The process was more complicated and time consuming because even an experienced carpet-weaver could make only a few square centimeters of carpet a day. These carpets were destined for the tents and houses of wealthier individuals and always commanded higher prices. The nomads also made felt carpets by ramming and rolling unprocessed wool into a firm material and then applying brightly colored ornamental appliqués. These carpets can still be found in central Asia, but the technique is rarely used in modern Turkey.

Initially, the Turkic carpet-weavers used the wool of sheep, goats, and camels as the primary sources of raw material for their carpets. Most of the Anatolian carpet-makers decorated their work with geometric patterns, such as triangles, rhombuses, hexagons, and rectangles. Symbolic tribal marks were also incorporated by the weavers into their carpets. Since the Middle Ages, many of the weavers started combining different materials, for example, wool piles on cotton warps, or mixing wool and silk to create a relief surface or even exclusively used silk (silk piles on silk warps). Some masters also started incorporating their individual signatures, signs of specific guilds or places of carpet weaving into the overall design.

Today, Turkish carpets could be differentiated from region to region due to the variations in carpet-weaving traditions, the tribal affiliations of the carpet-weavers, and the demands in the local markets. Every region in Anatolia has been producing carpets of their own style, design, and motif; quite often they would also be made of different materials and sizes. The most famous carpets came from Antalya, Bergama, Hereke, Kars, Ladik, Milas, and some other areas.[3]

For example, Antalya is well-known for its carpets made by the descendents of the seminomadic Yoruk tribes, who settled in villages around this region. They produced medium and small carpets usually made of wool colored with natural dyes. The most distinctive patterns used in their carpets came from ancient nomadic traditions including stylized sheep eyes, knife tips placed along the borders of the carpets, and various symbols of female fertility. The main section of these carpets often depicted a stylized double *mihrab* with geometrical motifs in and around it.

The carpets from the Kars region in northeastern Turkey are recognized for their unique design and warm combination of navy blue, red, and cream. The most common motif on the borders of these carpets is a stylized running dog. The main section often encompasses a large stylized cruciform with rectangular ornament in the middle flanked by geometric patterns shaped as tall cypress or spruce trees.[4]

The carpet-makers from the town of Ladik claim that this place is the oldest carpet-making center in Anatolia, and that it has produced high-quality carpets since the fourteenth and fifteenth centuries. The weavers in Ladik also used wool to produce high-density carpets (up to 200,000–250,000 knots per square meter) with natural dyes. Many of these carpets were destined for the palaces of Seljuk sultans and their generals. They were also widely used to cover floors in mosques in Konya and other cities. In fact, several of the oldest surviving carpets from Anatolia were found in Konya. The most popular design patterns of Konya carpet-weavers were flower motifs and dark red, blue, and cream colors.

The carpets from the town of Hereke, southeast of Istanbul, have been traditionally distinguished by their high quality, luxuriousness, and large sizes because they were often produced for the palaces of the Ottoman sultans and Ottoman dignitaries. The Hereke workstations were specifically designed to create masterpieces fit for the royal family. Traditionally, the large Hereke carpets were made of sheep or camel wool, silk, or a combination of silk and wool. Sometimes, it took many years to produce very high density beautiful carpets of up to 1 million knots per square meter. Often sultans personally commissioned such carpets and selected the design and the motifs. In the nineteenth century, these carpets sometimes depicted humans and animals.

CERAMICS AND TILES

The Turks began settling in Anatolia in large numbers in the eleventh to fourteenth centuries, gradually abandoning their Spartan nomadic traditions and accepting new concepts of life, comfort, and luxury, and bringing to life their own preference for high art and culture. In the words of Walter Denny, an expert in Ottoman art, the Ottomans created "a complex, distinctive and highly developed imperial Islamic artistic tradition that blended many strains, from ancient nomadic Turkic art forms, to the distant but powerful Chinese visual tradition, to the many artistic styles assimilated by the Ottomans as they conquered the Islamic and European World."[5]

Ceramics was one of the innovations that the Turks began using in their everyday life, including expensive glazed items produced at local workshops

Examples of traditional Turkish pottery. Courtesy of the author, 2007.

or imported from Persia or Byzantine. Eventually, the wide usage of ceramics fostered support for the establishment of local workshops that produced various forms of kitchenware from inexpensive pottery for ordinary people to expensive pieces produced for nobility and royal families.

Experts traditionally differentiate ceramics of the Seljuk era and of the Ottoman period.[6] In general, during the Seljuk era the pottery was simpler and displayed Persian and central Asian influences because many masters traveled from those regions along the Great Silk Road all the way to Konya. It was Konya that became one of the most established centers of pottery production in the Seljuk Empire. Among other most renowned centers of early ceramics manufacturing were Iznik, Kutahya, and some other places.

During the Ottoman era, the middle class and elite developed tastes for exquisite and expensive goods, including high-quality decorated ceramics. The pottery makers discovered a rich variety of chemicals that generated bright and vivid colors and introduced new techniques of underglaze painting. They produced a large number of dishes, jugs, egg-shaped vases, flasks, and mugs that were beautifully painted by the best artists in the country and were made exclusively for the upper classes of the Ottoman society and for export.

A potter demonstrates his skills working with clay.
Courtesy of the author, 2007.

Notwithstanding the achievements in ceramics, the artists of the Seljuk and Ottoman states became renowned around the world for elevating the design and production of tiles to the level of the exceptionally elaborate art that would be associated with the heavenly garden "epitomized [in] the Ottoman artistic concern with light, a central Islamic metaphor for God."[7] During the early Seljuk era, the architects were using a combination of glazed and unglazed bricks to decorate their monumental buildings. Eventually, the craftsmen began working with a separate building material that was used for ornamentation purposes—tiles. Initially, the colors of the tiles were limited to blue, white, or black. Often each tile was of a single color, and these tiles were used to create elaborate mosaics decorating entrances to and domes of mosques, *madrasahs*, and palaces.

During the Ottoman era, the concept of decorating with tiles changed radically. The Ottoman architects used square and rectangular tiles that in combinations of four, six, or more (always an even number) formed beautiful large-scale panels. These tiles were hand painted with flowers, leaves, various abstract patterns—because depiction of humans and animals was not allowed—or with Quranic verses. The manufacturers produced tiles of various colors, including popular blue and deep blue, green, lilac, and deep red. The production of such tiles became a very complex process because many tile panels resembled jigsaw puzzles consisting of hundreds, and in some cases thousands, of pieces that had to be designed, hand painted, and produced for large public projects around the Ottoman Empire.

The artists and manufacturers developed their skills to perfection, and were able to produce works of impressive quality and design. It is still debatable, though, how much the Ottoman tile-makers were influenced by Persian, Central Asian, and Chinese tile-making traditions. Nevertheless, modern experts do agree that the Ottomans mastered their own distinctive style and artistic approaches that still amaze visitors in Istanbul, Bursa, and other cities and towns around the country.

CALLIGRAPHY AND MINIATURE PAINTING

Calligraphy, or the art of fine handwriting, can be found around modern Turkey everywhere—from the walls of old and new mosques and *madrasahs* to the libraries and museums, from numerous bookshops to souvenir stores, and from books in the hands of collectors to the miniature lockets on the necklaces of children and adults alike. The art and culture of handwriting was born in the first centuries of the Islamic caliphate, as a huge number of calligraphers in the language of the new religion—Arabic—emerged in the Muslim world. For more than a millennium the Arabic script was widely used in all parts of the Muslim world and Arabic often was the language of art, science, and theological discourse. In the absence of printed technologies that were practically unknown in Asia Minor until the seventeenth and eighteenth centuries, there was a considerable demand for people who could quickly write letters and documents and decorate various books and scrolls both for elite and statesmen and for mass audiences.

The demand for high-quality and expensive handwritten books and scripts grew steadily as the wealthy stratus of Muslim society and the royal families learned to appreciate the art of calligraphy. The demand was fulfilled by highly skilled professional handwriters who applied their artistic creativity and imagination and perfected their writing skills by creating beautiful manuscripts that were often embellished in paint and gilt. Such manuscripts were pieces of art in themselves and were often commissioned by individual patrons, royal librarians, scholars from prestigious *madrasahs*, or by wealthy families.

The early Turks discovered the art of calligraphy during their conquest of central Asia and Persia. Fascinated and impressed by the beautiful artistic works of famous calligraphers, they brought the art of handwriting to Anatolia. By the thirteenth century, hundreds of calligraphers were employed in Konya by Seljuk rulers. Later, the Ottomans made Istanbul one of the world's leading centers of calligraphy.[8] From the early eras many wealthy patrons ordered books completed by the calligraphers to be decorated. The classic decoration (or illumination) included stylized wing triangles, hexagons, and so on, called *rumi*; special serried curves called *munhani*; floral motifs called *hatayi*; clouds called *bulut*; decoration of the page preceding the manuscript called *zahriye*; and decoration of the final section of the manuscript called *hatim*.[9] Among the floral motifs pictures of roses and tulips were most popular.

The art of hand-painted miniatures arrived in Turkey hand in hand with the popularity of books, which was to some extent influenced by the pre-Islamic Persian and Chinese traditions. However, the advent of Islam during the Middle Ages brought certain restrictions as to what was allowed to be painted. The Muslim artists are not to depict humans or even animals and landscapes because Islamic traditions explicitly state that artistic depiction of God's creatures represents idolatry and worship of earthy subjects, which is one of the gravest sins in Islam.

Yet, not all artists agreed with these restrictions and the objects they depicted evolved over time.[10] In general, Muslim artists avoided painting humans, animals, and landscapes in public spaces and focused on miniature paintings in books and scripts. Initially, calligraphers decorated their works with extraordinary but abstract patterns and beautiful intertwined lines. Eventually, some of them began testing new territories and crossing lines by depicting real and fantastic animals, landscapes, and even humans,[11] that in Thomas Arnold's words displayed "the influence of Hellenic art . . . [and] other elements that are distinctively oriental, especially the style of the ornaments, the hunting scenes, and the type of some of the female figures."[12] The liberal attitudes of the Seljuks and Ottomans led to a gradual change and softer interpretation of the ban that allowed the artists decorate books with miniature paintings depicting scenes from the lives of the royal courts, battlegrounds, or from historic chronicles, legendary stories, and fairy tales.[13]

The distinctive features of the Seljuk and Ottoman era miniature paintings include two-dimensional organization of the scene and positioning of objects in the picture. There is also great attention to details, landscape, architecture, interior design, and people's clothing, yet the humans are depicted with characteristically flat faces and almond-shaped eyes. Miniature paintings with deep and rich colors seamlessly blended with ornaments and calligraphy of the handwritten manuscripts and represented the extension of the artistic decoration of the books, rather than individual pieces of art. Late in the Ottoman era, some artists began experimenting with the Western concepts of painting and moved beyond simply decorating books, producing pictures, panels, and other works.

Many scholars believe that the Persian school of miniature painting, particularly from the city of Tabriz, had a profound influence on the Ottoman art of the miniature.[14] One of the most influential artists was Kamaliddin Behzad (1455–c. 1533), whose painting style had a significant impact on the development of miniature art in both the Persian and Ottoman empires. Originally from the city of Herat, where Behzad learned the art of miniature painting and created his works, he moved to Tabriz in the early sixteenth century. There he produced impressive miniatures depicting court life and various other scenes as part of numerous books' decorations. The Ottoman sultans, awed by his works and by works of his students, invited hundreds of Persian artists, calligraphers, bookbinders, and book illustrators to Istanbul in the early sixteenth century,[15] where they began working at the so-called Persian Academy of Painting (*Nakkaskhane-i Irani*). Yet, the Ottoman artists who worked closely with the miniature painters from Persia developed their own style and approach to miniature painting and calligraphy.[16]

Among the great examples of the Ottoman calligraphy is a copy of the Quran prepared by the famous calligrapher, Ahmed Karahisari Mushaf-i Serif (c. 1468–c. 1556). The work on this copy of the Quran, which is considered to be among the largest in the world, was started in the mid-sixteenth century and was probably completed by a student of Ahmed Karahisari. This lavishly decorated and beautifully illustrated in classic calligraphy and floral ornamentation copy is on display in the library of the Topkapi Palace Museum.

The Ottoman sultans introduced an important innovation that shaped the Turkish miniature painting for many centuries. Beginning with Suleyman the Magnificent (1520–1566), each sultan employed an official royal historiographer whose role was to regularly produce illustrated volumes of the official Ottoman history and the deeds of the ruling sultans. The effect of this decision on miniature painting was twofold. On the one hand, it promoted the development of a school of secular book decoration. On the other hand, the royal miniature painters created large collections of miniatures that vividly depicted the portraits of the rulers, the court life, social structures, battles, architecture, and the everyday life of the subjects of the state. For example, royal miniaturist Nakkas Osman (?–c. 1590s), with the help of his assistants, produced his acclaimed *Surname* (c. 1582) that covered the most important events during the reign of Murad III (1574–1595) illustrating the book with hundreds of beautiful and intricate miniatures. He also contributed to the two-volume history *Hunername* (*Book of Accomplishments*).[17] Another gifted miniature painter was Abdullah Buhari (?–c. 1760s) who created many remarkable landscapes and portraits of women (including early nude images) and was also known for his inno-vative approach in attempts to create three-dimensional paintings, which brought his work very close to the artistic expressions of his Western con-temporaries.

JEWELRY AND METAL

The Seljuk and Ottoman era craftsmen left an impressive heritage of fine jewelry and metalwork. Goldsmiths developed impressive techniques in fine metalwork, rolling silk-thin gold and silver wire to decorate all kind of lux-ury items—from women's jewelry to books, bow cases, sables, and tableware. Many masterpieces of that era inevitably display different cultural influences as for centuries Anatolia was a key trading region on the Great Silk Road where goods, including jewelry and weaponry, traveled freely. The Ottoman Empire accumulated so much wealth that many people were able to afford luxurious artwork made of bronze, silver, or gold, thus, stimulating the mar-ket for fine jewelry and metalwork. Many features made Ottoman jewelry tradition quite unique and different from European jewelry, but two of them stand out and are worth noting. First, the Ottoman artisans did not hesitate to mix various metals in one piece of work; this was in sharp contrast with the European jewelry tradition of preferring the same metal in one item. Second, the Ottoman jewelers showed preference to intricate floral motifs, and rarely depicted animals or birds.[18]

Customarily, young Turkish women received pieces of jewelry as gifts from their parents, grandparents, and relatives, so by the age of marriage a girl would have an impressive set of jewelry. On the day of her wedding, her collection would easily compete with any jewelry exhibition with all the pieces imaginable—amulets, armlets, bandeaux, bracelets, bangles, brooch pins, belts, buckles, buttons, chains, earrings, forehead jewelry, garlands, neck-laces, panache, pendants, rings, and many other pieces. She would proudly display her wealth to her female friends, relatives, and future in-laws to show off her status, social position, and noble line of ancestry because the heirloom treasures had been in the same family for five to seven generations or even longer. Not only did the jewelry play an esthetic role in society, it was also a kind of a personal banking account or safety net for difficult times, recession, or in the case of divorce.

Like in many other areas around the world, silver was the metal of choice as it was affordable for most ordinary people. Wealthy families also could afford and did use silverware at home—from elaborately decorated trays and vessels to incense burners, nice buckets, lamps, flasks, and other items.

In the meantime, gold was popular among the upper classes, and precious stones were popular among the royal dynasties and truly rich families. Some historical chronicles claim that Sultan Selim and Sultan Suleiman mastered goldsmith skills while they were princes-in-waiting to a degree that they decorated their own weaponry—swords, bow cases, and daggers. Traditionally, in Muslim society, it is strongly discouraged for men to adorn themselves with gold. However, it was perfectly acceptable to possess expensively decorated weaponry, horse caparisons, and aigrettes. In fact, many officers and generals received expensive sables, swords, and daggers, and later pistols and guns from their commanders for exceptional service during numerous military campaigns.

Examples of exceptionally fine and richly decorated metalwork could be found in the treasury section of the Topkapi Palace in Istanbul. The turban ornament—aigrette (*sorguç*)—is probably one of the more typical decorations used by the Ottoman sultans and princes to show their power and status. For example, the centerpiece of the eighteenth-century sultan's aigrette, displayed in the treasury section of the Topkapi Palace, bears a large emerald and a smaller ruby, surrounded by diamonds and topped by rows of diamonds and pearls that end with tufts of plumes. Four 5- to 6-inch (15–18 centimeters) gold chains decorated with diamonds and emerald droplets extend to the left and right of the centerpiece and their ends would be pinned to the turban. Another example of the metalwork is the full armor of Sultan Mustafa III (1757–1774), which consists of a helmet, protective gear, sable, two shields, gold-plated gloves, and a decorated belt with large buckles. An interesting example of such fine work is a Quran binding, which is made of gold encrusted with polychrome enamels combined into the intricate flowery motif.

MODERN ART

Painting

Being in the forefront of the cultural exchange between the Muslim world and the West, the Ottomans became quite open to Western influences in the modern era. Although the Ottoman artists still refrained from making sculptures or depicting humans in their publicly displayed paintings in accordance with the Islamic traditions, they began experimenting with mural paintings for private collectors from early eras. The mural art gradually evolved from floral and abstract motifs to the painting of realistic landscapes and scenes from the everyday life of the royal courts and the Ottoman elite.[19]

In art, there were no boundaries—there were always exchanges.[20] In the seventeenth and eighteenth centuries, there emerged numerous groups of painters (*nakkash*) and portraitists (*musavvir*) in Istanbul, despite vociferous disapproval from the conservative Islamic scholars (*ulema*).[21] Among the most noticeable of these new artists was Abdulcelil Celebi (Levni) (?–c. 1733) who became a royal court painter working on portraits of the Ottoman rulers for the official genealogy (*Silsilname*) and who created an invaluable collection of drawings of the seventeenth century Ottoman court. His works represent the beginning of the transformation of the traditional Ottoman artistic approaches under Western influence. The Ottoman officials felt themselves culturally close to their Western counterparts to the degree that they even commissioned various albums with pictures of their subjects—men and women depicted in the Western style—for distribution among foreign dignitaries and diplomats.[22]

There is no clear-cut timeframe, however, for the transformation of the classic Ottoman art, that for centuries has been under a strong Islamic influence, to the modern art linked to Western traditions.[23] Some experts trace those transformations to the eighteenth and nineteenth centuries, others push the date even further back to the late seventeenth century. Others highlight that there was never an impassable wall between the Ottoman and European traditions because both cultures learned from each others' best achievements for centuries.[24] It was a process that could be exemplified in a development of the art of painting in Turkey.

In the late eighteenth and early nineteenth centuries, many Western painters became fascinated and even obsessed with the exotic features of the Ottoman culture and life, mesmerizing and vivid art, and with the sexuality of the Ottoman court, harems, and women. For more than a century, probably starting with Napoleon's campaign in Egypt and ending with World War I, many western European and Russian artists regularly traveled to the Ottoman Empire.[25] Among these artists, often called Romantic orientalists, were Jean Auguste Dominique Ingres (1780–1867), John Frederik Lewis (1805–1876), Edward Lear (1812–1888), Ivan Aivazovski (1817–1900), Jean-Léon Gérôme (1824–1904), Paul Desiré Trouillebert (1829–1900), and many others.

By the mid-nineteenth century, members of the Ottoman Court invited many Western painters to reside in Istanbul, and even appointed some of them as royal court painters.[26] Among the most prominent of them was Fausto Zonaro (1854–1929) who resided in Istanbul's trendy Beshiktash area for many years and created an impressive collection of several hundred works. His incredible oil paintings depicted in the classic style the life of the royal family, Ottoman elite, military, and everyday life of Istanbul and left a strong imprint on the cultural landscape of the country.[27]

One of the effects was that the Ottomans felt a need to establish their own schools of painting. Like their Western counterparts, many nineteenth- and early twentieth-century Turkish painters attempted to organize themselves into artistic groups that brought together like-minded people with similar artistic and often political views.[28] As a first step in creating a Turkish painting school was the introduction of painting classes in military schools, such as the Military School of Engineering (*Mühendishane-i Berri-i Humayun*). The next step was the opening of the Ottoman School (*Mektebi Osmani*) in Paris where many young painters were sent for study and training. These schools produced a whole generation of painters who excelled in landscape painting, although they had little interest in figural painting. The life of Ahmed Ali (Seher Ahmet Pasha) (1841–1906) might be a good example. He was sent to Paris and lived there for about eight years and was mentored by such famous French artists as Gustave Boulanger (1824–1888) and Jean-Léon Gérôme (1824–1904). Ahmed Ali went into the annals for organizing one of the first ever group exhibitions in Turkey in 1873 and for his influential personal exhibition in 1902. He left a series of impressive landscapes and still-life paintings that inspired a whole generation of painters in his native land.

The Fine Art Academy (*Sanayi-i Nefise Mektebi*) was founded in 1883. It brought together many gifted individuals and gave them an opportunity to exchange ideas and support each other in various ways. Among the painters of this early period (sometimes also called Turkish Primitives), we can mention Hoca Ali Riza (c. 1864–1930),[29] whose rich collection of landscape paintings of the places in and around Istanbul and ruins of historic sites, as well as pencil drawings of his contemporaries work is quite remarkable.[30]

In the 1910s and 1930s, several artistic groups came to live in Turkey. For example, the Association of Ottoman Painters (later The Association of Turkish Painters) was established in 1909. Among the interesting artists of this period we can mention Sami Yetik (1876–1945), whose notable works included realistic-style battle scenes in his *Recapturing the Village* (1917) and panoramic *Market Place* (1917).

The Turkish scholars also highlight the contribution of the group called 1914–Generation to the development of artistic traditions in the country. The representatives of this group often worked in a sharp realistic style similar to that of their counterparts in Russia and Germany. For example, Ruhi Azel (1880–1931) worked in the "revolutionary" style powerfully depicting the determination and hard work of ordinary people in *The Stone Breaking* (1924) and *Welcoming Ataturk in Istanbul* (1927). Avni Lifij (c. 1889–1927) painted the horrific impact of wars on peaceful life of people in his *Day of Distress*

(1917) and *Allegory* (1917) as well as a realistic depiction of the hard work of ordinary people in *Municipal Works in Kondikoy—Istanbul* (1916).

Many Turkish painters experimented with different styles and genres. One such an example is Cemal Tollu (1899–1968), who was a member of Group-D (active in the 1930s and 1940s)—an informal artistic society that brought together an eclectic group of young artists.[31] He left an impressive legacy of about 100 works, mainly oil on canvas in various styles including numerous portraits and landscapes of Anatolia.

The government initiated the Painting for Revolution campaign, which became an important benchmark in developing the Turkish school of painting in the 1930s because it commissioned works that depicted the War of Independence, the struggle for new life, and changes in society. From 1938 to 1944, the government also sponsored the Provincial Tours for Painters campaign that commissioned ten artists every year to travel to various remote towns and cities in Turkey to work on the topic of their choice and to promote interest in the visual arts among the local population.

One of the distinctive features of post–World War II Turkish painting has been that these painters—although they were fully aware of the trends and various techniques in Western art—rarely followed strict academic norms and rules, and experimented with different styles and approaches over time.

Initially, the art of painting was dominated entirely by men, but gradually many women joined the ranks. Among the first such women was Mihri Hanim (1886–1954)[32] who taught art at the teachers' training school for girls for many years and whose portraits of writer Tevfik Fikret (c. 1915), commander Mustafa Kemal (c. 1923), and others impressed contemporaries for their realism and vigor. Another female painter was Mufide Kadri Hanim (1889–1911). She left an impressive heritage of beautiful and romantic landscapes and portraits. Celile (Ugur Aldim) Hanim (1883–1956) focused on female individual and group portraits, which scandalized Turkish society because they were mainly nude representations of her female contemporaries, such as *A Gipsy Girl* and *Bath for Ladies*.

RECENT TRENDS

On the eve of the twenty-first century, the powerful forces of globalization and market-oriented economy increasingly began reshaping the artistic landscape in Turkey. Global culture often annihilates the unique national artistic traditions and taste, as the global mass pop culture makes inroads into everyday life, not only in the form of entertainment of ordinary people, but also by affecting everyday life, culture, and traditions. Many Turks complain that the days when beautiful kitchen porcelain and silverware, samples of Ottoman classic era books, calligraphy, and jewelry were kept in the families from generation to generation are gone. Many craftsmen claim that truly Ottoman and Turkish art pieces, which, in the past, found ways into the homes of many people, were replaced by cheap, tasteless, and motionless mass-produced objects that surround people in their everyday lives.

Some experts claim that traditional art became excessively commercialized. Many craftsmen in the cities and even remote towns and villages abandon their unique traditions, centuries-old, best-kept secrets and techniques, and the true "Turkish" authenticity in favor of adjusting their work to the taste of an average foreign tourist. Although, in fact, it was the rise of mass tourism, both international and domestic, that opened many isolated places to new trends and people's curiosity. These tourists created a huge demand for traditional art because a *kilim*, a carpet, or a piece of ceramics often was a must-have souvenir for those who visited various places around the country.

Other experts disagree with these statements by pointing out that Turkish artisans have always been eager to learn from the best examples of their colleagues and counterparts from the East and West and synthesized the best foreign traditions. In addition, they point out that tourism brings necessary demand for traditional Turkish art by providing employment to thousands of craftsmen, weavers, and artists. The argument goes that there have always been artists who produced for the mass market and there have always been artists who created masterpieces for true art-lovers and the elite.

However, the simple truth is somewhere in between, as contemporary Turkish art became an inseparable part of the modern global culture being represented in unique ways in various artistic styles and genres. Many young Turkish artists who work in modern pop and kitsch style became known far beyond Turkey. For example, Selcuk Demirel (1954–) has been drawing for various Turkish newspapers and magazines for several decades and has achieved international acclaim for his satirical and comic depiction of mass pop culture and life.[33]

NOTES

1. Quoted in Metin And. *Turkish Miniature Painting*, 4th ed. Istanbul: Milet Publishing Limited, 1987, p. 28.

2. Sergei Rudenko. *Frozen Tombs of Siberia: The Pazyryk Burials of Iron Age Horsemen.* Translated with a preface by M. W. Thompson. Berkeley: University of California Press, 1970.

3. There are many ways to classify the Turkish carpets, and different experts use different approaches. For example, see Nazan Ölçer et al. *Turkish carpets from the 13th–18th Centuries: Rare Carpets Selected from the Collections of Museum of Turkish*

and Islamic Arts, Istanbul, Vakiflar Carpet Museum, Istanbul, State Museums of Berlin-Museum of Islamic Arts, Budapest Museum of Applied Arts, Konya Mevlana Museum, Heinrich Kirchheim: Together with Paintings from State Museums of Berlin-National Gallery, Warsaw National Museum, and The National Gallery, London. Istanbul: Ahmet Ertug, 1996.

4. For a study of carpet motifs, see Christopher Alexander. *A Foreshadowing of 21st Century Art: The Color and Geometry of Very Early Turkish Carpets.* New York: Oxford University Press, 1993.

5. Walter Denny. *Gardens of Paradise: 16th-Century Turkish Ceramic Tile Decoration.* Istanbul: Ertug and Kocabiyik, 1998, p. 13.

6. For an overview of the ceramics from the Ottoman era see Walter B. Denny. *Iznik: The Artistry of Ottoman Ceramics.* London and New York: Thames & Hudson, 2004.

7. Ibid., p. 14.

8. For a research on Ottoman calligraphy, see M. Ugur Derman. *Letters in Gold: Ottoman Calligraphy from the Sakıp Sabancı Collection, Istanbul.* New York: Metropolitan Museum of Art. Distributed by H. N. Abrams, 1998.

9. Mine Esiner Ozen. *Türk Tezhip Sanatı* [Turkish Art of Illumination]. Istanbul: Gozen kitap ve yayınevi, 2003, pp. 3–5.

10. For an interesting overview, see Sir Thomas W. Arnold. *Painting in Islam. A Study of the Place of Pictorial Art in Muslim Culture.* 2nd ed. Oxford: Oxford University Press, 1928, reprint: Piscataway, NJ: Gorgias Press, 2004.

11. For the evolution of the approach to painting in the Muslim world and the interaction between Muslim and non-Muslim painters, see Sir Thomas W. Arnold. *Painting in Islam. A Study of the Place of Pictorial Art in Muslim Culture.* 2nd ed. Oxford: Oxford University Press, 1928, reprint: Piscataway, NJ: Gorgias Press, 2004, pp. 52–70.

12. Ibid., p. 57.

13. Metin And. *Turkish Miniature Painting.* 4th ed. Istanbul: Milet Publishing Limited, 1987.

14. Norah Titley. *Persian Miniature Painting and Its Influence on the Art of Turkey and India.* London: The British Library, 1983.

15. Ibid., p. 134.

16. Metin And. *Minyatürlerle Osmanlı-İslâm Mitologyası* [The methodology of the Islamic Ottoman miniature]. Istanbul: Akbank, 1998.

17. Gunsel Renda et al. *A History of Turkish Painting.* 2nd ed. Seattle and London: Palasar SA in association with University of Washington Press, 1988, p. 31.

18. For some discussions of jewelry traditions see Isık Bingo. *Ancient Jewelry.* Ankara: Turkish Republic Ministry of Culture, 1999. Also: http://www.turkishculture.org/pages.php?ChildID=&ParentID=10&ID=46&ChildID1=46.

19. For details, see Gunsel Renda et al. *A History of Turkish Painting*, pp. 69–85.

20. For an example of a research on such exchanges, see Karin Adalh, ed. *The Sultan's Procession. The Swedish Embassy to Sultan Mehmed IV in 1657–1658 and the Ralamb Paintings.* Istanbul: Swedish Research Institute in Istanbul, 2006.

21. Esin Atıl. *Levni and the Surname: The Story of an Eighteenth-Century Ottoman Festival.* Istanbul: Kocbank, 1999, p. 31.

22. Ibid., pp. 22–24.

23. Gunsel Renda et al. *A History of Turkish Painting,* pp. 88–91.

24. Ibid., pp. 89–92.

25. Lynne Thornton. *Women as Portrayed in Orientalist Painting.* Paris: ACR Edition, 1985) and Roger Benjamin, Lynne Thornton et al. *Orientalism: Delacroix to Klee.* Sydney: Art Gallery of New South Wales, 1997.

26. Omer Tasledn and Ilona Baytar. *Osmanlı Sarayı'nda oryantalistler* [Orientalists at the Ottoman place]. Istanbul: BMM Milli Saraylar Daire Başkanlıgi, 2006.

27. Osman Ondes and Erol Makzume. *Ottoman Court Painter Fausto Zonaro.* Istanbul: Yapı Kredi Kültür Sanat Yayıncılık, 2003 and Gérard-Georges Lemaire. *The Orient in Western Art.* Cologne, Germany: Konemann Verlagsgesellschaft, 2008.

28. For evolution of the artistic thought, see *Osmanlı Ressamlar Cemiyeti'nden Guzel Sanatlar Birligi'ne, 1909–1991* [From the Society of Ottoman Painters to the Association of Fine Arts, 1909–1991]. Istanbul: Alarko Egitim-Kultur Vakfı, 1992.

29. Other sources list different dates for the life of Hoca Ali Riza—1857–1939.

30. Sennur Aydın et al. *Hoca Ali Rıza: Hazırlayanlar* [Hoca Ali Rıza: pictures]. Istanbul: Yapı Kredi Yayınları, [s.n.] 1988.

31. For discussion of his works, see Veysel Ugurlu, ed. *Cemal Tollu: Retrospektif* [Cemal Tollu: Retrospective]. Istanbul: Yapı Kredi Yayınları, 2005.

32. For details of her life and artistic accomplishments, see Taha Toros. *Ilk Kadin Ressamlarimiz* [The First Lady Artists of Turkey]. Istanbul: Akbank, 1988, pp. 9–18.

33. Selcuk Demirel. *Goz Alabildigine* [As Far as the Eye Can See]. Istanbul: Yapı Kredi Yayınları, 2003.

7

Architecture

One of the most striking features of all Islamic architectural monuments is their focus on the enclosed space, on the inside as opposed to the outside, the façade, or the general exterior articulation of a building.[1]
—Ernst J. Grube, scholar and expert on Islamic architecture

IT IS NOT an exaggeration to say that contemporary Turkey is both a museum under an open sky and an exhibition hall for studying the evolution of architectural thought through observation of the world's most celebrated masterpieces. Nearly all of the architectural styles that may be found in textbooks are represented here. At the center of this exposition is, of course, the classical Ottoman architecture. Among the best and most famous examples of this are the magnificent Suleymaniye and Blue Mosques in Istanbul. Many cities around the country also boast classical Ottoman-era structures. Assemblages of medieval public complexes—mosques sporting sky-scraping minarets, *madrasahs* (religious colleges), *khanaqas* (Sufi lounges), *hammams* (Turkish baths), caravanserais (medieval inns), and the splendid palaces of sultans, *beis*, and wealthy individuals—are spread around nearly every major city and town symbolizing both the achievements of the Ottoman state and tastes of its rulers.

Indeed, the towering signature-style, pencil-shaped Ottoman minarets guard the domed square structures, and these are adorned with numerous half-domes and porticoes, and always include domed cloisters, courtyards, and buttresses. Baked bricks and elaborately cut stones assembled in stern symmetrical patterns shape the monumental public buildings. Sky-blue tile works (blue is the ancient color of the Turkic tribes) envelope many public and religious buildings, and symbolize the significance of the Turks as saviors and guardians of the Muslim world and Islamic heritage.

The splendid masterpieces of Seljuk and Ottoman architecture in Konya, Bursa, Izmir, Istanbul, and other centers represent the most impressive architectural achievements of the medieval era. Nevertheless, the architectural heritage of Anatolia is even more impressive because it naturally incorporates the styles and construction elements of diverse civilizations from centuries of coexistence. Many Ottoman buildings stand alongside ancient and early medieval sites, buildings, and ruins of early civilizations—from naturalistic Hittite sphinxes, demons, and elegant ancient Greek agoras to grand Roman and Byzantine temples and monuments. In fact, on many occasions, construction workers of later periods used foundations, bricks, stone works, or sites of earlier buildings and were often inspired by examples from previous eras in designing and constructing their works. Visitors and students thus find that the modern architectural heritage of Turkey is not exclusively Ottoman and Islamic; rather it represents examples from many civilizations that existed on Anatolian soil.[2]

Unfortunately, Kronos, the god of time, was not always kind to the architectural heritage of this land. Many fine examples of early architecture disappeared forever in the course of numberless wars and military campaigns. Due to the economic and financial difficulties of the eighteenth and nineteenth centuries, the Ottoman government significantly reduced funds for the maintenance, restoration, or preservation of many religious and public buildings and complexes. In 1923, after the devastation of World War I and the War of Independence, the Turkish Republic emerged an extremely poor state, wholly focused on rebuilding its economy and constructing a new way of life that included modern public buildings and public housing, and the provision of food for its people. For decades, it had few resources with which to maintain many of its historical sites, despite their world-heritage value. Only in the last quarter of the twentieth century, which brought economic stabilization and a meteoric rise in international tourism, and thus revenue, did the government begin allocating significant resources into the restoration and maintenance of a significant number of the country's architectural sites.

In today's Turkey, the architectural achievements of the past coexist with contemporary styles of architectural expression, and in the modern quarters of Ankara, Antalya, and many other cities, one finds a full range of styles and designs from early twentieth-century cubism to functionalism and neoclassicism.

ANCIENT ARCHITECTURE

For modern Turks the historical heritage of the Anatolian lands, from ancient temples to the grand mosques of the Ottoman era, is an intrinsic part
of their national identity, in the sense of both their "Turkishness," and the
Turkish culture.[3] It is unlikely that any town guides in Turkey or students
of Turkish architecture would dream of beginning their introduction to the
topic without mentioning the ancient civilizations that flourished on the
territory of the modern state, and also the various important environmental and political aspects that affected construction and design through the
centuries.

The first of these factors is the climate of each specific area. Anatolia's climate is probably as diverse as that of the continental United States, ranging
from pleasantly mild subtropical conditions in Antalya to extremes of cold
in the snow-covered mountain areas of the eastern and northeastern parts of
east Anatolia. Most of western Anatolia and the Aegean region, where many
civilizations flourished, usually enjoy long, dry, and sunny summers, cooling
moderately during the windy winters.

The second factor is that many centuries ago Anatolia lost most of its pris-
tine forests and experienced a shortage of construction-quality timber. Thus,
for centuries various types of stone, which abounds in the region, and clay,
which was used to make sun-dried and fired bricks, became the materials of
choice. In addition, in some of the central parts of Anatolia and in the Black
Sea region, people often, and with great skill, adapted many of the caves and
grottos on the hill sides as dwellings and public buildings, and even as places
of worship.

The third factor is that from earliest days, successive rulers over the land
displayed their military supremacy, geopolitical importance, and wealth by
building everything at a grand scale—from public complexes to royal palaces
and centers of worship.

Among the most renowned and oldest examples of ancient architecture
are the temples and fortresses of the Hittite civilization (eighteenth to eighth
centuries B.C.). Especially famed are the ruins of the Eflatunpinar Monument (near Beysehir and Konya) and Ivriz Rock Monument (near Eregli and
Konya), which testify to the active use of local materials, such as large stone
blocks, for carving out silhouettes of deities and kings. The Eflatunpinar Monument, for example, probably represents the ruins of a large temple of the early
Hittite era, with carvings of simplified representations of demons and deities.
The Ivriz Rock relief is part of what was originally a very large, complex and
elaborate stone work depicting kings, gods, and various elements of everyday
life in the Hittite kingdom.[4] Further examples of the architecture of that era

may be found in Alacahoyuk, Bogazhoy, Govurkale, Karabel, and a number of other locations.

The Hellenic civilization of the sixth to second centuries B.C. left perhaps the most remarkable monuments, and for many centuries these had a profound effect on the architecture and art of regions as far afield as southern Europe, Asia Minor, and northern Africa. The Ionian confederation of cities and towns emerged after a century or two of struggles among the Urartian, Phrygian, Lydian, and Persian civilizations.[5] The Hellenic architecture in the Ionian region represents a significant departure from the Hittite tradition, introducing more elegant, complex, and airy structures. The most striking architectural remains of the Hellenic civilization can be found in and around the cities of Bergama (Pergamon) and Ephesus. Although in ruins now, most of the Hellenic agoras, temples, theaters, and commercial and living quarters were altered during the Roman period. Yet, the elegant temples with numerous columns, marvelous sculptures, and figures of gods, heroes, and famous citizens made of marble and stone of that era survived into modern times.

The Romans entered the political and cultural scene in the second century B.C., and their influence and dominance lasted many centuries. Although they did introduce many changes, there was continuity with the Roman architecture because the Romans had been under the influence of Hellenic traditions. In many cases, the Romans built larger public buildings and temples, believing that such monumentalism symbolized the power and might of their empire. In cities such as Pergamon and Ephesos, the Romans repaired the existing theaters, adding new sections and seats. One of the important innovations of the Roman era was buildings with two-story-high walls supported and decorated by columns. The Library of Celsus, built in Ephesus by order of Consul Gaius Julius Aquila in 114–117 A.D., and the Temple of Jupiter, constructed between 117 and 138 in Aezani (Cavdarhisar near Kutahya), are examples of such architectural works. Another innovation was the central heating system introduced in the Roman baths, which had hot air delivered through holes in the brick walls and floors of the buildings. During this period, many cities grew significantly as the Romans learned to build increasingly complex feats of engineering, in particular the aqueducts capable of bringing fresh water from many miles away.

The Byzantine period (the fourth to the fifteenth centuries) was perhaps the most enduring and productive period in the long history of Anatolian architecture. Despite its ups and downs, the Byzantine Empire invested significant resources into erecting public and especially religious buildings. One of the most remarkable examples is the Hagia Sophia Church (the Church of Holy Wisdom), which was built on the foundations of two earlier churches and was inaugurated by the Emperor Justinian in 537. The monumental style and dimensions of the Hagia Sophia evoke the power, influence, and eternal nature of the Eastern Orthodox Church and the Eastern Roman Empire. This monumental style was replicated many times in other parts of Anatolia, though the Hagia Sophia remained one of the largest churches in the world for many centuries. It was rebuilt and replanned on a number of occasions, yet, throughout the centuries, its original majestic beauty was preserved. The mosaics and frescos of this church are another characteristic feature of the Byzantine period. Most of them depicted religious events or the life and actions of the Byzantine royal family. Unfortunately, during the iconoclastic period (726–842), most of the pictorial art was destroyed because worshiping icons and other examples of figurative expression were prohibited. Only with the end of the iconoclastic period were new mosaics, frescos, and icons created for all major churches across the region.

The Fourth Crusade (1201–1204) brought devastation to Constantinople and the cities and towns in the surrounding area. Provoked by the great schism of 1054, by the political intrigues of the Venetians, and simply by greed, the Crusaders pillaged the city and dethroned the Byzantine Emperor. Tens of thousands of masterpieces and art works were stripped off of the public and religious buildings and carried away to the West. In addition, the Crusaders destroyed countless *objets d'art* of both the Roman and Byzantine periods, melting down bronze statues, relief objects, and even church doors into coins. In the late Byzantine period, the Eastern Roman Emperor recaptured Constantinople and its surrounding territory and attempted to restore some of the fortresses, churches, and public buildings. However, the resources were never adequate, and many buildings in Constantinople, Anatolia, and eastern Thrace fell into ruin or simply continued their long decay until the Ottoman conquest in 1453.

Islamic Architecture

Muslim rulers always tried to demonstrate the universalism and centrality of Islam, the youngest of the Abrahamic religions, by strategically placing Islamic symbols as the focal point of the landscape in conquered territories. New religious ensembles were constructed in all captured cities and towns, or old churches and important sites were converted into or gave ways to mosques. Islamic architecture itself carried an important message to the people; it stood, in the words of Robert Hillenbrand, as "[a] Muslim response to the splendors of Classical and Christian architecture around them, and an assertion of the power and presence of the new faith."[6] The development of the Turks' architectural ideas is an inseparable part of architectural heritage of Islam.

Its unique representation is also, in the view of some scholars, considered to be one of the most audacious and distinctive legacies of Islamic civilization. Many rulers—from the Seljuks to the Ottoman sultans—built rich and magnificent monuments, which arose in the sandy deserts and oases and captured the imaginations of travelers, who in turn generated endless legends of the immense wealth of the region.

One of the signature features of the region's architectural forms that developed after the Muslim conquest was the enclosed courtyard. The courtyard was a standard feature of both religious and secular buildings. Another distinctive element was a special portal usually built in front of mosques, mausoleums, or *madrasahs*. These portals designated the main entrance and signified the doorway to the place where Muslims could think about God without being interrupted by earthy problems. A third notable element was the dome—at first conical and later egg-shaped—large or small, which contributed enormously to the visual effect and created a lively sense of space inside. Such domes were sophisticated pieces of engineering; even today, designing and building such structures, especially the largest ones, presents a serious technological challenge.

Islamic architects have typically built their mosques with a minaret and water fountain, a *madrasah*, and a hostel with a kitchen; this combination traditionally constituted a single complex to serve the local Muslim community. Mosques have been, as a rule, rectangular, with an egg-shaped dome at the top. Islamic teaching prohibits representative art, portraiture, or erection of statues within or near a mosque, but it does not oppose beautification by other means—ornamental or floral motifs created with tiles, bricks or carved limestone, or *Kufi* writings of Quran verses. The same rules apply to the interior decorations of Islamic religious buildings. One of the most important structures of every mosque is the *mihrab*, an arch-shaped niche in the wall. The *mihrab* serves two purposes: it shows the direction to Ka-aba (in Mecca), and it improves the acoustics as it gives resonance to the voice of the Imam, amplifying his tones for all worshippers during the prayer. Unlike the altar in the Christian world, the *mihrab* must be kept simple and empty at all times— no pictures or sculptures are allowed and the religious ideas are represented by symbols and abstractions rather than by concrete forms. A common decoration in many mosques includes the Muslim rosary, which has ninety-nine beads deriving their names from the ninety-nine names of Allah, as described in the Quran.

A traditional accompaniment to every mosque has always been the minaret. These are slim and tall, usually cylindrical, with stairs inside and at the top a small room with open, arched windows, which is crowned with an egg-shaped or pointed dome. Unlike the massive bell towers in the churches of the Christian world, the minaret never holds a bell; instead, the faithful are called to prayer by the cry of a *muezzin*. Minarets are built to be visible from afar, standing therefore as landmarks indicating the direction for all devoted Muslims to take five times a day.

Before entering a mosque, the first stop is at a water fountain where worshippers are required to cleanse themselves before prayer. Every functioning mosque has an ablution fountain with running water, usually located in the center of the courtyard or close to the main entrance.

Islamic educational institutions—the *madrasahs*—were very often (but not always) built next to a large mosque, as modest building complexes with classrooms, offices and square inner courtyards lined with small, simple lodging cells (*hujra*). The courtyard was traditionally formed by rectangular buildings of two and sometimes three stories. Students and resident scholars lived in cells arranged along the intermediate walls two or more levels high. They usually studied under the open sky, sitting in small circles on the carpet that was spread around the courtyard in summer or in various rooms in winter. The kitchen provided food for students, travelers, and people in need, as well as to all members of the local community during the fasting month. The *madrasah* usually operated under the benevolent sponsorship of rulers, merchants, local communities, and special trust endowments (*waqf*).

The members of Sufi orders (dervishes) lived in seclusion from the temporal world in special monastic-style complexes (*khanaqas* also called *tekke*). These buildings were very austere, with no lavish decorations and were designed solely to provide year-round accommodation and a spiritual environment for group and individual contemplation. The typical complex included a living room, library, kitchen, and a hall for group meditation. Despite this isolation, by the sixteenth to the nineteenth centuries, the dervish orders had grown significantly in political power, acquiring strong influence in the courts of the Ottoman rulers, as many sultans, generals, and officers in the elite janissary corps were themselves members of Sufi brotherhoods.

Turbes (also *kumbets*—Turkish for mausoleums) were built in various sizes; they usually adhered closely to the classical architectural designs of the early Islamic era, and consisted of two parts: a tomb chamber (*gurkhana*) and a prayer chamber (*ziaratkhana*). Muslim tradition originally prohibited erecting any structure above the grave of a believer. This custom was strictly followed until the early ninth century, when one of the Caliphs ordered to build a mausoleum for himself and thus set a precedent. Thereafter, Islamic mausoleums usually followed an established custom and symbolism. Unlike the *Munhals* of India, the Turks did not build grand, lavish mausoleums in the style of the Taj Mahal, preferring modest stand-alone tombs that symbolized the infinitesimal status of human beings in Allah's universe. These structures

The interior of Jalaluddin Rumi Mausoleum (Mevlana Turbesi) in Konya. Courtesy of the author, 2007.

were most often designed to immortalize the deeds and achievements of the foremost political rulers, or to honor the most respected and popular Sufi leaders or saints (Rumi Mausoleum). Some rulers or wealthy individuals had mausoleums built in remembrance of their favorite and/or most important family members.

The architectural legacy of the Turks can be tentatively subdivided into three periods.

The early period is represented by the architecture of the eleventh to the fourteenth centuries,[7] and can be distinguished by several features. One is the introduction and wide use of fire-baked bricks in the construction of monumental Islamic public buildings. Another is a specific decorative style acquired under central Asian and Persian influences. In addition, religious buildings typically had a single dome and often resembled a heavily fortified medieval castle. During this era, major external decorations were formed by positioning of fire-baked bricks in mathematically perfect geometrical patterns, and by stalactitic, honeycomb-style ornamentation of the *muqarnas* (corbels) of the religious buildings. Many monuments of this early period have survived to the present, especially in eastern and central Anatolia.

The Caravanserai in Aksaray (c. 1229) is a classic example of numerous medieval inns built in Anatolia to service travelers of the Great Silk Road. This huge and luxurious complex was probably built at the order of Kayqubad I. It was designed as a series of galleries around a rectangular central courtyard attached to a huge domed hall. The complex consists of a large praying room, a *hammam* (bath), workshops, and a series of small private chambers and horse stables lined up around the courtyard. The inn proper was protected by high, windowless external walls adorned with buttresses. As in all caravanserais, a single entrance led to the complex and was fortified against marauders.

The Cifte Minare *Madrasah* in Erzurum (c. 1253–c. 1299) was built in 1253, but it was probably restored or expanded during a later period. This is a large, rectangular, two-storey complex. The main building has a portal, decorated in the Persian style, which forms the main entrance and is flanked by two tall fluted minarets. Across the courtyard from the main entrance, there is a small mosque, and several dozen small chambers are lined up in two levels on the both sides of the central court. The minarets are decorated with blue-glazed bricks, and the *muqarnas* are decorated with engraved trees and birds.

The Doner Kumbet (tomb) in Kayseri (c. 1276)[8] exemplifies the mausoleums of the Seljuk period. The lower part of the tomb is a cube-shaped structure, with thick walls that are divided into panels by ribs and arches. The conical dome is of a yellowish-brown color. It is decorated with carved geometrical motifs, but current thought among experts suggests that in the past it also sported carved images of human heads, lions, and eagles, which were at some stage destroyed. It is believed to have been dedicated to Princess Sah Cihan Hatun.

The Mosque and hospital in Divrigi (c. 1229) is another Islamic complex built in a classical rectangular shape. The assembly has a large decorated portal over the main entrance, a single, tall minaret, round in shape, and a mosque hall with four rows of four piers each. The two-story hospital is attached to the mosque. This complex displays some characteristics similar to the monumental architecture in Georgia (Caucasus) in that it emulates a heavy medieval castle built of large stone blocks. It is believed to have been built by the architect Ahmet of Tiflis (present-day Tbilisi).

The second period is traditionally associated with the rise of the Ottomans, and is represented by the architecture of the fourteenth and fifteenth centuries. This architectural period is characterized by marble-paved central halls and high-rising crowning domes, usually on a drum-shaped structure, or solid stone base. As building technology and architectural thought evolved over time, many decorators began using intricately carved terracotta with turquoise monochrome glazing. During this era, too, beautifully glazed polychromatic tiles became a widely used element of exterior decoration. The architects of this period favored egg-shaped domes, and conical domes gradually disappeared from the scene. In addition, the interior upper corners of many buildings were adorned with large, elaborate, and beautiful honeycomb-like *muqurnas*.

The Great Mosque in Bursa (late fourteenth century) is an excellent example of the arrival of a new style and of elaborate engineering work. This mosque has an intricate combination of twenty small and quite elegant domes supported by twelve massive piers, representing a significant departure from earlier preferences for a single dome and more weightily built constructions. The piers are decorated with large-scale calligraphy. The gracefully decorated entrance is flanked by two tall minarets, although these are modern replacements for the original minarets that were lost to an earthquake in 1855.

The Hatum Imareti in Iznik (c. 1388) is an example of a fourteenth-century hospice, with kitchens, hospital, living facilities, and prayer chambers. This is

The architectural details of a traditional building from the Ottoman era. Courtesy of the author, 2007.

a spacious, T-shaped structure with a stylishly elevated, five-domed pavilion-entry that leads to the central domed area. The building is flanked by two smaller domed rooms. It has a very modest exterior that is decorated mainly with geometrically positioned bricks and stones and two graceful columns at the entry.

The Green Turbe (tomb) in Bursa (c. 1421) is a typical mausoleum of the early Ottoman era, sited next to the splendor of the Green Mosque. This octagonal tomb has a projecting portal and was built of green glazed bricks. The exterior wall is divided into sections by ribs and arches. The dome is egg-shaped and its design and construction create an impression of weightlessness. The *mihrad* captivates the onlooker's attention, decorated as it is with green and blue ceramic tiles and two honeycomb-styled niches, richly ornamented with floral motifs.

The Ak Madrasa in Nigde (c. 1409) was built as a traditional, rectangular two-story complex. Its main entrance is highlighted by a high-rising portal decorated with inscriptions and geometrical motifs; this gives way to an open central court. The portal divides the building's front wall symmetrically, and a pair of pointed arches on the second level rest on reused Byzantine-era columns. Some dozens of small chambers line up on the two levels on both sides of the central court, and these open out to a small mosque.

The third period is the Islamic architecture of the fifteenth to the eighteenth centuries. The works of this period reflect the triumph of the Ottomans, as they attained the status of one of the world's leading powers, rival to the kingdoms and empires of continental Europe in wealth and might. This development inspired many grand projects in major urban centers all around the country, including, especially, the jewel of the young superpower—Istanbul. Architectural thought at this time involved creating buildings on a very large scale while developing a feeling of more open and freely illuminated space, symbolic of the seemingly limitless power of the Ottomans. The builders opted for unmitigated grandeur in the public buildings, used expensive materials in their construction, and adorned them with lavish decorations. The architects were taking ever further the project of synthesizing the architectural traditions of the Muslim Middle East and the Mediterranean; which was manifested with unparalleled clarity in the works of the Empire's supreme architect: Mimar Sinan (c. 1492–1588).[9]

The Suleymaniye Mosque in Istanbul (1557) is one of the most recognized grand mosques of the Ottoman era and is one of Mimar Sinan's masterpieces.[10] It was built between 1550 and 1557 on a headland of the Golden Horn. The huge complex is built on a rectangular foundation. The large 53-meter-high dome is surrounded by about 500 smaller domelets and semidomes and is raised on elegant columns. The complex distantly resembles a pyramid, symbolizing the immense power and eternal glory of the Empire and its ruler—Suleiman (Turkish for Solomon) the Magnificent (1494–1566). This is an extremely complicated building; it is both an artistic and technological *tour de force*, with great attention to detail in the design and construction, and groundbreaking engineering solutions to the problems the work presented. The ornamentation of the building includes Iznik tiles, terracotta, carved marble, and glazed mosaic. Blue, green, and yellow frescos create a symmetrical decoration topped with Quranic verses in oversized *Kufi* script. The interior is lighted by a series of well-positioned windows that create a feeling of open space. The complex originally hosted seven *madrasahs*, a hospital, *hammam*, hostel, kitchen, shops, piazza, tombs, and a fountain. In addition, it has four lofty, pencil-shaped minarets symbolizing the royal patronage of the mosque.

The Hoseki Nurrem Hammam in Istanbul (c. 1556) was, for many years, the largest bathhouse in the city. The ensemble was built by Sinan. It is divided into two separate sections—one for men and one for women—with the entrances on opposite sides of the long rectangular building. The men's section is adorned with a triple-domed portico that leads to the main square hall. Small open cells line up to host changing areas, private rooms, laundry areas, and cafeterias. The main domed courtyard contains a huge marble massage platform and numerous arched sections with water fountains. The women's entrance is more modestly marked. It leads to a square hall and sections are organized similarly to the men's. The building is very discreetly ornamented, and, yet, it is elegant and well considered.

The Sultan Ahmat Complex in Istanbul (early seventeenth century) was built by architect Sedefkar Mehmet Agha between 1609 and 1617, a few decades after Sinan's Suleymaniye. This complex also consists of a main high-rising dome resting on four heavy columns complemented by a series of domelets and semidomes that cover the prayer area. The open central court is flanked by a series of half-open galleries with elegant thin columns creating a sense of openness and natural light. The building's exterior features numerous windows that provide a flood of light inside the main hall. The complex is lavishly decorated with blue tiles (hence it is traditionally known as the Blue Mosque) and is furnished with six elegantly decorated minarets.

In the eighteenth and nineteenth centuries, the Ottoman architects continued working intensively on new public projects, focusing on secular buildings, such as offices for government officials and ministries, mansions for wealthy individuals, workshops, and factories. However, financial constraints meant that those buildings and complexes were smaller in scale. There was also an attempt to blend the traditional Ottoman style with European baroque and rococo.[11]

RESIDENTIAL HOUSING

As in many other parts of the world, the mass residential architecture has been adapted to the local climate and traditional lifestyle.[12] People have long used the local materials, which are the most widely available. A rural house is traditionally organized around an inner courtyard. The high outer walls are interrupted by only a single door, and they completely shelter the house and courtyard, transforming the house into a small fortress. This feature illustrates the continuity of central Asian and Persian traditions and a synthesis of the traditions of Anatolia and the Balkans. The walls protected the household from thieves and marauders and provided the space to accommodate large extended families. Until the mid-twentieth century it was not uncommon for three or four generations to live together in such a household. The building's typically dull exterior was often fully counterbalanced by picturesque decorations inside, including expertly carved doors and pilasters inside the houses and above the galleries around the courtyards. The domesticated animals—sheep, cows, horses—were usually sheltered under the same roof of the building but in a separate section.

There were several types of typical settler housing. For instance, in the valleys and oases of central Anatolia the houses were made of sun-dried clay bricks covered with plaster. Distinctive features of this style also included a flat roof and a lack of windows or fancy decoration on the outer walls. Another type of housing, which is found in the mountains and forested areas in north and northeastern parts of the country, used rocks and wood more extensively. Yet another style was prevalent in the wealthy western regions of Anatolia and eastern Thrace, where wealthy individuals invested in the construction of a widely renowned style of Turkish *konaks* (mansions) with high ceilings, large windows, and gable roofs.[13]

In the eighteenth and nineteenth centuries, the Ottoman elite discovered the value of cottage-style, single- and multifamily stand-alone houses with small gardens, orchards, or cultivated areas attached. Standardized European-style, rectangular, fully detached houses with gable roofs and large windows were widely introduced throughout the region. Also, local governments made a considerable effort to ensure that the major streets of the cities and towns were wide enough to accommodate increased traffic. It became obligatory to plant trees, especially poplar, mulberry, and certain fruit trees, along the roads within and between the towns, forming endless lines of wooded land.

The traditional Ottoman house did not contain much furniture. In keeping with custom in a number of Middle Eastern countries, the furniture often consisted of a low table about half a meter (20 inches) high, at which people sat on floor mats and cushions or on low stools. In addition, practically every room contained trunks of various sizes. Many people kept a small box and bookstand for the sacred book, the Quran. Wealthy families could have small bookshelves or trunks for other books and for paperwork. Piles of mats and blankets were used instead of beds because people usually slept on the floor during the winter and on special wooden platforms in the courtyard or backyard in summer. European-style furniture, including beds, tables and chairs, sofas, and so on, were appearing in some private houses by the eighteenth and nineteenth centuries, but traditional furniture prevailed well into the mid-twentieth century.

In the past, all traditional houses were strictly divided into male and female sections and common areas, where family members dined together or received guests. Wealthy families provided separate rooms for every wife and often for every female family member, and the female area was inaccessible to male guests and even relatives. Entering women's rooms is still considered a highly offensive act, especially for outsiders. Very poor rural families, on the other hand, shared their far more modest houses not only with family members, but also with their animals, from which they were often separated by only a thin wall.

MODERN ARCHITECTURE

The architectural landscape in Turkey underwent fundamental changes in the twentieth century. During the Ottoman era, the new trend was most visible in the cities and towns around Istanbul, Bursa, and other large centers, and was still limited in other parts of the country. The authorities built several new cities to host new industries, such as textile, glass, munitions, and metal factories, workshops, and so on, but construction was frozen for nearly a decade from the beginning of World War I through the War of Independence (1914–1923).

The government of the new Turkish Republic believed that the narrow, zigzagging streets of the cities and towns, and the chaos of the oriental bazaars, should give way to Western-style models. Urban architects and engineers laid out modern landscaping and architectural planning for both new and old cities. In the process they destroyed many established residential houses and public buildings. In a number of cases, old districts were completely bulldozed to give way to new multiapartment buildings, factories, sport and art centers, and schools, and new, wide streets were designed for the new mode of transportation that began arriving in the country en masse only in the 1930s and 1940s—the automobile. The exemplar of this approach to transforming the country's architectural environment is apparent in the building of the new capital—Ankara. The city planners tried to compensate for the lack of diversity, color, and architectural fantasy in the newly built urban centers by the scale of their investment in the erection of Western-style apartments and office buildings, and by the prolific planting of trees and bushes.

The first waves of large-scale construction came in the mid-1920s and in the 1940s, as many public and residential buildings were built, along with numerous factories and industrial plants. In most cases, their architecture reflected a combination of classicism and constructivism. During this period, many government and cultural buildings were built in the neoclassical, monumental style.

The beginning of mass urbanization in the region in the 1950s and 1960s brought a new type of housing—three- to four-story buildings with small apartments, usually of one or two bedrooms. The government initiated large-scale construction of apartment buildings not only in the major urban areas, but also in small towns, particularly in the vicinity of new large industrial projects. During this era, several notable Turkish architects emerged: for example, Emin Onat and Orhan Arda designed the Ataturk mausoleum and architectural complex around it in Ankara (1953) in European monumental style.

In the 1970s and 1980s, many industrial centers were significantly enlarged; and numerous multistory apartment buildings were built, especially in rapidly growing urban centers, such as Ankara, Istanbul, and Izmir, in order to accommodate people who poured in from rural areas and small towns in search for jobs and better opportunities, thus creating very large residential districts. Most of these dwellings were built of brick, and later of concrete, reinforced concrete and large panels in a solid but faceless style.

Throughout the twentieth century, the cities and towns of Turkey always maintained one venerable institution—oriental bazaars. The bazaars and retail districts have always been part of the urban life and provided everything— foods ranging from exotic oriental fare to fresh fruits and vegetables, and goods from locally made souvenirs to handicraft items to consumer goods, and, of course, the place to leisurely drink famous Turkish coffee or tea.

RECENT TRENDS

The architectural landscape in Turkey has experienced a new series of fundamental changes in the early 2000s as part of the worldwide real estate boom. Economic liberalization freed private initiatives and channeled large inflows of private and public investment funds into the construction sector, including

The state of techno-art: the newly built headquarters of the *Zaman* newspaper in Istanbul. Courtesy of the author, 2007.

private housing construction. By the early 2000s, Turkish cities had changed beyond recognition, with new government and private office buildings, new prestigious hotel skyscrapers that housed international chains, such as Hyatt, Holiday Inn, Marriott, Renaissance, Sheraton, and others. In addition, hundreds of small and large retail stores and European- and Asian-style restaurants, coffeehouses, clubs, and service centers have appeared in all large cities and towns.

A major shift took place in the conceptualization of the symbolic meaning of public architecture. Constructivism, modest and often colorless pragmatism, and mass and cheap construction were all abandoned. Experimental forms and designs came in to fashion. Some of these new construction projects were often very expensive, both in basic design and ornamentation. Many buildings were lavishly decorated and have integrated modern technologies from wireless Internet to solar panels and computerized climate control.[14] To ensure that the newly built architectural complexes and modern infrastructure would attract international business and tourism, the government invited the leading construction and design companies from France, Italy, the United States, and elsewhere to the country.

Private housing also took off, as wealthy individuals raced to the suburbs to build single-family houses and cottages that were often designed in popular classical Mediterranean style. Most of these new constructions display an eclecticism that has more to do with wealth and desire to show off than with traditional styles. However, in many provincial centers, the upper-middle class has turned back to the traditional *konak* style of the early eighteenth and nineteenth centuries.

Yet, the picture is less rosy in the small towns, especially in remote areas, as the extravagant development in the major cities has not arrived to the provinces. The worldwide real estate craze of the early 2000s reached even the most remote areas. To the horror of the conservationists, these cities and towns began changing due to the new construction that brings comfortable modern housing and business offices but extinguishes the old charm of the traditional Turkish towns and villages.

The global real estate crisis and credit crunch of 2008 have had a negative impact on the construction sector of the Turkish economy and slowed down some projects; yet, Turkish businessmen claimed that the impact has been relatively mild and short lived.[15]

NOTES

1. George Michell et al., eds. *Architecture of the Islamic World: Its History and Social Meaning, with a Complete Survey of Key Monuments.* London: Thames and Hudson, 1978, p. 7.

2. Numerous civilizations and states that controlled large territories in southern Europe, Asia Minor, the Caucasus, and northern Africa had their centers and capitals in Anatolia. However, the author here limits discussion to the architecture within the territory of present-day Turkey.

3. Interview with a school teacher in Ephesus, June 2 and June 6, 2007.

4. For more coverage of the Hittite Kingdom, see Trevor Bryce. *The Kingdom of the Hittites.* New York and Oxford: Oxford University Press, 2006 and Archibald Henry Sayce. *The Hittites: The Story of a Forgotten Empire.* New York: Adamant Media Corporation, 2005.

5. The Ionians were not, of course, the only influence on the region's architecture; the Urartian, Phrygian, Lydian, and Persian civilizations also had a great impact on the development of the architecture of the period, but space limitations prevent their discussion here.

6. Michell et al., eds. *Architecture of the Islamic World*, p. 7.

7. For details, see Henri Stierlin. *Turkey from the Selcuks to the Ottomans (Taschen's World Architecture).* Köln and New York: Taschen, 1998.

8. Other sources indicate that it was probably built in 1267.

9. For Mimar Sinan's autobiography see Gülru Necipoglu, Howard Crane, and Esra Akin, eds. *Sinan's Autobiographies: Five Sixteenth-century Texts.* Boston: Brill, 2006.

For a discussion of Mimar Sinan life, see Guulru Necipoglu, Arben N. Arapi and Reha Guna *The Age of Sinan: Architectural Culture in the Ottoman Empire.* London: Reaktion, 2005.

10. On the architectural legacy of Mimar Sinan, see John Freely and Augusto Romano Burelli. *Sinan: Architect of Suleyman the Magnificent and the Ottoman Golden Age.* London and New York: Thames and Hudson, 1992.

11. For discussion, see Renata Holod, Ahmet Evin, and Suha Özkan, eds. *Modern Turkish Architecture.* Ankara: Chamber of Architects of Turkey, 2005 and Sibel Bozdoğan, *Modernism and Nation Building: Turkish Architectural Culture in the Early Republic.* Seattle, WA: University of Washington Press, 2001.

12. In this review, I cover the housing of mainly the eighteenth and nineteenth centuries because this period has been better studied by local and Western scholars. For detailed research, see Ahmet Turhan Altıner and Cüneyt Budak. *The Konak Book: A Study of the Traditional Turkish Urban Dwelling in its Late Period.* Istanbul: Tepe, 1997.

13. For a detailed discussion, see Godfrey Goodwin. *A History of Ottoman Architecture.* London: Thames and Hudson, 1971, pp. 428–453.

14. Vercihan Ziflioglu. "Turkish Duo Ride Global Architecture Trend." *Turkish Daily News.* October 27, 2007. http://www.turkishdailynews.com.tr/article.php?enewsid=85472.

15. "Turkish Finance and Industry Leaders Seek Way Out of Crisis." *Today's Zaman.* October 27, 2008 http://www.todayszaman.com/tz-web/detaylar.do?load=detay&link=156951 (accessed on October 27, 2008).

8

Gender, Courtship, and Marriage

It is a world in which all the senses feast riotously upon sights and sounds and perfumes; upon fruits and flowers and jewels ... and upon yielding flesh, both male and female, whose beauty is incomparable....

It is the world of ... a legendary Constantinople.[1]

—B. Rehman, literary critic

IN *CONVERSION IN Erzurum*, her memoirs about the years in Turkey as a Peace Corps volunteer in the 1960s, Dr. Susan Fleming Holm describes the immense diversity in the status of women in Turkey and the variety of customs that regulate the social and family relations, dress code, and fashion.[2] What was true then, evidently, still applies to the dynamic environment of the world of the Turkish women. Yet, the customs and traditions that regulate the lives of the women in today's Erzurum or, say, Bursa or Antalya, are still oceans away from each other—it is as if these cities belonged to different universes. And there is Istanbul—an effervescent city with untamed energy, a place of impossible contrasts and cultural diversity. On the very same streets or on the waterfront in the trendy Beshiktash district in Istanbul, a casual observer would meet women fully covered by long conservative dresses and headscarves as well as women who choose to have the minimum amount of fabric for their miniskirts or opt for bold, low-cut jeans.

Despite this display of freedom, emancipation, and westernization, the position of women in Turkey is not that simple and straightforward. The constitutional and legal frameworks clearly guarantee the rights of the women,[3]

A Turkish girl in traditional headdress. Courtesy of the author, 2007.

and there are female members of the parliament, female doctors, engineers, and heads of large corporations and ministries. Yet, in a complex Turkish society that is subdivided into hundreds of social and regional groups and strata, the position of women within their families, communities, and in society is also determined by a legion of traditional rules and norms. Even today, in some places, the centuries-old communal and tribal traditions oblige women to live in seclusion and punish them heavily for talking to a man without explicit permission from the male members of her family. Therefore, it should not come as a surprise that a senior politician in Ankara, the center of Turkish modernization and urbanization, can publicly suggest that women should keep themselves busy by managing their kitchens and housework, but not politics. But one has to remember that even in Western societies it took nearly a century to establish legal equality of men and women in the workplace, in the courts, and in society. It took them many more decades to close the gap between the formal declaration of equality in the national constitutions and actually implementing it.

The emancipation of women and westernization are topics that are still hotly talked about at all levels of Turkish society, from private kitchens and family gatherings to parliamentary debates and constitutional court discussions. In the country, where the social roles are strictly prescribed and closely guarded, even the public dress code often is still considered to be a political and social statement and might be at the center of public discussions in major newspapers and political talk shows on television. Should women wear a headscarf or should they not? Should the state make a decision for women on wearing a particular dress or should it not? Should the state regulate family relations or should these relations remain a private matter? Should a man be punished for taking a second wife? Or should these issues remain a private decision of the extended family? These and myriad other questions firmly remain on the agenda not only in Turkey, but even more so in the Turkish communities in Paris, Munich, and Vienna.

FROM HAREMS TO THE REVOLUTION

Throughout the nineteenth century, the Western world was been fascinated by the exotics of the Ottoman Empire. Numerous travelers visited the land with one goal in mind—to discover and assess the "otherness" of this oriental society. There, they found the world so exotic, the traditions and lifestyles so unusual, and customs that regulated the relations in society so unlike the Western mindset. On their return, many of them published both sensationalist and serious works and memoirs; and this body of literature greatly contributed to the formation of the most influential schools that dealt with the non-Western world—schools of oriental research.[4] A significant number of these publications focused on the lives of the "oriental" women and, more specifically, on the most erotic aspects of their lives that were of interest to the Western general public and serious readers alike—polygamy, harems, and slavery.

For Western writers, polygamy (*cok eslilik* in Turkish) has always been one of the clearest symbols of the decadent oriental regimes, a sign of oppression of women and a hidden form of slavery. Conventional stereotypes often portrayed oriental marriages as unions without love, prearranged for the highest bidder for a beautiful young girl. Quite frequently, part of these stereotypes were the marriages that crossed age barriers, when an old man could and would marry on his will a woman of any age, even as young as his own granddaughter. In romantic depictions of the Ottoman and Middle Eastern lives by Westerners, the oriental Juliet was always separated from her Romeo to become someone else's second, third, or even fourth wife because of the strong traditions of prearranged marriages and polygamy, which, in the opinion of these Western authors, silenced the women's will and took away their freedom of choice.[5]

Many contemporary Western scholars still debate the accuracy of the Western scholars' historical, cultural, and social representation of gender, courtship and family life in the Middle East, in general, and in the Ottoman society, in particular.[6] Many recent studies have seriously criticized these oversimplified descriptions of Ottoman society from several positions—from the legal and religious defense of the traditional norms and views on the status of women in society to the cultural and feminist attacks on orientalism and claimed that those descriptions represent conceptual misunderstanding and misinterpretation of the "other" societies.

According to some Turkish scholars who look at polygamy from an Islamic legal point of view, the truth is that Muslim men, indeed, have rights to have many wives, and in Islamic law (*Shariah*) the number of wives is limited to four. Even then, there are so many conditions that it makes it quite difficult to marry any woman beyond the first wife. A man has to fulfill his social duty helping members of his community by marrying a widow or an orphan who needs protection and help. Some scholars also suggested looking at polygamy in the historical context, pointing out that during the medieval-era wars, thousands and tens of thousands of men were killed in battle; therefore, the only way to protect widows and women who were left behind was through polygamy.

Yet, the battle among scholars still goes on, as those who have criticized polygamy have never put down their pens. They pointed out that the intentions were always honest and practical, but in reality there always were the wealthy members of society who abused their power and influence and had young wives and numerous concubines under their will, ignoring the legal and social preconditions. Recently, there was also an attempt to quantify the polygamy phenomenon in Ottoman society. A study conducted by Professors Alan Duben and Cem Behar came to the conclusion that only between 2 and 3 percent of all married Muslim men in nineteenth-century Istanbul had more than one wife.[7]

The system of *harems* (translated as forbidden or private from Arabic) in the Ottoman land was a single source of speculation, eroticized stereotypes, and misinterpretation. In the orientalist and feminist literature, harems were an eroticized space where a single oriental man had access to as many women as he wished. In such a depiction, widely publicized in numerous paintings, travel stories, and oriental tales, these beautiful women indulged themselves in golden-cage-like settings, learning only a single important skill—pleasing their master's sexual desires. Gradually, scholars began deconstructing the simplified and eroticized description of harems by highlighting that the latter enforced sexual segregation in Turkey and downsized women's public space to their households or palaces.

Some scholars, who have studied the harem system in depth, argue that these views were rooted in masculine misconception and fantasies of European men who ignored the social function of harems. Many studies have highlighted that the institution of the harem was a distant cousin of the British one, as it operated under a similar motto "my home is my fortress"; and that the harems were initially created as a part of extended family units and of the

Islamic concept of sexual segregation. Historically, harems were a structured system that organized the women's living quarters of an extended family (not necessarily always polygamous). Over time, the harem system evolved in different places according to local historical and social circumstances, becoming a part of the Muslim social order.[8] In the preindustrial domestic division of labor in the Ottoman State, the harems became a powerful point of matriarchal pillar of family.

Then there was the Ottoman institution of domestic slavery, creating a single institution that provided moral and political justification for claiming the superiority of Western social norms and systems. Yet, one has to remember that only in the nineteenth century did the industrialized and rapidly liberalizing West proclaim slavery a crime. The United States, one of the last Western bastions of state-sanctioned slavery, abolished it at the price of a terrible civil war. In 1865, in the Ottoman land, slavery was formally outlawed, but it survived in different forms and incarnations well into the twentieth century.

Lucy Garnett, who visited Istanbul early in the twentieth century, observed in her book published in 1909:

Inseparable...from the harem system is the institution of domestic slavery, ... slave women...are the absolute property of their owners....The demand for slaves for the service in Turkish households is practically perennial.[9]

It is very difficult to quantify the extent to which slavery survived in the Ottoman Empire in the second half of the nineteenth and into the early twentieth centuries. Officially, the slave market was closed in Istanbul by the mid-nineteenth century. However, the black market and shadow slave trade survived, and demand for female slave housekeepers, babysitters, and skillful handicraft masters was still quite high. There were many ways through which women could end up in the hands of slave dealers. Sometimes marauding criminal gangs ambushed frontier villages and towns, taking away young women and men and selling them on the black market. Another way was the deceptive acquisition of young boys and girls from desperately poor but large families with promises to give the children education or good jobs in prosperous Istanbul, Bursa, or Izmir. There was also a cruel buying out of children, especially young girls, from their parents for cash, or as a debt repayment.

Yet, as with many social institutions, slavery was very complex. Ottoman and Turkish scholars, and some of their Western colleagues, have been regularly highlighting some principal peculiarities in the institution of slavery that made it very different, say, from eighteenth- and early nineteenth-century U.S. slavery. One of the most contrasting differences was that most of the slaves in

the Ottoman Empire were not destined for inhuman exploitation on planta-
tions. Slave status in the empire was not permanent, and many of the slaves
were freed within a few years. They and their children were not strictly segregated from other strata of society. Many female slaves were freed to become
wives of members of Ottoman nobility, thus, obtaining an equal status in
society. Many former slaves and their descendants achieved prominence and
power in the Ottoman society attaining ministerial positions of the *pashas* or
governing positions in various provinces. Yet, for every such *pasha* or governor,
there were thousands of poor slaves who lived in terrible conditions, locked
in the hardship of manual labor for long hours and without proper rights to
defend themselves.

In the nineteenth-century Ottoman Empire, many traditional institutions
came into conflict with the realities of the rapidly changing world. As in western Europe centuries earlier, the views of conservatives who called for preserving the existing social institutions collided with the views of those who called
for modernization and change. Among many issues that these intellectuals
and policy makers debated was the status of women, who remained one of
the most unprotected and suppressed groups in society.

During the era of reforms (Tanzimat), the Ottoman Western-oriented elite
envisioned emancipation within the modernization and westernization frameworks. However, there were many groups in society who fiercely resisted any
reforms, even changes in the dress code or marriage law. They perceived these
attempts as a social and political challenge to the existing status quo and established social norms, morality, and sexuality.

WOMEN AND ATATURK'S REFORMS

Not only did the collapse of the Ottoman Empire, five long years of conflict, and of the War of Independence bring the existing political order to an
end, but they also exposed an acute crisis of the social institutions and political and intellectual impotence of the ruling elite. The political crisis in the
state went hand in hand with the economic downturn and steep recession
that invited misery and poverty to practically every family around the country, and, particularly, it negatively affected women. The government and the
last sultan's entourage were blamed for financial mismanagement, incompe-
tence, and widespread corruption that had virtually bankrupted the country.
In this atmosphere of decadence and pessimism, many groups of society began turning their anger and frustration against the existing institutions and
values. One implication was that many social groups that kept silent before,
including women, began to be actively involved in politics, keenly heeding
new ideas that were coming from outside of the country—from liberalism

and feminism to anarchism and radical nationalism. Several women even actively participated in revolutionary movement and the War of Independence.

The establishment of the Turkish Republic in October 1923 radically transformed the political situation around the country, and there were widespread expectations about changes in political and social areas. There was an understanding that the new government would also be obliged to improve the position of women in Turkish society. Women at that time, especially from the upper classes and intellectual elite, were promoting the Western concept of emancipation of women, but their discussions did not leave their small circles.

The new elite, led by Mustafa Kemal, came to power fully aware of the crisis and expectations in society. They decided to introduce a proactive policy in which the state and its agencies would actively promote state-endorsed agendas and intervene in all aspects of the life of the society. The Cultural Revolution project launched by the government also included the policy of emancipation of women through the greater involvement of women in all aspects of life—cultural, social, and political. As the first step, the ruling party fully endorsed the equality of women. The government announced that not only would it guarantee equality, it would also prioritize the efforts to change the status of women in society.

From the very beginning, the policy of the emancipation of women and the state-sponsored feminism targeted the elimination of the seclusion of women. Polygamy was abolished and women were granted full support and equal treatment in the civil code. It was strongly encouraged that women could and should have a strong presence in public life, and could appear in public without asking permission of the male family members. As a next step, women received rights and were strongly encouraged to receive Western-style education in all fields, including science, jurisprudence, and technical subjects. These efforts paid off in greater involvement of women in the work force, the rise in the number of dual-income families, and women with independent financial means.

Unlike their Bolshevik counterparts in revolutionary Russia, the Turkish government officials did not recruit women massively into the ruling political party or government institutions, and they never used the force and power of the government apparatus to enforce its policies on women's issues. They chose a more gradual approach, although they did sponsor the creation of a women's organization that promoted awareness of the rights of women in the Turkish Republic and the ideas of equality of the sexes. The Kemalist government actively supported and widely publicized its every step in the emancipation of women—the opening of the first coeducational schools; graduation of the first female doctors, engineers, lawyers, and fighter pilots; and the election of the first women into the national parliament.

During the first decades, many groups in Turkish society were engaged in heated debates and exchanged furious comments on the issue of women's involvement in the public sector.[10] The government, for example, believed that it was making progress. The feminists and women's rights advocates, however, argued that the government was not doing enough for women. The conservatives were sure that the government was wasting large resources with little outcome, proving that women were incapable of working productively in the public sector. Through all these debates and discussions, slowly but surely, Turkish women witnessed significant changes in their lives. By the 1960s and 1970s, the dual-income families became a norm and women holding jobs in the public sector and in public offices did not raise eyebrows anymore in the country.

WOMEN IN PUBLIC LIFE

The election of Tansu Penbe Ciller in 1993 as the first female prime minister was very symbolic for Turkish society and for the feminism movement. Ciller became a role model and an inspiration for a whole generation of Turkish girls and feminist activists in the country and in the Middle East. After graduating from a college in Istanbul, she received her PhD from the University of Connecticut and completed her postdoctoral studies at Yale University. Marriage and two children did not deter her from taking high profile public positions, including the position of the president of Istanbul Bank, serving as a member of Parliament, the leader of the True Path Party and the minister in charge of economics. Her political career was darkened by accusations of corruption and mismanagement, however, these types of accusations are very common in Turkish politics. For nearly a decade, Ciller managed to work with the toughest people in Turkish politics, including Turqut Ozal, Suleyman Demirel, and Mesut Yilmaz.

The political life and career of Tansu Ciller clearly indicated that creating a public space for women in a country traditionally dominated by men has always been a daunting task. Although the Republican government declared the equality of women, granting them social, political, and economic rights and abolishing the most severe restrictions, the reality challenged their best intentions. The country remained rural as most of the people lived in villages and small towns, where the traditionalist view of women as housewives and mothers was enforced by myriads of social norms and "honor" actions.

Probably, the single most important institution that contributed greatly to improving the social status of women was the modern system of education that was created in the 1920s and 1930s. The introduction of coeducational schools and institutions of higher learning had, for the first time ever, opened mass education to a large number of Turkish women. The government also strongly encouraged the women to receive education, gradually making school compulsory for all children regardless of their sex and social status. This has been in sharp contrast to the practices in some Muslim countries where the education of girls was, and in some cases, is still perceived as unnecessary. The literacy rate among girls in Turkey increased from just about 10 percent in the 1930s and 1940s to between 80 and 90 percent in the early 2000s.

Although it sounds very normal for many twentieth-century European states, coeducation was a huge change for a very conservative society in Turkey. Gradually, it also became socially accepted that girls could live and study away from their parents in Turkish or foreign colleges and universities. Along with this acceptance came a greater involvement of young women in various sport activities including professional and semiprofessional sports, such as volleyball, basketball, and others.

The industrialization and government's enforcement of the equality policy led to the rise of mixed-gender working environments and dual-income families. A greater number of women have taken up with confidence positions in government and in private enterprises. This process began in the mid-1930s with the election of eighteen women to the national parliament. A few decades later, Firuzan Ikinciogullari was elected as the first female chairman of the Supreme Court.

Yet, Turkey is still full of contrasts as women in Istanbul and Ankara have firmly established their position in the postindustrial and postmodern twenty-first century, while the villagers in some areas in Kars, Diyarbakir, and Van still face the realities and practices of the preindustrial eighteenth and nineteenth centuries. These realities, in which many Turkish women live, are as distant from each other as Venus and Mars. In one world, young Turkish women, such as Azra Akin, can walk on stage in a bikini while participating in the Miss World pageant (in fact, Akin won the pageant in London in 2002). In the other world, young girls still face the threat of honor killing simply for a date before marriage. In fact, according to various sources, up to a dozen girls lose their lives every year as victims of this tradition.

DATING, MATCHMAKING, AND WEDDINGS

Duygu Asena's novel *Kadinin Adi Yok* (*Woman Has No Name*), published in 1987, took Turkish society by storm just for talking about a simple issue—the meaning of marriage, love, and sexuality for a woman in Turkish society. The story became a bestseller as it discussed the life of a woman who wanted to find her freedom and fight restrictive social traditions. It touched the nerves of so many people and provoked such a mixed response that twelve years later it was briefly banned from being reprinted. Yet, the message was so powerful that already in 1988, Turkish director Atif Yilmaz produced a movie based on the story.

As in many countries around the world, many Turkish Capulet families do not want give freedom to their Juliets to marry the Romeos of the Montague family. Therefore, in the public perception, young people of legal marriage age should follow centuries-old traditions and seek professional help of parents, close and distant relatives, especially those who have good and solid records in matchmaking. While the search is on, relatives, neighbors, and friends are often alerted to make sure that there is no dating or relations between the young offspring and an unknown stranger. Many groups in society are so obsessed with social status that they still prefer arranged marriages within specific social, regional, political, and financial circles. For example, a nationwide study conducted among married couples in 1997 revealed that 69 percent of respondents joined their union in arranged marriages and hardly met each other prior to marriage.[11] About ten years later, the percentage of such marriages fell to 46 percent.[12]

Indeed, during the last decade, an increasing number of young people skip through this social net and take initiatives into their own hands. They meet their soul mates in cinemas, colleges, and workplaces and date like young people in any other Western country do, although they are often more conservative in expressing their affection compared to their Western counterparts. Of course, young people know about the sexual revolution in the West and have seen *Sex and the City*, and they have heard about one-night stands (*tek gecelik iliski* in Turkish). Some of them even discuss it with each other, but not many of them experiment in such a way. Society strongly discourages, if not prohibits outright, sexual relations between the dating partners before marriage. In fact, until spring 2002, school officials in Turkey could even authorize testing unmarried girls for virginity, and some government officials even suggested that if female students at school did not pass the test, they should be expelled.[13]

A search for a potential partner has never been brief since the marriage is often perceived as one of the most important events in life and is taken very seriously. But once the partner is found or assigned—there is a very important ritual that everyone must pass—meeting the prospective in-laws and their relatives. As an American journalist explained: a man does not marry a Turkish woman, he usually marries her whole family.[14] These meetings have an important economic implication. Every family member and every relative whom the young prospective bride and groom meet is actually obliged to provide some form of social support and, what is even more important, financial support to start a new family.

A Turkish wedding. Courtesy of the author, 2007.

Nowadays, every family tries its best to organize a big and extravagant wedding, inviting as many relatives and friends as possible. One Turkish observer noted that "the concept of marriage as a ritual gradually left its place to that of a wedding ceremony as a sort of *spectacle* where society itself was the public."[15] Indeed, in Turkish society a wedding is not a personal matter of a bride and groom, but a matter for the whole clan, social group, or extended family members to come together and to show off their power, wealth, and solidarity.

As in many conservative societies, every adult man and woman is expected to be married and become a part of the vast social networks of relatives and closely knit kinships. According to a survey recently conducted in Turkey, only about 3 percent of men and women between the ages of 40 and 44 declared that they were never married.[16] The marriage rate in Turkey is quite high and very few people cohabit without officially registering their unions.[17] The latter group includes those who live in polygamous marriages, mainly in the remote rural places in the eastern provinces of the country. Polygamy, although legal and practiced in some Muslim countries, is officially banned in Turkey. Yet, about 1 percent of the men in the country have more than one wife.

Once married, people are expected to remain in the same union for the rest of their lives and have many children. The divorce rate in the country—11 percent—is probably the lowest in Europe, although, during the last decade, the country experienced a slight increase in this number.

It is no wonder that the average household in Turkey is about 5.0 persons (twenty-fourth place of fifty-three countries ranked in the survey), which is much higher than in the United States (2.8), the United Kingdom (2.3) or Sweden (2.1), but lower than Iraq (7.7), Kuwait (6.4), or Nicaragua (5.3).[18] The average size of a household in Istanbul is 3.9 persons; it is much higher—6.8 and 7.5—in Diayarbakir and Van provinces, respectively.

RECENT TRENDS

The entrepreneurial revolution launched by Turgut Ozal in the 1980s triggered an avalanche of changes that have been continuously affecting Turkish society in profound ways well into the twenty-first century. The rapid changes transformed the life of people in many areas reaching even the most remote and sleepy provinces in the east and northeast parts of the country, although there is still a huge gap between the lifestyles and social norms in the major urban centers and rural areas as well as between the generations. Nowhere else in Turkey are these changes more profound than in the major metropolitan triangle—Ankara–Izmir–Istanbul. Certainly, these economic and social changes have a greater impact on the lives of women there.

With the rise of private entrepreneurship, the emergence of large corporations, both national and international, there was a rapid growth in a financially independent, well-educated, and well-articulated class of women. Many of them became financially and socially independent enough to decide about their personal lives, choice of a partner,[19] marriages, and careers. Many young Turkish women's dreams of working internationally came true, and today young women comprise a considerable share among young Turkish graduates and PhD students heading to the United States, the United Kingdom, and other countries. They would probably like to build careers similar to the career of Guler Sabancı, chairwoman of Sabancı Holding, whom *Fortune* magazine named the world's ninth most powerful woman in 2008.[20]

The younger generation of Turks displays significant changes in their attitudes toward marriage and personal relations. In the largest cities, young people do not believe anymore that children are brought by a stork or bought in a hospital or bazaar, while the larger part of youth in conservative Konya, Kars, or Kayseri still probably believe otherwise. In a sign of change, the use of contraceptives reached 63.9 percent, on a par with Romania, Morocco, and Tunisia, although behind the United States, Nicaragua, Mexico, and Jamaica.[21]

The social and cultural changes prompted numerous intellectual debates across the country, which culminated in the so-called headscarf debate. According to Islamic tradition, women are obliged to show modesty and religious devotion by covering their hair with a scarf and wearing a dress that covers most of the body. However, for many years the practice of wearing a headscarf has been banned in all major public institutions and universities in Turkey, although not on the streets. Several political groups in the center, including the Justice Party (AK), announced their support for removing the ban. For some secularist groups, it is a clear indication that male-dominated political groups plan to regain control over the freedom of Turkish women and this would be one of many steps. On this issue, the Western-oriented as well as Islamist feminists became involved a fierce battle. The Islamic feminists have developed sophisticated arguments using references to and theological arguments of both Islamic tradition and Islamic law in defense of equality with men and the legal rights of Muslim women, while firmly defending their desire to wear the headscarf.[22]

Yet, despite all the changes and transformation, serious gender problems still exist in Turkey. For example, in the 2007 Global Gender Gap Index Turkey was in 121st place out of 128 behind Iran, Oman, and Egypt, down from 105th place in 2006. Although it is doing relatively well in the Health and Survival subindex (87th place), it is far behind in the Educational Attainment subindex (110th place) and the Economic Participation subindex (118th place).[23]

NOTES

1. Andrew Lang, ed. *The Arabian Nights Entertainments.* New York: Longmans, Green and Co., 1898. Cited in Alev Lytle Croutier. *Harem. The World behind the Veil.* New York: Abbeville Press, 1989, p. 173.

2. Susan Fleming Holm. "Conversion in Erzurum," In: Anastasia Ashman and Jennifer Eaton Gokmen, eds. *Foreign Women in Modern Turkey.* Emeryville, CA: Seal Press, 2006, pp. 46–55.

3. European Stability Initiative. *Sex and Power in Turkey. Feminism, Islam and the Maturing of Turkish Democracy.* Berlin-Istanbul: European Stability Initiative, 2007, pp. 3–5.

4. Robert Irwin. *For Lust of Knowing: The Orientalists and Their Enemies.* London: Allen Lane, 2006.

5. Caroline Finkel. "'The Treacherous Cleverness of Hindsight': Myths of Ottoman Decay," in Gerald MacLean, ed. *Re-Orienting the Renaissance: Cultural Exchanges with the East.* Basingstoke: Palgrave, 2005, pp. 148–174.

6. For example, see Edward Said. *Orientalism.* New York: Vintage Books, 1994.

7. Alan Duben and Cem Behar. *Istanbul Households. Marriage, Family and Fertility 1880–1940.* Cambridge: Cambridge University Press, 1991.

8. Leslie Pierce. *The Imperial Harem: Women and Sovereignty in the Ottoman Empire.* Oxford: Oxford University Press, 1993.

9. Lucy Garnett. *The Turkish People. Their Social Life, Religious Beliefs and Institutes and Domestic Life.* London: Methuen and Co., 1909, p. 211.

10. Şirin Tekeli, ed. *Women in Modern Turkish Society: A Reader.* London and Atlantic Heights, NJ: Zed Books, 1995.

11. *First European Quality of Life Survey: Quality of Life in Turkey.* Dublin, Ireland: European Foundation for the Improvement of Living and Working Conditions, 2007, p. 39. Available at http://www.esiweb.org/pdf/turkey_quality_of_life_in_turkey.pdf. (accessed on November 5, 2008).

12. Ibid., p. 39.

13. "Some Progress for Turkish Women," in *The New York Times*, June 19, 2002.

14. Private interview, Washington, DC, 2007.

15. Meltem Ahiska and Zafer Yenal. *The Person You Have Called Cannot be Reached at the Moment: Representation of Live Styles in Turkey 1980–2005.* Istanbul: Ottoman Bank Archive and Research Center, 2006, p. 223.

16. *First European Quality of Life Survey: Quality of Life in Turkey,* p. 39.

17. *First European Quality of Life Survey: Quality of Life in Turkey,* p. 9.

18. http://www.globalhealthfacts.org/topic.jsp?i=65 (accessed on November 5, 2008).

19. According to a series of studies conducted in Turkey about the current trends in marriages, an increasing number of Turkish women choose younger partners, as the number of marriages where a husband is younger than a wife nearly doubled during the last decade from 55,511 in 1997 to about 90,000 in 2006. See Omer Oruc. "Trend of Women Marrying Younger Men Worrying, Say Social Scientists." *Today's Zaman.* October 9, 2008. http://www.todayszaman.com/tz-web/detaylar.do?load=detay&link=155403 (accessed on November 5, 2008).

20. http://money.cnn.com/magazines/fortune/mostpowerfulwomen/2008/global/index.html For commentaries see http://www.todayszaman.com/tz-web/detaylar.do?load=detay&link=155379 (accessed on November 5, 2008).

21. http://www.globalhealthfacts.org/topic.jsp?i=72 (accessed December 5, 2008).

22. Yesim Arat. *Rethinking Islam and Liberal Democracy: Islamist Women in Turkish Politics.* Albany: State University of New York Press, 2005.

23. Global Gender Index: http://www.weforum.org/pdf/gendergap/index2007.pdf (accessed on November 5, 2008).

9

Festivals, Fun, and Leisure

One of the predominating instincts of the Osmanli Turks has ever been a passion for the picturesque in nature, a love of splendid sites, sparkling seas, leafy shades, cool fountains, and wide horizons.[1]

—Lucy M. J. Garnett, British writer

TWO PECULIARITIES STRIKE a foreigner visiting Turkey more than anything else—the feeling that festivals never end on the streets of the cities and towns and that the Turks seemingly never leave their favorite coffeehouses, bars, or restaurants. In a way, the streets of Istanbul very much resemble the streets of Rome or Madrid in the widespread love affair with the never-ending *siesta*. Many of Turkey's western neighbors may deny any closeness of the country's culture to that of Europe; yet, even the most uncompromising European Turkophobes would not deny that Turkey belongs to the leisure-loving Mediterranean culture. A careful observer would find a lot of similarities between Turkey and Greece, Italy, or Spain in the lifestyle and in the popular culture.[2]

Diversity is one of the determining features of modern Turkish culture. Each of the eighty-one provinces of the republic has its own unique cultural life, festivals, customs, and even cuisine. This diversity is further refined by the richness of the cultural heritage of various ethnic minorities and regional groups who, in one historical era or another, contributed to the cultural development of Anatolia. During the last fifty years, so many people moved from one place to another, especially from small and remote villages and towns to

Older residents resting, discussing community issues, and forming community opinions. Courtesy of the author, 2007.

the large urban centers, that some Turkish observers ironically remark that the Turks probably rediscovered their nomadic roots or reawakened their eternal love for changing places. Practically every migrant community felt obliged to continue celebrating their centuries-long festivals and holidays in their new homes by inviting new neighbors and even strangers to join the events.

Different generations view leisure and fun from different points of views. In sharp contrast to American traditions, the norms, expectations, and local public opinion prescribe strict behavioral patterns and social roles depending on the age, gender, and social status of a person. A fifty-year-old man is expected to be the cornerstone of family life and an authoritative figure in the community. Thus, he is obliged to spend time with his friends discussing the most important community events, conspiracies in politics, and oil-price manipulations over endless cups of coffee or tea in a local coffeehouse, his office (even during office hours), or in front of the TV, but not dancing in a discothèque or a club. A young person knows the rules as well. Of course, he knows that he is expected to say politely "yes, father" (*evet, dede*). After that he would probably act the way many young people in the United States would—he would most likely disappear with his friends, classmates, or girlfriends to enjoy the pleasures of globalization, consumerism, and global pop culture: from hanging around in dance clubs and disco bars to surfing the Internet or chatting on cell phones.

The lifestyle and leisure traditions in Turkey are also shaped by the high value placed on family bonds. A "family" in this country means many generations of close and distant relatives, cousins, nieces, and nephews—sometimes no less than several hundred in total. It is amazing how mothers and grandmothers, who are totally in charge of maintaining these relations and organizing extended family events, remember all those faces, names, locations, tastes, likes, and dislikes. Of course, there is also a long registry of events to attend, postcards to send, telephone calls to make, and marriages to arrange. Inevitably, it is an obligation for all family members, even for younger ones, to attend those events, dressing up in their best clothes, and flying from the farthest corners of Turkey or even the world to demonstrate family ties and to reconfirm or attain their social status within these communities.

All together, this mixture of local and national traditions, close-family events, and global influences merge into a vibrant festive lifestyle. Here, West meets East—secular traditions coexist with religious devotions and norms, and hip hop lives along with traditionalism.

FESTIVALS

Religious Festivals

As secular as it seems, Turkey, as a country, takes religious festivals seriously. During the republican era, the government vigorously promoted secularization of all aspects of life and zealously discouraged displaying religious devotion in public.[3] Yet, most people continue observing Islamic traditions, including Islamic festivals, in private, at the family and community levels. Even during the era of "Leaping into the future" (*cag atlamak*) of the 1980s and 1990s when the society underwent serious changes embracing modern Western culture from consumerism to the information and communication revolutions, affection toward religion did not weaken. In this regard, the Turks probably resemble the Japanese—they leaped forward into modernity without divorcing themselves from the traditional and religious symbols. For many Turks, the cultural symbols of the religion remain one of the important features of Turkishness. Even the most westernized Muslim Turks, both men and women, would put away their trendy clothes several times a year and put on something traditional and conservative to celebrate important Islamic festivals.

Since 1991, Islamic holidays have made a strong comeback and have become official public holidays on the national calendar. Islamic festivals are celebrated according to the lunar calendar that consists of twelve months, each between twenty-nine and thirty days. Because the lunar year is ten or eleven days shorter than the Gregorian calendar year used in Western countries, all events and festivals in the lunar calendar move back ten or eleven days every year.

Ramazan Bayrami (Ramadan)

Ramazan Bayrami (also *Ramadan* in Arabic) is the name of the ninth month in the Islamic calendar, and is one of the most important periods in the Islamic calendar. Prophet Muhammad began receiving messages from God during *Ramazan*. It is considered an essential duty for all devoted Muslims to celebrate this month by fasting from sunrise to sunset. They should not eat or drink during the daytime, although the Islamic doctrine allows for some exceptions (e.g., pregnant or nursing women, travelers, and certain other categories of people are allowed to abstain from fasting). All Muslims are expected to refrain from all wrongdoing, and fighting during this month. People break their fast after sunset in a special fast-breaking dinner ceremony called *iftar*: family members, friends, colleagues, or neighbors come together to share a prayer and then food while listening to a talk about Islamic values and religious duties from invited Muslim scholars (*ulema*). In a recent trend, these ceremonies have been adapted to the digital era: people simply watch televised *iftars* (*televole iftar*) or special DVDs while eating the special food ordered online or by phone. Children use this opportunity to visit other houses, and they are showered with small gifts from adults, usually sweets, toys, and lately with small amounts of money. Rich or simply successful people are strongly encouraged to share their fortune with all members of their communities by inviting them to their homes for the *iftars* or to give away food to the poor members of their communities. It became a tradition in Turkey that private individuals, businesses, and mosques invite not only their Muslim fellows, but also non-Muslims for the *iftars*.

As in all Muslim countries, businesses and public work in Turkey slow down during this time. In some areas during *Ramazan*, owners may close their food stores, restaurants, and coffeehouses for the daytime and open only later in the day. However, the rules are not as strict as in the Middle East, and many shops and food stores remain open, especially in the tourist areas.

Seker Bayrami

The day when Muslims celebrate the end of the fasting month, *Ramazan*, and organize the biggest feast of the season, is called *Seker Bayrami* (also *Eid-Al-Fitr* in Arabic). For families and often for businesses this means an open-door event during which people visit each other. It is strongly encouraged that all members of the community visit their neighbors; and even former and current business and political rivals and opponents must forget about their differences and come together for the feast. In Turkey, it is often expected that the wealthy members of the communities sponsor big feasts and invite all their neighbors and colleagues to share their fortune and success. The celebration usually continues for the whole day, sometimes long past midnight and is one of the largest and most loved holidays in the country.

Kurban Bayrami

This holiday (Eid-Al-Adha in Arabic) is celebrated in the twelfth month of the lunar calendar (the *zul-hajj* month) when Muslims commemorate the end of *Hajj*, the pilgrimage to the holy city of Mecca. It is linked to an event mentioned both in the Bible and the Quran, and is connected to the story about Ibrahim's (Abraham's) willingness to sacrifice his son Ismail (Isaac) in the name of God. At the last moment, an angel replaced Ismail with a sacrificial animal. During this holiday, people attend a prayer at a congregational mosque, then sacrifice a domestic animal (a sheep or goat, but never poultry); and, in the end, they organize a big feast for all relatives and close friends. Two-thirds of the meat is usually given to the poor, orphans, or persons with disabilities.

In the past, families bought a whole lamb or even several lambs and invited a special person to slaughter those animals. Today, it is acceptable to order the sacrifice by phone and to receive the "sacrificed animal" at home.[4]

Christmas

Traditionally, most of the Muslim Turks do not celebrate Christmas. Yet, today "Christmas trees" appear in many public places and on postcards under the name of a "New Year Tree" (*Yilbasi Agaci*). There are two regional festivals beloved by both children and adults that distantly relate to Christmas celebrations. The first one is the much celebrated St. Nicolas Festival in the place believed to be the home of a real historical figure, named Nicolas of Myra, in the city of Demre (formerly Myra). It is traditionally celebrated on December 24 with much fun and cheering to the delight of thousands of local and international spectators. Another holiday is the Pine Nut Festival celebrated on December 25 in Gaziantep.

Christian minorities—Orthodox Christians, Orthodox Armenians, Orthodox Syrians, and others, celebrate Christmas (called *Noel Bayrami* in Turkish) with major religious ceremonies. Between 2000 and 2008, public and government attitudes have significantly relaxed as Turkey has harmonized its legal system and its regulative politics toward religious minorities. With the recent increased assertiveness, the general public, too, has become more neutral toward the religious ceremonies conducted by churches, often perceiving them as other festivals that are losing their religious context and rather becoming more of cultural festivals on their own.

FOLK FESTIVALS

Travel guides in Turkey cheerfully compete with each other in an attempt to count the number of folk festivals in the country. Some claim that Turkey is a country of 100 festivals,[5] others take it to 200, and some reporters bravely play with the next round number—300. It is nearly impossible to count all of the local, regional, and national festivals because their number increases every year. Three factors play an important role in this process. The first is a growing interest in the family's local roots, as even affluent urbanites begin to research their dusty family albums and archives in search of the ancestors' hometowns in Konya, Kayseri, or Trabzon. The second is the growing commercialization of the festivals because these celebrations have become one of the driving forces of consumerism and a manifestation of the changing lifestyle of the people. The third is the increasing importance of international and domestic tourism for national and local economies.

As in many other countries, most of the local folk festivals evolved around major seasons of the year and often related to the activities of farmers. Some of these celebrations remain fairly local and small in scale and involve community feasts, folk singing and dancing, or simply visiting friends and relatives. Some of these festivals have achieved regional and national fame. Among them are the Apricot Festival in Malatya, the Cherry Festival in Aksu, the Golden Orange Festival in Antalya, the Rose Festival in Isparta, the Melon Festival in Diyarbakir, and some others.

There is also a group of festivals dedicated to famous literary, cultural, or historical figures. Among the most popular and noteworthy festivals is the Nasrettin Hoca Ceremonies in Aksehir honoring the famous comic and the subject of thousands of jokes and funny stories across the Turkic-speaking world. There are also other important cultural festivals and ceremonies, such as the Ertugrul Gazi Festival in Sogut, the Karacaoglan Festival in Mus, the Yunus Emre Ceremonies in Antalya, the Mevlena Rumi Festival in Konya, and many others.

Nevruz (also *nowruz,* translated as new day [from Farsi]) is a spring festival and the beginning of the New Year according to the ancient Iranian solar calendar (by convention usually fixed on March 21 or 22). It was celebrated as a major holiday in many places from the Middle East to Central Asia during the pre-Islamic times.[6] In Anatolia it was traditionally perceived as a spring and peace festival and was called *Sultan-i Nevruz, Nevruz Sultan,* or *Mart Bozumu* (harvest time in March), although it had a different meaning for different communities. For example, among the Tahtaci Turkomans of Anatolia, it was a day of remembering ancestors; among the seminomadic Yoruks tribes, it was the beginning of spring and moving from winter quarters to spring pastures in the mountain valleys; in Gaziantep and some other areas it is *Nevruz,* the day of wishes and called *Sultan Nevriz* after a pretty fairy (in other places— a bird) who flies from west to east and helps dreams come true by shaking her ankle bracelet.[7] It became quite politicized in Turkey during the twentieth century because, in the past, some Kurdish political activists have used this holiday to stage political rallies across the country; some of which were quite violent.[8] Thus, *Nevruz* was not celebrated in Turkey for many decades, and it was reestablished only after 1995. In a recent trend, Turkish authorities have attempted to depoliticize the event and turn it into another folk festival, especially because it has been a national holiday across all Turkic-speaking countries in Central Asia since the 1990s.

In present-day Turkey, *Nevruz* is widely celebrated by the Kurds and some people in eastern Anatolia. Local communities and local governments traditionally set up performances of various music and dance groups in major

Villagers celebrate a festival and perform a traditional Turkish folk dance (*zeibek*). Courtesy of the author, 2007.

public parks or central squares of towns and cities. Merchants set up outdoor food stores and large bazaars, and families visit each other or attend major community events. People believe that a cheerful *Nevruz* sets up a good mood and good luck for the whole year. Usually, during these days, young people of the opposite sex can socialize without being accused of breaking any social customs or taboos. In the evening, people start small bonfires on the streets or outskirts of their villages and young unmarried males have to show their bravery and cleanse themselves of their past sins by jumping over the fire. One of the important parts of the celebration is to visit parents and relatives and have the holiday meal together.[9]

OTHER PUBLIC HOLIDAYS

The government of Turkey commemorates five major national holidays: (1) National Sovereignty and Children's Day (April 23), (2) Commemoration of Ataturk, Youth and Sports Day (May 19), (3) Victory Day (August 20), (4) Republic Day (October 29), and (5) the New Year (January 1). These holidays are organized on a grand scale with military, sport, and public spectacles.

In addition, there are several informally celebrated days that became especially popular during the last few decades, for example, Father's Day, Mother's Day, Woman's Day (International Day of Women, March 8), Valentine's Day, Halloween, and some others.[10]

Republic Day is celebrated in the most splendid way, usually with a lot of public speeches, anniversary concerts, fireworks, and extensive discussions of the meaning of republican traditions for contemporary Turkey on the pages of all major newspapers. For several days, the streets in all major cities and towns across the country are decorated with national flags and national symbols.

Victory Day commemorates the Battle of Dumlupinar in the War of Independence. Millions of Turkish citizens display the Turkish flags and Turkish symbols to demonstrate the national unity and to remember those who lost their lives defending the independence of the country. During recent years, Valentine's Day has gained wide recognition in Turkey, especially among the younger generation. Turkish teenage boys, like teenage boys in many other countries, would try to do something "cool" or even outrageous in order to impress their girlfriends.[11] On this day, the young, and not-so-young couples, exchange dozens of text messages and pictures on their cell phones or spark a little or big romantic affair because everyone believes that Cupid is flying around sending a lot of his amorous arrows and hitting hearts of people regardless of their age or social status. Fueled with large marketing and sales advertising from large consumer-goods companies and retail outlets, the Valentine's Day holiday has achieved greater appeal across generations, gaining a Turkish flavor.

A New Year's Eve celebration is not as big as in the Western world, but it has become more popular during the last decade, especially in large cities. As in other European countries, many people across Turkey buy and decorate New Year's trees. The whole week before the New Year is a week for special New Year's concerts, and circus, theater, and ballet performances (usually the famous Nutcracker), and masquerades and wishing each other Happy New Year!—*Yeni Yilin Kutlu Olsun!* Children and parents find their presents under the New Year's tree on January 1, but not on Christmas Day,[12] as in many European countries and the Americas—therefore, these presents are called New Year's presents. December 31 is the day to make a lot of phone calls, visit friends, and finish shopping and cooking. It is also the day to be spent at the festive dinner tables with close family members and to be glued to the New Year's TV shows, concerts, interviews, and direct broadcasting from various cities and towns across the nation and the world.

FAMILY AND COMMUNITY CELEBRATIONS

Traditionally, leisure and entertainment activities in Turkey were built around family and community life. Weekends were usually spent with the extended families hosting guests or visiting relatives and indulging themselves with never-ending feasts and gossip about family and community members. People often went shopping in the local mom-and-pop stores to meet their neighbors (very much like shoppers in the United States in the pre-Wal-Mart era) and to local mosques to build a sense of spiritual community.

The arrival of the TV, packaged mass entertainment, and super malls have radically changed the concept of leisure and free time and now undermine the family and community bonds and traditions. However, traditional family values in Turkey show a great degree of resilience to the Western-style individualism and consumerism. Of course, Turkish society is very complex. On the one pole are the so-called White Turks (also Euro-Turks: affluent westernized urbanites) who, in public opinion, probably know more names of American pop stars and places than Turkish historical figures and cities. On the other pole are the so-called *maganda* (coarse and unrefined villagers) who, in public view, still live in the age of barbarity with their backward manners and views.[13] Yet, an average Turk strongly believes that being with their family and community is an important part of their culture and of their Turkishness.

Family Celebrations

Celebrating the most important family events is still a part of traditional culture across all strata of Turkish society. People usually rejoice at all possible events, such as the birth of a first child or first grandchild, a circumcision ceremony, building of a new home, and, of course, a wedding.

Weddings are probably the best examples of family celebrations in the country. A wedding is always the single most devastating event in the entire history of every family's banking account. Weddings are usually very large—it is not uncommon to get 100 to 200 or even 300 to 400 people, if neighbors and friends are counted, for a single event that might continue anywhere from just one or two evenings to three to five days. People always invite all close and distant relatives, neighbors, colleagues, and friends. For Westerners it might be quite unusual to invite a stranger or foreigner to a family event, but that is not the case in Turkey. The wedding is more than a simple family celebration. In a society that becomes increasingly obsessed with social status, identity, and lifestyle, it is an opportunity to show and reconfirm the social status and financial prosperity of the bride and groom's family and to win public status for the newlywed couple. As in the United States, it is also an excellent chance for professional and social networking.

Many celebrations are organized in a grand manner, with music, dance, and plenty of food and drinks. In a recent trend, some wealthy members of rural communities sponsor folk music and song concerts or local sports events (wrestling, horse racing, etc.). Such events need to be well-planned in advance, and many people are involved in the organizational process.

Bazaars

Turkey is famous for its bazaars—from the Grand and Spice bazaars to the Valide Hans in Istanbul to small shop districts in Konya and souvenir streets in Antalya. For tourists, the bazaars are places to find and take home souvenirs and mementos and to have a thrilling, truly "oriental" experience. These Turkish markets offer nearly everything for every possible taste—from unique local handicraft pieces, carpets, Ottoman-style tiles (if a person promises to buy—the sellers could find for him a tile that was "personally painted" by an Ottoman sultan) and ancient jewelry to locally made T-shirts and leather jackets and imported electronics and toys for children.

For the locals, the bazaars are often a way of life, as they mingle, meet friends and colleagues, gossip, show off wealth and success, or search for help or partnership there. In small towns, whole families dress up in their best clothes and go to a bazaar in the morning and come back in the evening, thereby combining shopping, socializing, and eating out in a day-long event. The bazaars often not only offer the freshest products and affordable prices, but also a beloved local exercise called bargaining (*pazarlyk*). *Pazarlyk* is a ritual all its own because it requires knowledge of market traditions and exceptional oratorical and artistic skills. Many people love bazaars for these colorful and emotional conversations and haggles, which have simply died out in the modern supermarkets and malls. Sometimes buyers and sellers sit quietly over a

A bazaar is the place that is most beloved by many Turks and tourists for its oriental flavor. Courtesy of the author, 2007.

cup of Turkish tea or coffee for hours discussing family issues, weather, or oil prices and strike a deal in the end by shaking hands after enjoying a long and friendly conversation. At other times, the negotiation might turn into a theatrical performance with strong emotions and dramatic gesticulations seemingly taken directly from Shakespearian dramas, including dramatic moves, dances, reciting examples of trade history of the last century, and serious arguments that depend on the size of the deal and regional background of the people involved. There is an anecdote that illustrates how to learn the origin of a person you met at the bazaar—just ask him: "How much is two times two?" If the answer is a straight and categorical "Four"—he is from Ankara; if the person replies—"well, it depends on the size of the deal . . ."—he is from Istanbul; if the person asks in return "Am I a buyer or seller?"—this person is definitely from Konya.

Coffeehouses

Traditional Turkish coffee (*kahve*) is a symbol of Turkish culture second only to Turkish carpets. Coffeehouses are so popular across the country that a single street in a town or city can host a dozen of them. There is fierce

The traditional Turkish café offers a great variety of food. Courtesy of the author, 2007.

competition not only among the coffeehouses, but between modernity and traditionalism in coffee drinking and serving patterns. The so-called new coffeehouses, often represented by the foreign chains such as Starbucks or Gloria Jean's, serve many types of coffee and offer design, music, and an environment for young people to hang together as they do in any city in Europe. In the meantime, the "old-style" traditional coffeehouses still honor sexual segregation by providing male and female sections (*haremlik-selamlik*) and offer a choice of classic Ottoman Turkish folk or religious music.[14]

In Turkish culture, not only is the traditional coffeehouse a place to eat and drink, it is also an important institution of social networking and socializing. It is also a kind of social club where, over a cup of coffee, people discuss community needs and development at the local level as well as major political, social, and economic actions. The coffeehouse is a place where local public opinion can be formed or influenced, family and personal reputations can be established or ruined, and new businesses accepted or rejected.

Meals

There is a joke in Turkey that half the country is ready to give up the European Union (EU) membership rather than go without *balik ekmek* or *kokerech*

(Turkish dishes).[15] Another half of the country is ready to give up the World Trade Organization (WTO) membership for an annual supply of *shish kebab*. Many people will take the risk of commuting halfway across a city, which is a serious adventure in Ankara and Istanbul during peak hours, in order to have his lunch with his friends in his favorite restaurant, where his cook Mehmet would prepare for him his beloved *kofte* and *dolma* and would serve him *baklava,* prepared in the style of the Ottoman sultans.

The national Turkish cuisine was enriched by influences from many other cultures, especially from the Caucasus, the Middle East, and the Balkans.[16] The country offers endless varieties of soups (*chorbas*), such as *yoghurt chorbasi* (yogurt soup)*, mercimek* (lentil soup), *balik chorbasi* (fish soup), *tavuk chorbasi* (chicken soup), and many others; *dolmas* (vegetables, such as cabbage leaves, eggplants, peppers, tomatoes, grape leaves, or zucchinis, stuffed with rice and meat); and juicy and spicy meat *kebabs* that every province and city offers in its own very special recipe. Like people in Central Asia, Turks use dairy products—various types of yogurts and yogurt drinks—with most of their meals. The local population does not eat pork because it is not permitted by Islamic traditions.

The love of food goes hand in hand with a very strong sense of hospitality. It is an old Turkish tradition to invite a guest or even a stranger to share food with the host family. It is quite normal to spend several hours eating dinner while discussing family affairs, gossips, and current events or simply teasing each other. Hosts usually offer several courses, in large quantities, and finish the meal with a cup of very strong Turkish coffee or tea, even if it is late in the evening.

An elderly woman prepares traditional Turkish food. Courtesy of the author, 2007.

During the last decade, the fast-food culture attempted to capture one of the last unconquered territories—Turkey—and to divert Turkish eating and drinking habits. This battle is still going on as the general public debates the "MacDonaldization" of Turkish culture. McDonald's, Burger King, Pizza Hut restaurants, and the like popped up in every significant city and town across the country. Top-notch international marketing specialists developed grand strategies to hypnotize a whole generation of young business people to lure them into sacrificing their long, magnificent, royal-like lunches for burgers and Coca-Cola. This change is often attractively packaged and presented as a shift from the "old and boring traditions" to the new excitement of experiencing a European or American lifestyle and a culture with an enticing motto— "New generation choose cola!" The knights of the Turkish kitchens and restaurants did not surrender and attempted to fight back with their own version of fast, and not so fast but authentic Turkish food and drinks, and their own Coca Cola–scale commercials about their product—the Cola Turka.[17] In fact, in 2007 and 2008, it became a kind of craze among young computer and IT wizards to produce their very own clip of Cola Turka and post it to YouTube.[18]

SPORTS

During the Ottoman era, both the nobility and commoners loved to observe traditional sports, including wrestling, oil-wrestling, fencing, weightlifting, horse racing, and other activities. There were many professional wrestlers, oil-wrestlers, and weightlifters whose names survived in the historical chronicles, although these sportsmen have never been organized into the Western-style professional leagues or teams. Hunting, especially with dogs, was popular among the rich landlords, local tribal leaders, and members of the royal entourage.

The Ottoman society became acquainted with the Western-style mass sports only in the second half of the nineteenth century, and for many years the sporting activities were limited to Istanbul and its boroughs. It took several decades before modern types of sports made strong inroads into the everyday lives of people, when the young Turkish Republic massively invested in sport facilities. Wrestling, boxing, and martial arts are among the most popular sporting activities, and as in many other countries, pictures of favorite champions hang on the walls of many teenage boys and girls. Basketball, volleyball, and baseball are among the mass sporting activities that have started at nearly every school, and there are numerous school, lyceum, and university competitions at every level. Surprisingly, college sports (or interuniversity sport activities) have very little popularity among the public and have never found their way to national television, such as in the United States.

The team representing the Ottoman Empire first participated in the Olympic Games in 1908, but it took a long twenty-eight years before the Turkish team won its first Olympic medals at the 1936 Olympic Games (one gold and one bronze medal). The most successful Olympic Games in Turkish Olympic history were in 1948 when Turkey won twelve medals. Since the 1980s and 1990s, government and private clubs began investing significantly in mass sport, creating large pools of local talent that are ambitious enough to challenge the major players in international competitions. For example, at the Beijing Summer Olympic Games in 2008 Turkey won eight medals—one gold, four silver, and three bronze medals, taking twenty-fifth place overall (just behind Argentina, Switzerland, and Mexico). This was a considerable improvement from the Summer Olympic Games in 2000 when Turkey won only five medals—three gold and two bronze, taking twenty-sixth place overall (just behind Belarus, Spain, and Canada).[19]

Soccer (*futbol* in Turkish) is the single most popular sport in the country, and most Turkish commentators recognize that daily routine simply stops in the country during major soccer tournaments, especially if a Turkish team is playing. To the great dismay of women, nearly every year, most Turkish men are firmly glued to their TVs when Turkish teams participate in major European cups. Large and small crowds of men gather at the home of a friend with the largest television set, and scream, jump, and cry with great emotion, very much like British, Spanish, or Mexican fans.

At present, there are thousands of soccer fields in the country, and there are probably hundreds of registered and unregistered soccer clubs. Men of all ages usually play soccer during weekends on soccer fields that are established in practically every city and town. Teenage boys often play soccer after classes end at school soccer fields, while adults come together a few times a month to play intercommunity or intertown formal and informal tournaments, usually at the community soccer fields. Women's soccer, however, is not popular in the country, and there are no professional women soccer teams.

The major Turkish teams are *Beshiktash* (established in 1910),[20] *Galatasaray* (established in 1905), and *Fenerbahce* (established in 1907). Turkey surprised the soccer world establishment in 2000 when *Galatasaray* won the European Cup, beating the British *Arsenal* in Denmark, and in 2002 when the Turkish National Team won third place in the World Cup in Korea. The Turkish team also performed extremely well in the UEFA EURO 2008 games by beating Switzerland and Croatia, but losing to a strong German team in the semifinals.

There is an immense entertainment and pop-culture industry that revolves around the sports superstars, especially in soccer. As in many Western countries, they receive front-page coverage in the gossip and celebrity sections of all the major Turkish newspapers and magazines. Very often, the victories in major sport events are widely televised and discussed and are proudly displayed to boost the national pride.

RECENT DEVELOPMENTS

The cultural changes of the last two decades in Turkey have been so profound that Chris Morris called them "The quiet revolution on the edge of Europe."[21] In the 1980s, state officials abandoned the idea of a centralized control over public events and left it to private individuals to decide what to celebrate and how. This development created opportunities for market forces to build a whole new entertainment industry for every taste and for every group of society.[22] Turkish private businesses invested heavily in the development of mass tourism and successfully attracted millions of domestic and foreign tourists. In this process, many folk and art festivals became increasingly business- and profit-oriented and tailored for international visitors. Even local governments tend to sponsor indigenous small-scale sport events and music and folk festivals in order to attract visitors and create new jobs in their hometowns.

The entertainment industry began promoting a new lifestyle linking health, leisure, and social status to body images and various forms of consumption. As in the United States, the Turkish media obsessively advertises extremely skinny bodies for women and sporty macho images for men as ideal symbols of success and prosperity. Thus, some urbanites increasingly abandon the traditional Turkish coffeehouses and family and community events for endless hours of exercises in fitness centers, prestigious golf courses, and sports clubs. They started unloading traditional Turkish cuisine in favor of various types of diet products and migrating to new trendy Western-style cafés and restaurants.

The older generation still sticks to the "authentic Turkish" traditions of lifestyle and leisure, but even the concept of "authentic traditions" is now disputed and is quickly evolving. For example, many generations of Turks patronize traditional Turkish baths (*hamams*), but Finnish (dry) saunas have become increasingly popular, especially in the newly built condominium, apartment, and hotel complexes. In the past, the *hamams* created a sense of community and were a favorite place to meet on weekends to relax, receive a massage, or just escape the weather extremes, and they have traditionally been strictly segregated into all-boy and all-girl clubs. In the most recent trend, to the dismay of the conservative members of society, some *hamams*, especially those that are attached to major hotel chains, began accepting both sexes.

The leisure and lifestyle habits of the younger generation also began shifting because of the impact of globalization and information revolution that arrived in Turkey of late. The Internet, text messaging, and chat networks attract many local geeks, who have formed vibrant virtual communities across the country, thus changing entertainment, dating, and socialization patterns. In the early 2000s, these new trends have been largely limited to Ankara and Istanbul, and to the immigrant Turkish communities in Europe and the Americas.[23]

Against this backdrop, groups of Turkish intellectuals and business people have been working on introducing an alternative concept of entertainment, leisure, and lifestyle combining the Islamic religious and spiritual notions and traditional family and community values with modern forms and channels of mass communication, including the Internet, TV, radio, and mobile phones.

NOTES

1. Lucy Gernett. *The Turkish People. Their Social Life, Religious Beliefs and Institutes and Domestic Life*. London: Methuen and Co., 1909, p. 1.

2. Gary Hoppenstand, Michael K. Schoenecke, John F. Bratzel, and Gerd Bayer, eds. *The Greenwood Encyclopedia of World Popular Culture*. 6 vols. Westport, CT: Greenwood Press, 2007.

3. Esra Ozyurek. *Nostalgia for the Modern: State Secularism and Everyday Politics in Turkey*. Durham, NC: Duke University Press, 2006.

4. About recent trends in celebrating religious holidays, see Meltem Ahiska and Zafer Yenal. *The Person You Have Called Cannot Be Reached at the Moment: Representations of Lifestyles in Turkey, 1980–2005*. Istanbul: Ottoman Bank Archives and Research Centre, 2006, pp. 404–408.

5. http://www.gototurkey.co.uk/index.php?menu_id=23&submen=23 (accessed December 5, 2008).

6. Sivas Hazirlayan and Sebnem Ercebeci. *Turk Dunyasında Nevruz. Dorduncu Uluslararası Bilgi Şöleni: 21–23 Mart 2001* [*Nevruz* in the Turkic World. Fourth Information/Knowledge Festival: March 21–23, 2001]. Ankara: Atatürk Kültür Merkezi, 2001.

7. For description of the celebration of *Nevruz* in different parts of Turkey, see http://www.kultur.gov.tr/EN/BelgeGoster.aspx?17A16AE30572D313 A781CAA92714FCE0A8F443AF43BC485E (accessed December 5, 2008).

8. For news coverage, see https://turkishdailynews.com.tr/archives.php?id= 27452 (accessed December 5, 2008).

9. Azize Aktaş Yasa. *Türk Kültüründe Nevruz v. Uluslar Arası Bilgi Şöleni Bildirileri: 15–16 Mart 2002* [Communiqué of the International Information Festival of the Nevruz in Turkic World: March 15–16, 2002]. Ankara: Ataturk Kultur Merkezi, 2002.

10. For a general discussion of the everyday life, see Meltem Ahiska and Zafer Yenal. *The Person You Have Called Cannot Be Reached at the Moment: Representations of lifestyles in Turkey, 1980–2005*. Istanbul: Ottoman Bank Archives and Research Centre, 2006.

11. Ali Akbar Mahdi, ed. *Teen Life in the Middle East.* Westport, CT: Greenwood Press, 2003. Kerry Mallan and Sharyn Pearce, eds. *Youth Cultures: Texts, Images, and Identities.* Westport, CT: Praeger, 2003.

12. Simah Zaim. "A New Year in Turkey." *Today's Zaman.* December 31, 2007, http://www.todayszaman.com/tz-web/detaylar.do?load=detay&link=130405 (accessed December 5, 2008).

13. For some discussions about *maganda*, see Meltem Ahıska and Zafer Yenal. *The Person You Have Called Cannot Be Reached at the Moment: Representations of Lifestyles in Turkey, 1980–2005,* pp. 31, 407.

14. Ibid., p. 289.

15. Ibid., p. 128.

16. For discussion of food traditions, see Algar, Ayla Esen. *The Complete Book of Turkish Cooking.* London: Kegan Paul International, 1995 and Peter Heine. *Food Culture in the Near East, Middle East, and North Africa.* Westport, CT: Greenwood Press, 2004.

17. The young and creative artists created a whole pop culture around the brand Cola-Turka. For an example of classic commercials, see http://www.colaturka.com.tr/anasayfa/index.html http://www.youtube.com/watch?v=UojhK_xxR0Y (accessed on October 16, 2008).

18. For example, see http://www.youtube.com/results?search_query=Cola+Turka&search_type= (accessed on October 16, 2008).

19. For detailed information about participation in the Olympic movement, see the National Olympic Committee of Turkey at http://www.turkishnoc.org/eng/s2-en.htm.

20. The *Beshiktash* was founded in 1903, but it was first officially registered seven years later in 1910.

21. Chris Morris. *The New Turkey: The Quiet Revolution on the Edge of Europe.* London: Granta, 2005.

22. For various local festivals, see Helene Henderson, ed. *Holidays, Festivals, and Celebrations of the World. Dictionary: Detailing Nearly 2,500 Observances from all 50 States and More than 100 Nations: A Compendious Reference Guide to Popular, Ethnic, Religious, National, and Ancient Holidays.* Detroit, MI: Omnigraphics, 2005.

23. Peter H. Stearns. *Consumerism in World History: The Global Transformation of Desire.* New York: Routledge, 2001.

Glossary

AKP (***Adalet ve Kalkınma Partisi*** **or** ***AK Parti***) A party formed in 2001 by a group of members of the banned *Welfare Party*. The AKP declares that it promotes a moderate conservative political agenda, but it demands that it address the religious needs of various Muslim communities in the country. Under the leadership of Recep Tayyip Erdogan, the party won the parliamentary elections in July 2007.

Alevi (**also** ***Elewi***) The name of a religious and subethnic community in Turkey, whose beliefs and practices are related to the Shi'a belief system.

Baba Father, grandfather, or ancestor; polite reference to the respected oldest member of an extended family; a saint or patron.

Bey (**also** ***beg***) The title used to refer to a tribal leader or to a prince in early Turkic society. During the Ottoman era, the title referred to the senior military officer and to the military commander at the province level; in the late Ottoman era, it was usually used in addressing an army officer. In modern Turkey, the title is sometimes used with the name of a male person to highlight his honorary position in society or to convey respect (*Ahmet-bey*).

Beylik A semi-independent principality established by a powerful warlord or given as a reward by a sultan for service.

Caliph (**from the Arabic** ***Khalifa*** **or successor**) The title that was used, in the early Islamic era in reference to the supreme spiritual and political leaders, who were considered to be successors of Prophet Muhammad.

Caravanserai A traditional guesthouse or inn in the cities and towns along major routes and mountains passes.

Dervish The term that refers to a member of Islamic mystic orders (*Sufis*) who emphasizes the development of a personal spirituality and has committed himself to the ascetic life.

Devsirme The policy of the systematic recruitment and conscription (often by force) of non-Muslim children into the Ottoman Empire's regular troops and the state institutions.

Divan The Ottoman Council of State that, under the leadership of the Grand Vizier, fulfilled the functions of the Cabinet of Ministers.

Etatism The term used for the policy of centralized economic planning and state control over the economic and political development of Turkey. The policy was introduced by Mustafa Kemal Ataturk to promote speedy economic development of the country.

Ghazi The term used in reference to warriors who fought against the enemies of the Islamic world. It is also sometimes used as a respectful reference to those who gave their lives fighting for a just cause.

***Grand Vizier (Sadr-i Azam* in Turkish)** The chief minister and advisor to sultans in the Ottoman and Middle Eastern states who chaired the Council of State (*Divan*) and whose administrative position was distantly similar to the position of a prime minister.

Dastan An epic created both in verses and prose that presents a historic, heroic, or romantic story.

***Hadith* (traditions)** The collection of observations of the life and deeds of Prophet Muhammad by his companions, which were verified and codified into the corpus of Islamic tradition and is an authoritative source of wisdom in Islamic thought.

Hajj The pilgrimage to Mecca (one of the tenets of Islam), which is a required duty for all Muslims who are able to go.

Hijab A headscarf worn by Muslim women; the term also refers to a veil dressing that covers a woman's hair, arms, and feet.

Imam-Hatip An Islamic scholar or clergyman who leads Muslims in their daily prayers and oversees the work of the mosques and the *madrasah*. He also interprets Islamic law and provides consultations on spiritual and some community issues.

Iwan A vaulted hall or space that is walled on three sides, with one entirely open end, which is usually in the form of an arch.

Janissaries Members of elite infantry units in the Ottoman army. The Janissary corps was abolished by Sultan Mahmud II in 1826.

***Jihad* (campaign, holy battle)** One of the central concepts in Islam, which obliges Muslims to spread and strengthen Islam in the world. According to the Islamic scholarly interpretation of the concept, Jihad can be performed in four ways:

by heart, by sword, by hand, and by tongue. It should be directed against evil desires, actions, or enemies.

Kanun   Set of laws introduced by the Ottoman sultans that were used in the Ottoman state along with the *Shariah* law to regulate the work of the state institutions and the lives of the subjects of the state.

Kemalism   The official ideology of the ruling elite in the modern Turkish Republic that include the so-called "Six Arrows": (1) Etatism, (2) Nationalism, (3) Populism, (4) Republicanism, (5) Revolutionism, and (6) Secularism.

Koran   See *Quran*

Kurban Bayrami **(also called** *Eid Al-Adha* **in Arabic)**   The Islamic festival celebrated in remembrance of Ibrahim's (Abraham's) near sacrifice of his son, Ismael, and God's sparing of Ismael's life in recognition of Ibrahim's faith.

Madrasah   An Islamic school that provides postprimary religious education; a theological seminary and law school that provides Islamic religious education and is usually attached to a mosque; a building where the boarding students of Islamic seminaries stay.

Mihrab   An arch-shaped niche in the wall that shows the directions to Ka-aba (in Mecca).

Muezzin   A person who calls Muslims for obligatory prayers five times a day.

Murid   A student of an Islamic school or follower of an individual Islamic teacher or a Sufi leader.

Namaz   Prayer.

Nevruz **(also** *nowruz*)   An ancient spring festival and the beginning of the New Year according to the ancient Iranian solar calendar (by convention it is usually fixed on March 21 or 22). It is widely celebrated in some countries in the Middle East, in the central Asian Republics, and in some parts of Turkey.

Ozan   A popular bard, who sings and improvises traditional folk songs or epics; a respected member of the community to whom people traditionally turn for political advice, foretelling, or entertainment.

Pasha   A senior military officer during the Ottoman era.

PKK (*Partiya Karkeren Kurdistan,* **also called KADEK)**   The militant Kurdish organization founded in the 1970s with the goal to defend the political and social rights of the Kurdish population and to establish an independent Kurdish State or Kurdistan.

Quran **(also** *Koran*)   The holy book of Islam. Muslims believe that it was revealed by Allah to Prophet Muhammad.

Ramazan **(also** *ramadan*)   The ninth month in the Islamic calendar; a time of fasting and atonement for sins.

Seker Bayrami **(also known as Ramazan Bayrami or** *Eid-Al-Fitr* **in Arabic)**   The Islamic festival that celebrates the end of the month-long fast of Ramadan.

***Shariah* (also *Seriat*)**   The Islamic legal system practiced in Muslim societies. It is based on four fundamentals: (1) the Quran, which is the message revealed by Allah to Prophet Muhammad; (2) the *Hadith* (Sunna), which is the recorded story of the life and deeds of Prophet Muhammad; (3) the *Ijma*, which are the universal decisions agreed on by Islamic scholars; and (4) the *Qiya*, or legal precedent. The *Shariah* imposes a strict regulation of public and private aspects of life according to divine revelation.

Sheikh   An esteemed religious person; a Sufi teacher or authority.

Sheyhulislam   The title of the highest ranking Islamic official in the Ottoman State who is appointed by the Sultan, is entrusted to interpret the *Shariah* law, and who administers the execution of the judicial rulings.

***Sublime Porte* ("Gate of the Eminent," or *BabıAli* in Turkish)**   (1) The residence of the Ottoman central government and the Grand Vizier. The name derives from the name of the gate to the office buildings occupied by the Grand Vizier and his staff members in the Topkapi Palace (Istanbul). (2) In the nineteenth century, the name was often used as a synonym for the Ottoman Foreign Ministry.

***Sufism* (also known as *tasawwuf*)**   A mystical movement in Islam that emphasizes the development of a personal spirituality and an internal comprehension of divinity and is organized into mystic orders under the leadership of recognized spiritual leaders.

Sultan   The ruler of a Muslim state who asserted absolute political sovereignty, without claiming overall spiritual or political leadership over the entire Muslim world—the position reserved for a caliph. During the Ottoman era, the term was used to refer to the head of the Ottoman state.

Tanzimat   The series of reforms initiated and implemented by the government in the Ottoman state between the Rose Garden Decree in 1839 and the introduction of the Constitution in 1876.

Topkapi   The royal palace in Istanbul, the residence of the Ottoman sultans, and the *Divan* (Ottoman Council of State) during the Ottoman classical era.

Ulema   The highly respected and knowledgeable Islamic scholars and jurists entrusted to interpret the Islamic legal system and explain the meaning of the Quran and the *Hadith*.

Ummah   The term used to refer to the entire Muslim community.

Vaqf   The Islamic endowment established to support a specific charitable, educational, or religious purpose.

***Young Turks* (*Jon Turkler* in Turkish)**   The name given to a group of young Ottoman dissidents and young military officers who staged the revolution in 1908.

Selected Bibliography

INTERNET SOURCES

Acik Radio (Radio Station): http://www.acikradyo.com.tr/.
Anatolian News Agency (in English): http://www.aa.com.tr/en/news/39/.
Ankara University: http://www.ankara.edu.tr/.
Ataturk University: http://www.atauni.edu.tr/.
ATV (TV Channel): http://www.atv.com.tr/.
Bogazichi University: http://www.boun.edu.tr/.
Central Intelligence Agency World Factbook: Turkey: https://www.cia.gov/library/
    publications/the-world-factbook/geos/tu.html.
Cihan News Agency: http://www.cihanvideo.net/.
CNN Turk (TV Channel): http://www.cnnturk.com/.
Columbia University: Internet resource page of Turkey: http://www.columbia.edu/
    cu/lweb/indiv/mideast/cuvlm/Turkey.html.
Cumhuriyet Newspaper: http://www.cumhuriyet.com.tr/.
Directorate General of Press and Information, Office of the Prime Minister: http://
    www.byegm.gov.tr/.
Doing Business in Turkey: http://www.buyusainfo.net/docs/x_3776730.pdf.
Dunya Online: http://www.dunyagazetesi.com.tr/.
Energy Information Administration: Country Analysis Briefs: Turkey:http://www.
    eia.doe.gov/emeu/cabs/Turkey/Background.html.
Gateway Turkey: http://old.developmentgateway.org/countryprofile/?country_iso=tr.
Hurriyet Newspaper (in English): http://www.hurriyet.com.tr/english/.
Insight Turkey Magazine: http://www.insightturkey.com/.

International Religious Freedom: http://www.state.gov/g/drl/rls/irf/2007/90204.
    htm.
Istanbul University: http://www.istanbul.edu.tr/.
Library of Congress, Country Profile, Turkey: http://lcweb2.loc.gov/frd/cs/profiles/
    Turkey.pdf.
Middle East Technical University: http://www.metu.edu.tr/.
Milli Gazete Newspaper: http://www.milligazete.com.tr/.
Milliyet: http://www.milliyet.com.tr/.
Ministry of Culture and Tourism: http://www.kultur.gov.tr/.
National Library of Turkey: http://www.mkutup.gov.tr/.
New Anatolian Newspaper: http://www.thenewanatolian.com/.
Parliament of Turkey: http://www.tbmm.gov.tr/index1.htm.
Permanent Mission of Turkey to the UN: http://www.un.int/turkey/.
President of Turkey: http://www.cankaya.gov.tr/.
Prime Minister of Turkey: http://www.basbakanlik.gov.tr/.
Radical Newspaper: http://www.radikal.com.tr/.
Sabah Newspaper (English website):http://english.sabah.com.tr/.
Samanyolu (TV Channel): http://www.stv.com.tr/.
Today's Zaman (in English): http://www.todayszaman.com/.
Turkey News Agency (TNA): http://www.turkishnewsagency.com/.
Turkey Post: http://www.turkey-news.com/.
Turkey Times: http://www.wn.com/turkeytimes.
Turkish Daily News: http://www.turkishdailynews.com.tr/.
Turkish Herald: http://www.theturkishherald.com/.
Turkish Historical Society: http://www.ttk.gov.tr/.
Turkish Press: http://www.turkishpress.com/.
Turkish–United States Business Council: http://www.turkey-now.org/.
UNESCO in Turkey: http://www.unesco.org.tr/.
UNESCO World Heritage: http://whc.unesco.org/en/statesparties/tr.
United Nations in Turkey: http://www.un.org.tr/UN2/.
U.S. Department of State's International Information Programs: http://usinfo.state.
    gov/eur/.
U.S. Embassy in Ankara: http://turkey.usembassy.gov/.
Vatan Newspaper: http://www9.gazetevatan.com/.
World Public Opinion: http://www.worldpublicopinion.org/.
Yeni Safak Newspaper: http://www.yenisafak.com.tr/.
Zaman Newspaper (English website): http://www.zaman.com.tr/.

ANNUAL REPORTS AND YEARBOOKS

Federal Research Division. *Turkey: A Country Study.* Whitefish, MT: Kessinger Pub-
    lishing, 2004.
Gunumuz Turkiyesinde Kim Kimdir [Who's Who in Turkey]. Istanbul: Profesyonel,
    2006.

International Business Publications. *Turkey Business and Investment Opportunities Yearbook.* Washington, DC: International Business Publications, 2004.

International Business Publications. *Turkey Recent Economic and Political Developments Yearbook (World Strategic and Business Information Library).* Washington, DC: International Business Publications, 2007.

International Institute for Management Development. *IMD World Competitiveness Yearbook 2006.* Lausanne, Switzerland: International Institute for Management Development, 2006.

Organization for Economic Cooperation and Development. *OECD Economic Surveys: Turkey, 2006.* Paris: Organization for Economic Cooperation and Development, 2006.

Ozga, Jenny, et al. *World Yearbook Education 2006: Education and Policy (World Yearbook of Education).* London, Routledge, 2006.

Stockholm International Peace Research Institute (SIPRI). *SIPRI Yearbook 2001 (Stockholm International Peace Research Institute's Yearbook): Armaments, Disarmament, and International Security.* London: Routledge, 2003.

Turkey. London: Economist Intelligence Unit (quarterly, from 1992 onward).

Turkey. United Nations Development Program (UNDP) (annually).

Turkey. Europa World Yearbook. London, Europa Publications (annually).

Turkey. Freedom in the World: The Annual Survey of Political Rights and Civil Liberties. Piscataway, NJ: Transaction Publishers (annually from 1992 onward).

Turkey: Recent Economic Development. Washington, DC: International Monetary Fund, 1995; 1996; 1997, 1998.

Turner, Barry, ed. *The Statesman's Yearbook 2001: The Politics, Cultures, and Economies of the World (Statesman's Year-Book).* New York and London: Palgrave Macmillan, 2004.

United Nations. *Statistical Yearbook for Asia and the Pacific 2004. Annuaire Statistique Pour l'Asie et le Pacifique.* New York: United Nations Publications, 2006.

U.S. Department of State. *Country Reports on Terrorism.* Washington, DC: U.S. Department of State (annually).

BIBLIOGRAPHIES

Aydin, Mustafa, and M. Nail Alkan. *An Extensive Bibliography of Studies in English, German, and French on Turkish Foreign Policy (1923–1997).* Ankara: SAM, 1997.

Faroqhi, Suraiya. *Approaching Ottoman History: An Introduction to the Sources.* Cambridge: Cambridge University Press, 2000.

Harding, Cigdem Balım. *Turkey.* Oxford, England and Santa Barbara, CA: CLIO Press, 1999.

Hartesveldt, Fred van. *The Dardanelles Campaign, 1915: Historiography and Annotated Bibliography (Bibliographies of Battles and Leaders).* Westport, CT and London: Greenwood Press, 1997.

Icimsoy, A. Oguz, and Hamza Kandur. *A Bibliography of Books in English on Turkey, 1700–1990*. Istanbul: Librairie de Péra, 1995.

Ilter, Erdal. *Turk-Ermeni Ilidkileri Bibliyografyasi* [Bibliography of Turkish-Armenian Relations]. Ankara: Ataturk Yuksek Kurumu, Ataturk Kultur Merkezi Baskanligi, 2001.

Kornrumpf, Hans-Jurgen. *Osmanische Bibliographie, Mit Besonderer Berucksichtigung der Turkei in Europa*. Leiden, Brill, l973.

Koroglu, Erol. *Ottoman Propaganda and Turkish Identity: Literature in Turkey during World War I (Library of Ottoman Studies)*. London: Tauris, 2007.

Laciner, Sedat. *Turkiye ve Dunya: Ingilizce Turkiye ve Turkler Bibliyografyasi* [Turkey and the World: A Complete English Bibliography of Turkey and Turks]. Istanbul: Kaknüs Yayınları, 2001.

Meho, Lokman I., and Kelly L. Maglaughlin. *Kurdish Culture and Society: An Annotated Bibliography (Bibliographies and Indexes in Ethnic Studies)*. Westport, CT and London: Greenwood Press, 2001.

Penfold, P. A. *Maps and Plans in the Public Record Office: Europe and Turkey*. London: Stationery Office, 1999.

Suslu, Azmi, et al. *Ataturk ve Turkiye Cumhuriyeti Konusunda Yurtdısında Yayinlanmis Kitaplar Bibliyografyasi* [Ataturk and the Turkish Republic: Bibliography of Books Published Abroad]. Ankara: Ataturk Arastirma Merkezi, 2000.

DICTIONARIES

Akdikmen, Resuhi. *Langenscheidt New Standard Dictionary: Turkish-English/English-Turkish*. New York: Langenscheidt, 2006.

Bayerle, Gustav. *Pashas, Begs, and Effendis: A Historical Dictionary of Titles and Terms in the Ottoman Empire*. Istanbul: Isis Press, 1997.

Blau, Joyce. *Kurtce-Turkce, Kurtce-Fransizca, Kurtce-İngilizce sozluk: Dictionnaire Kurde-Turc-Français-Anglais.* [Kurdish-Turkish-French-English Dictionary]. Istanbul: Sosyal Yayinlari, 1991.

Clauson, Gerard. *An Etymological Dictionary of Pre-Thirteenth-Century Turkish*. Oxford: Clarendon Press, 1972.

Gates, Charles. *Turkish-English, English-Turkish Dictionary and Phrasebook*. New York: Hippocrene Books, 2002.

Haig, Kerest. *Dictionary of Turkish-English Proverbial Idioms; With Interpretations and Translations. (Turkce-Inglizce siyve misalleri gosteren sozluk). A Collection of 2250 Proverbs, Sayings and Idiomatic Expressions Peculiar to the Turkish Language.* With an alphabetical index and a preface by Malcolm Burr. Amsterdam: Philo Press, 1969.

Iz, Fahir, and H. C. Hony. *The Oxford English-Turkish Dictionary.* Oxford and New York: Oxford University Press, 1992.

Jaeckel, Ralph, and Gulnur Doganata Erciyes. *A Dictionary of Turkish Verbs: In Context and by Theme. Ornekli ve Tematik Turkce Fiiller Sozlugu.* Washington, DC: Georgetown University Press, 2006.

Mitler, Louis. *Ottoman Turkish Writers: A Bibliographical Dictionary of Significant Figures in Pre-Republican Turkish Literature.* New York: P. Lang, 1988.

Okcugul, Vasif. *Yeni Turkce-İngilizce Okul Lugati* [Etymological dictionary Turkish-English]. Istanbul: Kanaat Yayınları, 1972.

Ovacik, Mustafa. *İngilizce-Turkce Hukuk Sozlugu* [English-Turkish Law Dictionary]. Ankara: Banka ve Ticaret Hukuku Araştırma Enstitusu, 1986.

Oztopcu, Kurtulus. *Dictionary of Turkic Languages: English, Azerbaijani, Kazakh, Kyrgyz, Tatar, Turkish, Turkmen, Uighur, Uzbek.* London: Routledge, 1996.

Yurtbas, I. Metin. *A Dictionary of Turkish Proverbs.* Ankara: Turkish Daily News, 1993.

ENCYCLOPEDIAS AND REFERENCE BOOKS

Agoston, Gabor, and Bruce Masters. *Encyclopedia of the Ottoman Empire.* New York: Facts on File, 2007.

Azim Nanji. *The Muslim Almanac: A Reference Work on the History, Faith, Culture, and Peoples of Islam.* Detroit, MI: Gale Research, 1996.

Cotterell, Arthur. *The Penguin Encyclopedia of Ancient Civilizations.* New York: Penguin, 1989.

Gocgun, Onder, ed. *Turk Dunyasi Edebiyat Tarihi* [The History of the Literature of the Turkic World]. Vols. 1–6. Maltepe, Ankara: Ataturk Kultur Merkezi Baskanligi, 2001–2004.

Heper, Metin. *Historical Dictionary of Turkey.* 2nd ed. Lanham, MD: Scarecrow Press, 2002.

Isik, Ihsan. *Encyclopedia of Turkish Authors: People of Literature, Culture and Science.* Ankara: Elvan Publishing, 2005.

Islam ansiklopedisi: Islam alemi cografya, etnografya ve biyografya lugati [Encyclopedia of Islam: Islamic World Dictionary of Geography, Ethnography, and Biography]. Istanbul: Milli egitim basimevi, 1940–1988.

Levinson, David, and Karen Christensen, eds. *Encyclopedia of Modern Asia.* 6 vols. New York: Charles Schribner's Sons, 2002.

Motyl, Alexander J., ed. *Encyclopedia of Nationalism: Leaders, Movements and Concepts.* Vol. 2. San Francisco: Academic Press, 2001.

Pope, Arthur Upham and Phyllis Ackerman, eds. *A Survey of Persian Art from Pre-Historic Times to the Present.* 16 vols. London, New York: Oxford University Press, 1938–.

Rubin, Don, et al. *World Encyclopedia of Contemporary Theatre: Asia/Pacific.* London: Routledge, 2001.

Tural, Sadik, ed. *Turk Dunyasi Edebiyatcilari Ansiklopedisi* [The Encyclopedia of Turkic World Literature]. Vols. 1–5. Ankara: Atatürk Kultur Merkezi Baskanlıgi Yayınları, 2002–.

READERS, MEMOIRS, AND COLLECTIONS OF DOCUMENTS

Barker, John. *Syria and Egypt under the Last Five Sultans of Turkey: Being Experiences, during Fifty Years, of Mr. Consul-General Barker. Chiefly from His Letters and Journals.* London: Tinsley, 1876.

Basgoz, Ilhan. *Turkish Folklore Reader (Uralic & Altaic).* London: Routledge, 1997.

Bournoutian, George A. *Russia and the Armenians of Transcaucasia, 1789–1889: A Documentary Record.* Costa Mesa, CA: Mazda Publishers, 1998.

Brassey, Lady Annie. *Sunshine and Storm in the East, or Cruises to Cyprus and Constantinople. A Diary.* 1880. Reprint. Piscataway, NJ: Gorgias Press, 2005.

Buxton, Charles Roden. *Turkey in Revolution. Memoirs.* London: Fisher Unwin, 1909.

Clarke, Kenneth, and Mary, eds. *A Folklore Reader.* New York: A. S. Barnes, 1965.

Edib, Halide. *Memoirs of Halide Edib.* 1926. Reprint. Piscataway, NJ: Gorgias Press, 2005.

Elcin, Sukru, et al., eds. *Turk Dunyasi Edebiyat Metinleri Antolojisi* [The Anthology of the Literature of Turkic World]. Vols. 1–5. Maltepe, Ankara: Ataturk Kultur Merkezi Baskanlıggi, 2001–2004.

Gettleman, Marvin E., and Stuart Schaar, eds. *The Middle East and Islamic World Reader.* New York: Grove Press, 2003.

Haggis, Jane, and Susanne Schech. *Development: A Cultural Studies' Reader.* Malden, MA: Blackwell Publishing Limited, 2002.

Lewis, Bernard. *Music of a Distant Drum: Classical Arabic, Persian, Turkish, and Hebrew Poems.* Princeton: Princeton University Press, 2001.

Lewis, Reina. *Feminist Postcolonial Theory: A Reader.* London: Routledge, 2003.

Lewis, Reina, and Nancy Micklewright. *Gender, Modernity and Liberty: Middle Eastern and Western Women's Writings: A Critical Sourcebook.* London: I. B. Tauris, 2006.

Pasha, Djemal. *Memories of a Turkish Statesman, 1913–1919.* 1922. Reprint. New York: Arno Press, 1973.

Ramsay, William Mitchell. *The Revolution in Constantinople and Turkey: A Diary.* 1909. Reprint. Boston: Adamant Media Corporation, 2002.

Sabanci, Sakip. *This is My Life. Memoirs.* Saffton Walden, UK: World of Information, 1988.

Tekeli, Sirin, ed. *Women in Modern Turkish Society.* London: Zed Books, 1995.

Tietze, Andreas. *Turkish Literary Reader (Uralic & Altaic).* London: Routledge, 1997.

Upward, Allen. *The East End of Europe: The Report of an Unofficial Mission to the European Provinces of Turkey on the Eve of the Revolution.* Chestnut Hill, MA: Adamant Media Corporation, 2002.

TRAVEL AND DESCRIPTIONS

Bowman, Anna Dodd. *In the Palaces of the Sultan.* 1903. Reprint. Piscataway, NJ: Gorgias Press, 2004.

Curzon, George. *Persia and the Persian Question.* Reprint. London: Cass, 1966.

De Kay, James, E. *Sketches of Turkey in 1831 and 1832. By an American.* New York: Harper, 1833.

Frances Wood. *The Silk Road: Two Thousand Years in the Heart of Asia.* Berkeley, CA: University of California Press, 2003.

Friedman, Block. *Trade, Travel, and Exploration in the Middle Ages: An Encyclopedia (Garland Reference Library of the Humanities).* London: Routledge, 2000.

Gibb, H. A. R. *Ibn Battuta Travels in Asia and Africa, 1325–1354.* London: Routledge, 1929.

Halid, Halil. *The Diary of a Turk.* London: Black, 1903.

Hogarth, David. *Accidents of an Antiquary's Life.* London: Macmillan, 1910.

Komroff, M. *Contemporaries of Marco Polo, Consisting of the Travel Records to the Eastern Parts of the World of William of Rubruck (1253–1255); The Journey of John of Pian de Carpini (1245–1247); The Journal of Friar Odoric (1318–1330) & the Oriental Travels of Rabbi Benjamin of Tudela (1160–1173).* New York: Boni & Liveright 1928.

MacLean, Gerald M. *The Rise of Oriental Travel: English Visitors to the Ottoman Empire, 1580–1720.* New York: Palgrave Macmillan, 2004.

Madden, Richard Robert. *Travels to Turkey, Egypt, Nubia, and Palestine.* London: Whittaker, Treacher, 1833.

Pardoe, Julia. *Beauties of the Bosphorus.* London: Virtue, 1838.

Pease, Lorenzo Warriner. *The Diaries of Lorenzo Warriner Pease: An American Missionary in Cyprus and his Travels in the Holy Land, Asia Minor and Greece.* Edited by Rita C. Severis. Aldershot, Hants, England and Burlington, VT: Ashgate, 2002.

Porter, James. *Turkey; Its History and Progress: From the Journals and Correspondence of Sir James Porter, Fifteen Years Ambassador at Constantinople.* Reprint. [s.l.]: Elibron Classics, 2000.

Ramsay, William Mitchell. *The Revolution in Constantinople and Turkey: A Diary.* London: Hodder and Stoughton, 1909.

Rockhill, W. ed. *The Journey of William of Rubruck to the Eastern Parts of the World, 1253–55, as Narrated by Himself, with Two Accounts of the Earlier Journey of John of Pian de Carpine.* London, Printed for the Hakluyt Society, 1900.

Sakaoglu, Necdet. *Osmanli Kentleri ve Yabancı Gezginler* [Ottoman Cities through the Eyes of Foreign Travelers]. Istanbul: Ray Sigorta Şişhane, 1996.

Spencer, Edmund. *Travels in the Western Caucasus, Including a Tour through Imeretia, Mingrelia, Turkey, Moldavia, Galicia, Silesia, and Moravia, in 1836.* London: H. Colburn, 1838.

Tozer, Henry Fanshawe. *Researches in the Highlands of Turkey; Including Visits to Mounts Ida, Athos, Olympus, and Pelion, to the Mirdite Albanians, and Other Remote Tribes: With . . . Superstitions of the Modern Greeks.* Reprint. Chestnut Hill, MA: Adamant Media Corporation, 2001.

Vamberi, A., *Ocherki i kartiny vostochnykh nravov* [The Essays on the Oriental Traditions]. St. Petersburg: [s.n.] (in Russian).

Whitfield, Susan. *Life along the Silk Road.* Berkeley, CA: University of California Press, 2001.

CHAPTER 1

Andrews, Peter Alford, ed. *Ethnic Groups in the Republic of Turkey.* With the assistance of Rüdiger Benninghaus. Wiesbaden, Germany: Reichert, 1989.

Bisaha, Nancy. *Creating East and West: Renaissance Humanists and the Ottoman Turks.* Philadelphia: University of Pennsylvania Press, 2004.

Braude, Benjamin, and Bernard Lewis. *Christians and Jews in the Ottoman Empire: The Functioning of Plural Society.* 2 vols. London and New York: Holmes and Meier Publishers, 1982.

Brown, Carol, ed. *Imperial Legacy: The Ottoman Imprint on the Balkans and the Middle East.* New York: Columbia University Press, 1996.

Davidson, Roderic. *Reforms in the Ottoman Empire, 1856–1876.* Princeton, NJ: Princeton University Press, 1973.

Erdem, Harkan. *Slavery in the Ottoman Empire and Its Demise, 1800–1909.* New York: St. Martins Press, 1997.

Faroqhi, Suraiya. *Ottoman Empire and the World around It.* London and New York: I. B. Tauris, 2004.

Faroqhi, Suraiya. *The Cambridge History of Turkey.* Cambridge: Cambridge University Press, 2006.

Finkel, Caroline. *Osman's Dream: The History of the Ottoman Empire.* New York: Basic Books, 2006.

Gokay, Bulent. *A Clash of Empires: Turkey between Russian Bolshevism and British Imperialism, 1918–1923.* London: I. B. Tauris, 1997.

Goodwin, Jason. *Lords of the Horizons: A History of the Ottoman Empire.* New York: H. Holt, 1999.

Gunter, Michael M., and Mohammed M. A. Ahmed, eds. *The Kurdish Question and the 2003 Iraqi War.* Costa Mesa, CA: Mazda, 2005.

Hale, William. *Turkish Politics and the Military.* London: Routledge, 1993.

Haniooglu, Sukru. *The Young Turks in Opposition.* New York and Oxford: Oxford University Press, 1996.

Hourani, Albert, ed. *The Modern Middle East.* London: I. B. Tauris, 1993.

Ihsanoglu, Ekmeleddin, ed. *History of the Ottoman State, Society and Civilization.* Istanbul: IRCICA, 2001.

Inalcik, Halil, and Donald Quataert. *An Economic and Social History of the Ottoman Empire.* 2 vols. Cambridge: Cambridge University Press, 1997.

Jenkins, Gareht. *Context and Circumstance: The Turkish Military and Politics.* (Adelphi Papers). London: Routledge, 2005.

Jwaideh, Wadie. *The Kurdish National Movement: Its Origins and Development.* Syracuse, NY: Syracuse University Press, 2006.

Kayali, H. *Arabs and Young Turks: Ottomanism, Arabism, and Islamism in the Ottoman Empire, 1908–1918.* Berkeley, CA: University of California Press, 1997.

Khoury, Dina Rizk. *State and Provincial Society in Ottoman Empire: Mosul, 1540–1834*. Cambridge: Cambridge University Press, 1998.

Kinross, Patrick Balfour. *Ataturk: The Rebirth of a Nation*. London, Weidenfeld and Nicolson [1964].

Levi, Avigdor, ed. *The Jews of the Ottoman Empire*. Princeton, NJ: Darwin Press, 1994.

Lewis, Bernard. *The Emergence of Modern Turkey*. 3rd ed. New York: Oxford University Press, 2002.

Macfie, A. L. *The Eastern Question 1774–1923 (Seminar Studies in History)*. London and New York: Longman, 1996.

Mansel, Philip. *Constantinople: City of the World's Desire, 1453–1924*. London: John Murray, 1995.

Marcus, Aliza. *Blood and Belief: The PKK and the Kurdish Fight for Independence*. New York: New York University Press, 2007.

McCarthy, Justin. *The Ottoman Turks: An Introductory History to 1923*. London: Longman, 1997.

McCarthy, Justin. *Death and Exile: The Ethnic Cleansing of Ottoman Turks*. Princeton, NJ: Darwin Press, 1995.

Saray, Mehmet. *The Russian, British, Chinese and Ottoman Rivalry in Turkestan*. Ankara: Turk Tarikh Kurumu, 2003.

Shaw, Stanford Jay. *History of the Ottoman Empire and Modern Turkey*. 2 vols. New York: Cambridge University Press, 1977.

Shaw, Stanford Jay. *Between Old and New: The Ottoman Empire under Sultan Selim III*. Cambridge, MA: Harvard University Press, 1971.

Uslu, Nasuh. *The Cyprus Question as an Issue of Turkish Foreign Policy and Turkish-American Relations, 1959–2003*. New York: Nova Science Publishers, 2003.

Wheatcraft, Andrew. *The Ottomans*. London: Viking Press, 1993.

CHAPTER 2

Arberry, Arthur John. *Sufism, an Account of the Mystics of Islam*. London: Allen & Unwin, 1963.

Atasoy, Yildiz. *Turkey, Islamists and Democracy: Transition and Globalisation in a Muslim State (Library of Modern Middle East Studies)*. London: I. B. Tauris, 2005.

Azim Nanji. *The Muslim Almanac: A Reference Work on the History, Faith, Culture, and Peoples of Islam*. Detroit, MI: Gale Research, 1996.

Berkes, Niyazi. *The Development of Secularism in Turkey*. London: Routledge, 1999.

Cagaptay, S. *Islam, Secularism and Nationalism in Modern Turkey: Who Is a Turk?* (Routledge Studies in Middle Eastern Politics). New York: Routledge, 2006.

Fethullah, Gulen. *Key Concepts in the Practice of Sufism: Emerald Hills of the Heart*. 2 vols. Rutherford, NJ: Fountain, 2004.

Fethullah, Gulen. *Toward a Global Civilization of Love and Tolerance*. Somerset, NJ: The Light, Inc., 2004.

Foltz, Richard. *Religions of the Silk Road: Overland Trade and Cultural Exchange from Antiquity to the Fifteenth Century*. New York and London: Palgrave Macmillan, 2000.

Hall, Manly. *Twelve World Teachers: A Summary of Their Lives and Teachings.* Los Angeles, CA: Philosophical Research Society, 1996.

Hasluck, Frederick William. *Christianity and Islam under the Sultans.* Edited by Margaret M. Hasluck. 1929. Reprint. Mansfield Centre, CT: Martino Publishing, 2006.

Karpat, Kemal. *The Politicization of Islam: Reconstructing Identity, State, Faith, and Community in the late Ottoman State.* New York: Oxford University Press, 2001.

Mardin, Serif. *Religion and Social Change in Modern Turkey: The Case of Bediuzzaman Said Nursi.* Albany, NY: State University of New York, 1989.

The Meaning of the Holy Qur'an. (Translation and commentary by Abdullah Yusuf Ali). 7th ed. Beltsville, MD: Amana Publications, 1995.

Olsson, Tord. *Alevi Identity: Cultural, Religious and Social Perspectives (Transactions (Svenska Forskningsinstitutet I Istanbul), V. 8.).* London: Routledge Curzon, 1998.

Saktanber, Ayse. *Living Islam: Women, Politics and Religion in Turkey.* London: I. B. Tauris, 1998.

Toynbee, Arnold J. *The Western Question in Greece and Turkey: A Study in the Contact of Civilizations.* 2nd ed. London: Constable, 1923.

Unal, Ali, and Alphonse Williams. *Advocate of Dialogue: Fethullah Gulen.* Rutherford, NJ: Fountain, 2000.

Yavuz, Hakan. *Islamic Political Identity in Turkey (Religion and Global Politics).* New York: Oxford University Press, 2003.

CHAPTER 3

Andrews, Walter, et al, eds. *Ottoman Lyric Poetry: An Anthology (Publications on the Near East).* Expanded ed. Seattle, WA: University of Washington Press, 2006.

Basgos, Ilhan. *Bilmece: A Corpus of Turkish Riddles.* (University of California publications. Folklore studies). Berkeley, CA: University of California Press, 1973.

Gibb, Elias J. W. *A History of Ottoman Poetry.* Vols. I–VI. London: Luzac and Company, 1900–1909.

Gibb, Elias J. W. *A History of Ottoman Poetry.* Edited by Edward Browne. reprint. Whitefish, MT: Kessinger Publishing, 2007.

Gocgun, Onder, ed. *Turk Dunyasi Edebiyat Tarihi* [The History of the Literature of the Turkic World]. Vols. 1–6. Maltepe, Ankara: Ataturk Kultur Merkezi Baskanligi, 2001–2004.

Halman, Talat, ed. *Contemporary Turkish Literature: Fiction and Poetry.* London: Associated University Press, 1982.

Halman, Talat, ed. *Modern Turkish Drama: An Anthology.* Minneapolis: Bibliotheca Islamica, 1986.

Hikmet, Nazim. *Poems of Nazim Hikmet.* Translated from Turkish by Randy Blasing and Multu Blasing. Revised and expanded ed. New York: Persea Books, 2002.

Kalafat, Yasar. *Turk dunyasi karsilastirmali Turkmen Halk Inanclari: Afganistan, Ozbekistan, Turkmenistan, Nahcivan-Azerbaycan, Kafkasya, Iran, Irak, Anadolu, Makedonya*. Cankaya, Ankara: Avrasya Stratejik Arastirmalar Merkezi Yayinlari, 2000.

Karantay, Suat, ed. *Short Dramas from Contemporary Turkish Literature*. Istanbul: Bagazci University Press, 1993.

Lewis, Geoffrey, trans. *The Book of Dede Korkut (Penguin Classics)*. Reprint. New York: Penguin Classics, 1974.

Lewis, Geoffrey, trans. *The Turkish Language Reform: A Catastrophic Success (Oxford Linguistics)*. New York: Oxford University Press, 2002.

Menemencioglu, Nermin, ed. *Penguin Book of Turkish Verse (Penguin Poets)*. Harmondsworth, UK: Penguin Books, 1978.

Mitler, Louis. *Contemporary Turkish Writers: A Critical Bio-Bibliography of Leading Writers in the Turkish Republican Period up to 1980*. Richmond, UK: Curzon Press, 1997.

Pamuk, Orhan. *The Black Book*. New York: Vintage, 2006.

Pamuk, Orhan. *Istanbul: Memories and the City*. New York: Vintage, 2006.

Piterberg, Gabriel. *An Ottoman Tragedy: History and Historiography at Play (Studies on the History of Society and Culture, 50)*. Berkeley, CA: University of California Press, 2003.

Reichl, Karl. *Singing the Past: Turkic and Medieval Heroic Poetry (Myth and Poetics)*. Ithaca and London: Cornell University Press, 2000.

Reichl, Karl. *Turkic Epic Poetry: Traditions, Forms, Poetic Structure*. New York and London: Garland Publishing, 1992.

Silay, Kemal. *An Anthology of Turkish Literature*. Bloomington, IN: Indiana University Press, 1996.

CHAPTER 4

Bali, Rıfat N. *The Turkish Cinema in the Early Republican Years*. Beylerbeyi-Istanbul: Isis Press, 2007.

Dakovic, Nevena, et al, ed. *Gender and Media*. Ankara: Med-Campus, 1996.

Daldal, Asli. *Art, Politics and Society. Social Realism in Italian and Turkish Cinemas*. Istanbul: Isis Press, 2002.

Donmez-Colin, Gonul. *Turkish Cinema*. Istanbul: Reaktion Books, 2008.

Eickelman, Dale F., and Jon W. Anderson, eds. *New Media in the Muslim World: The Emerging Public Sphere*. Bloomington, IN: Indiana University Press, 2004.

Eleftheriotis, Dimitris, and Gary Needham, eds. *Asian Cinemas: A Reader and Guide*. Honolulu: University of Hawai'i Press, 2006.

Freedom House. *Freedom of the Press: A Global Survey of Media Independence*. Piscataway, NJ: Freedom House, 2005.

Hachten, William, and James F. Scotton. *The World News Prism: Global Media in an Era of Terrorism*. Ames, Iowa: Iowa State Press, 2002.

Inanoglu, Turker. *5555 Afisle Turk Sinemasi* [5555 Posters of Turkish Cinema]. Istanbul: Kabalci Yeyinevi, 2004.

Kosnick, Kira. *Migrant Media: Turkish Broadcasting and Multicultural Politics in Berlin.* Bloomington, IN: Indiana University Press, 2007.

Nowell-Smith, Geoffrey, ed. *The Oxford History of World Cinema.* Oxford; New York: Oxford University Press, 1996.

Ozguc, Agah. *Turk Sinemasinda Cinselligin Tarihi* [The History of Sexuality in Turkish Cinema]. Istanbul: Kabalci Yeyinevi, 2000.

Parkinson, David. *The History of Film (World of Art).* New York: Thames & Hudson, 1996.

Price, Monroe, ed. *Media Reform: Democratizing the Media, Democratizing the State (Routledge Research in Cultural and Media Studies).* London: Routledge, 2001.

Scognomillo, Giovanni. *Erotik Turk Sinemasi* [Turkish Erotic Cinema]. Istanbul: Kabalci Yeyinevi, 2002.

Shary, Timothy, and Alexandra Seibel, eds. *Youth Culture in Global Cinema.* Austin, TX: University of Texas Press, 2007.

CHAPTER 5

And, Metin. *Culture, Performance, and Communication in Turkey.* Tokyo: Institute for the Study of Languages and Cultures of Asia & Africa, 1987.

And, Metin. *A History of Theatre and Popular Entertainment in Turkey.* Ankara: Forum Yayinlari, 1964.

And, Metin. *A Pictorial History of Turkish Dancing: From Folk Dancing to Whirling Dervishes–Belly Dancing to Ballet.* Ankara: Dost Yayinlari, 1976.

Bartok, Bela, and Jake Highton. *Turkish Folk Music from Asia Minor.* Princeton, NJ: Princeton University Press, 1976.

Danielson, V., ed. *The Middle East (Garland Encyclopedia of World Music, Volume 6).* London and New York: Garland, 2001.

Ekmekcioglu, Ismail, et al. *Turk Halk Oyunlari.* Istanbul: Esin Yayinevi, 2001.

Faroghi, Suraiya. *Subjects of the Sultan. Culture and Daily Life in the Ottoman Empire.* London and New York: I. B. Tauris Publishers, 1995.

Feldman, Walter. *Music of the Ottoman Court: Makam, Composition and the Early Ottoman Instrumental Repertoire.* Berlin: Verlag, 1996.

Kaufmann, Walter. *Musical Notations of the Orient: Notational Systems of Continental East, South and Central Asia.* Bloomington, IN: Indiana University Press, 1988.

Levin, Theodore. *The Hundred Thousand Fools of God. Musical Travel in Central Asia.* Bloomington, IN: Indiana University Press, 1996.

Lewis, Bernard. *Music of a Distant Drum: Classical Arabic, Persian, Turkish, and Hebrew Poems.* Princeton, NJ: Princeton University Press, 2001.

Oztuna, Yilmaz, ed. *Turk Musikisi Ansiklopedisi* [An Encyclopedia of Turkish Music]. 2 vols. Istanbul, Milli Egitim Basimevi, 1969–1976.

Piken, Laurence. *Folk Musical Instruments of Turkey.* London: Oxford University Press, 1975.

CHAPTER 6

Alexander, Christopher. *A Foreshadow of 21st Century Art: The Color and Geometry of Very Early Turkish Carpets.* New York: Oxford University Press, 1993.

Altun, Ara, ed. *The Story of Ottoman Tiles and Ceramics.* Istanbul: Creative Yayincilik, 1997.

And, Metin. *Turkish Miniature Painting.* Istanbul: Dost Yayinlari, 1987.

Atasoy, Nurhan, and Julian Raby. *Iznik: The Pottery of Ottoman Turkey.* London: Thames and Hudson, 1994.

Atil, Esin. *Ceramics from the World of Islam.* Washington, DC: Smithsonian Institution, 1973.

Bahari, Ebadollah. *Bihzad, Master of Persian Painting.* Foreword by Annemarie Schimmel. London and New York: I. B. Tauris Publishers, 1996.

Bland, David. A *History of Book Illustration: The Illuminated Manuscript and the Printed Book.* 2nd ed. Berkeley, CA: University of California Press, 1969.

Bloom, Jonathan. *Paper before Print: The History and Impact of Paper in the Islamic World.* New Haven, CT: Yale University Press, 2001.

Bogolyubov, A. A. *Carpets of Central Asia.* Ramsdel: Crosby Press, 1973.

Ferrier, R.W., ed. *The Arts of Persia.* New Haven, CT: Yale University Press, 1989.

Glassie, Henry. *Turkish Traditional Art Today.* Bloomington, IN: Indiana University Press, 1993.

Grube, Ernst J. *The Classic Style in Islamic Painting: The Early School of Herat and its Impact on Islamic Painting of the later Fifteens, the Sixteenth, and Seventeenth Centuries; Some Examples in American Collection.* Venice, Italy: Edizioni Oriens, 1968.

Grube, Ernst J., et al. *Architecture of the Islamic World: Its History and Social Meaning, with a Complete Survey of Key Monuments.* London: Thames & Hudson, 1995.

Hillenbrand, Robert. *Islamic Art and Architecture.* London: Thames and Hudson, 1999.

Hull, A., et al. *Living with Kilims.* London: Thames and Hudson, 1995.

Lindisfarne-Tapper, Nancy, and Bruce Ingham. *Language of Dress in the Middle East.* London: Curzon Press, 1997.

Maritz, Iten. *Turkish Carpets.* New York: Kavindasha International, 1977.

Martin, F. R. *The Miniature Painting and Painters of Persia, India and Turkey, from the 8th to the 18th Century.* London, B. Quaritch, 1912. Reprint. South Asia Books, 1993.

Pinar, Selman, ed. *A History of Turkish Painting.* Seattle, WA: University of Washington Press, 1988.

Sumner, Christina, et al. *Beyond the Silk Road: Arts of Central Asia.* Haymarket, Australia: Powerhouse Publishing, 1999.

Sweetman, John. *The Oriental Obsession: Islamic Inspiration in British and American Art and Architecture, 1500–1920.* Cambridge, UK: University of Cambridge Press, 1988.

Tapper, Richard, and K. McLachlan. *Technology, Tradition and Survival: Aspects of Material Culture in the Middle East and Central Asia.* London and Portland, OR: Frank Cass, 2003.

CHAPTER 7

Altun, Ara. *An Outline of Turkish Architecture in the Middle Ages.* Istanbul: Arkeoloji ve Sanat, 1990.

Blair, Sheila, and Jonathan Bloom. *The Art and Architecture of Islam, (1250–1800).* New Haven, CT and London: Yale University Press, 1994.

Bozdogan, Sibel. *Modernism and Nation Building: Turkish Architectural Culture in the Early Republic (Studies in Modernity and National Identity).* Seattle, WA: University of Washington Press, 2002.

Celik, Zeynep. *The Remaking of Istanbul: Portrait of an Ottoman City in the Nineteenth Century.* Seattle, WA: University of Washington Press, 1986.

Eldem, Sedat Hakki, ed. *Turk Evi: Osmanli Donemi* [Turkish House: Ottoman Period]. 5 vols. Istanbul: Turk Anit Cevre Turism Degerlerini Koruma Vakfi, 1984–1985.

Goodwin, Godfrey. *A History of Ottoman Architecture.* 4th ed. London: Thames and Hudson, 2003.

Hattstein, Markus, and Peter Delius, eds. *Islam: Art and Architecture.* Cologne: Konemann, 2001.

Hillenbrand, Robert. *Islamic Art and Architecture (The World of Art).* London: Thames and Hudson, 1999.

Kiel, Machiel. *Studies of the Ottoman Architecture of the Balkans: A Legacy in Stone.* Aldershot, UK: Variorum, 1990.

Kuban, Dogan. *Muslim Religious Architecture.* 3 vols. Leiden: E. J. Brill, 1974–1985.

Kuran, Apdullah. *Sinan: The Grand Old Master of Ottoman Architecture.* Photographs by Ara Guler. Washington, DC: Institute of Turkish Studies, 1987.

Lifchez, Raymond, ed. *The Dervish Lodge: Architecture, Art and Sufism in Ottoman Turkey.* Berkeley, CA: University of California Press, 1992.

Michell, George, Ernst J. Grube, et al. *Architecture of the Islamic World: Its History and Social Meaning, with a Complete Survey of Key Monuments.* London: Thames and Hudson, 1978.

Necipoglu, Gulru. The Topkapi Scroll—Geometry and Ornament in Islamic Architecture (Sketchbooks & Albums). Santa Monica: Windsor Books International, 1996.

Oktay Aslapa. *Turkish Art and Architecture.* New York, Praeger, 1971.

Sozen, Metin. *The Evolution of Turkish Art and Architecture.* Translated by M. Quigley-Pinar. Istanbul. Haset, 1987.

CHAPTER 8

Acar, Feride, and Ayse Gunez-Ayata, eds. *Gender and Identity Construction: Women of Central Asia, the Caucasus and Turkey.* Leiden and Boston: Brill, 1999.

Arat, Yesim. *Rethinking Islam and Liberal Democracy: Islamist Women in Turkish Politics.* New York: State University of New York Press, 2005.

Arat, Zehra, ed. *Deconstructing Images of the Turkish Woman.* New York: St. Martin's Press, 1998.

Caner, Ergun Mehmet. *Unveiling Islam: An Insider's Look at Muslim Life and Beliefs.* Grand Rapids, MI: Kregel Publications, 2002.

Caner, Ergun Mehmet. *Voices behind the Veil: The World of Islam through the Eyes of Women.* Grand Rapids, MI: Kregel Publications, 2004.

Croutier, Alev Lytle. *Harem: The World behind the Veil.* Reprint. New York: Abbeville Press, 1989.

Garnett, Lucy M. J. *The Women of Turkey and Their Folklore.* 2 vols. London: D. Nutt, 1890–1891.

Goodwin, Godfrey. *The Private World of Ottoman Women.* London: Saqi Books, 1997.

Goody, Jack. *The Oriental, the Ancient, and the Primitive: Systems of Marriage and the Family in the Pre-industrial Societies of Eurasia.* Cambridge and New York: Cambridge University Press, 1990.

Hambly, Gavin. *Women in the Medieval Islamic World: Power, Patronage, and Piety.* New York: St. Martin's Press, 1998.

Hanim, Melek. *Thirty Years in the Harem, or, the Autobiography of Melek-Hanum, Wife of H. H. Kibrizli-Mehemet Pasha.* 1872. Reprint. Piscataway, NJ: Gorgias Press, 2005.

Jenkins, Hester Donaldson. *Behind Turkish Lattices: The Story of a Turkish Woman's Life.* 1911. Reprint. Piscataway, NJ: Gorgias Press, 2005.

Kagitcibasi, Cigdem, ed. *Sex Roles, Family and Community in Turkey.* Bloomington, IN: Indiana University Turkish Studies, 1982.

Kandiyoti, Deniz, ed. *Women, Islam and the State.* London: McMillan, 1991.

Lewis, Reina. *Rethinking Orientalism: Women, Travel, and The Ottoman Harem.* New Brunswick, NJ: Rutgers University Press, 2004.

Pierce, Leslie. *The Imperial Harem: Women and Sovereignty in the Ottoman Empire.* New York: Oxford University Press, 1993.

Vaka Brown, Demetra. *The Unveiled Ladies of Istanbul (Stamboul).* 1923. Reprint. Piscataway, NJ: Gorgias Press, 2005.

CHAPTER 9

Ahiska, Meltem, and Zafer Yenal. *The Person You Have Called Cannot Be Reached at the Moment: Representations of Lifestyles in Turkey, 1980–2005.* Istanbul: Ottoman Bank Archives and Research Centre, 2006.

Algar, Ayla Esen. *The Complete Book of Turkish Cooking.* London: Kegan Paul International, 1995.

Batmanglij, Najmieh. *Silk Road Cooking. A Vegetarian Journey.* Washington, DC: Mage Publishers, 2002.

Foster, Dean. *The Global Etiquette Guide to Asia.* New York and Toronto: Wiley, 2000.

Garnett, Lucy M. J. *The Turkish People: Their Social Life, Religious Beliefs and Institutions and Domestic Life.* Reprint. New York: AMS Press, 1982.

Ghillie, Basan. *Classic Turkish Cookery.* London: I. B. Tauris, 1997.

Hazirlayan, Sivas, and Sebnem Ercebeci. *Turk Dunyasinda Nevruz. Dordonco Uluslararasi Bilgi Soleni: 21–23 Mart 2001* [Nawruz in the Turkic World. Fourth Information/Knowledge Festival: March 21–23 2001]. Ankara: Ataturk Kultur Merkezi, 2001.

Henderson, Helene, ed. *Holidays, Festivals, and Celebrations of the World Dictionary: Detailing Nearly 2,500 Observances from all 50 States and More than 100 Nations: A Compendious Reference Guide to Popular, Ethnic, Religious, National, and Ancient Holidays.* 3rd ed. Detroit, MI: Omnigraphics, 2005.

Hoppenstand, Gary, Michael K. Schoenecke, John F. Bratzel, and Gerd Bayer, eds. *The Greenwood Encyclopedia of World Popular Culture.* 6 vols. Westport, CT: Greenwood Press, 2007.

Kandiyoti, Deniz, and Ayse Saktanber. *Fragments of Culture: The Everyday of Modern Turkey.* London and New York: I. B. Tauris, 2002.

Katz, Solomon H. *Encyclopedia of Food and Culture.* New York: Charles Schribner's Sons, 2002.

Mahdi, Ali Akbar, ed. *Teen Life in the Middle East.* Westport, CT: Greenwood Press, 2003.

Mallan, Kerry, and Sharyn Pearce, eds. *Youth Cultures: Texts, Images, and Identities.* Westport, CT: Praeger, 2003.

Morris, Chris. *The New Turkey: The Quiet Revolution on the Edge of Europe.* London: Granta, 2005.

Ozyurek, Esra. *Nostalgia for the Modern: State Secularism and Everyday Politics in Turkey.* Durham, NC: Duke University Press, 2006.

Robertson, Carol. *Turkish Cooking: A Culinary Journey through Turkey.* San Francisco, CA: Frog Ltd., 1996.

Stearns, Peter H. *Consumerism in World History: The Global Transformation of Desire.* New York: Routledge, 2001.

Stearns, Peter H. *Global Outrage: The Impact of World Opinion on Contemporary History.* Oxford, England: One World, 2005.

Yasa, Azize Aktas. *Turk Kulturunde Nevruz v. Uluslar Arasi Bilgi Soleni Bildirileri: 15–16 Mart 2002* [Communiqué of the International Information Festival of the Newruz in Turkic World: March 15–16, 2002]. Ankara: Ataturk Kultur Merkezi, 2002.

Index

About the Author

RAFIS ABAZOV is Adjunct Assistant Professor, School of International and Public Affairs/Harriman Institute, Columbia University. He has written four books, including *Culture and Customs of the Central Asian Republics* (Greenwood, 2007).

Recent Titles in
Culture and Customs of Europe